STRATEGIC CORPORATE COMMUNICATION

A Global Approach for Doing Business in the New India

Paul A. Argenti

MCGRAW-HILL

New York   Chicago   San Francisco   Lisbon   London   Madrid
Mexico City   Milan   New Delhi   San Juan   Seoul
Singapore   Sydney   Toronto

The **McGraw·Hill** Companies

1 2 3 4 5 6 7 8 9 0 DOC/DOC 0 1 5 4 3 2 1 0 9 8

ISBN   978-0-07-154991-2
MHID   0-07-154991-9

This publication is designed to provide accurate and authoritative information in regard to the subject matter covered. It is sold with the understanding that neither the author nor the publisher is engaged in rendering legal, accounting, futures/securities trading, or other professional service. If legal advice or other expert assistance is required, the services of a competent professional person should be sought.

—From a Declaration of Principles jointly adopted
by a Committee of the American Bar Association
and a Committee of Publishers

McGraw-Hill books are available at special quantity discounts to use as premiums and sales promotions, or for use in corporate training programs. To contact a representative, please visit the Contact Us pages at www.mhprofessional.com.

This book is printed on acid-free paper.

Library of Congress Cataloging-in-Publication Data

Argenti, Paul A.
   Strategic corporate communication: a global approach for doing business in the new India / by Paul A. Argenti.
      p. cm.
   Includes bibliographical references and index.
   ISBN 0-07-154991-9 (alk. paper)
   1. Corporations—Public relations—India.   2. International business enterprises—Public relations—India.   3. Communication in management.   I. Title.
   HD59.6.I4A74 2009
   658.4′5—dc22
                                                                            2008011672

To my mother,
Elenora Argenti

Contents

Preface

This book grew out of a sabbatical in 2004 that took me to India. During that time, I was fortunate to visit with many of the companies that I have written about here. I also realized that many of the things that I learned might be useful to executives in India and around the world. As a result, in 2007 I published a book geared to the Indian market that focused exclusively on corporate communication in India.

Soon after the book was published, however, several people who had read the book mentioned to me that it would be useful to executives who were doing business in India. As a result, I have rewritten the book to include more U.S. and global examples and to look at the subject from the perspective of someone doing business in India.

Much of the thinking for this book comes out of more than 25 years of work developing the field of study referred to in this book as *corporate communication*. While the term itself is not new, the notion of it as a functional area of management equal in importance to finance, marketing, and production is more recent. In the last 25 years, senior managers at a growing number of companies throughout the world have come to realize the importance of an integrated communication function. During those 25 years of work I published five editions of a textbook on the subject in the United States.

In this preface, I would like to talk a bit more about my expertise, what this book is all about, and why I think everyone involved in organizations today needs to know about this important discipline.

AUTHOR'S EXPERTISE

For the last 25 years, I have been a professor of management and corporate communication at the Tuck School of Business at Dartmouth College. Prior to that, I taught at the Columbia and Harvard Business Schools. I have also taught as a visiting professor at the Helsinki School of Economics in Finland, the International University of Japan, Erasmus University in the Netherlands, and Singapore Management University. I was also fortunate to be one of the founders of the Hanoi School of Business.

The tradition of teaching communication has been a long one at Tuck, but as at most schools, the focus was always on skills development, including primarily speaking and writing. The first development in the evolution of this field was an interest among businesspeople in how to deal with the media. Since this mostly involved applying oral presentation skills in another setting, the members of the faculty who taught communication were a logical choice for taking on this new task.

So when I began teaching the first management communication course at Tuck in 1981, I was asked to include a component on dealing with the media. I became interested in this through my study of marketing at Columbia and had already written a case on the subject, which appears in earlier editions of this book.

Over the years, my interest in the subject grew beyond how companies deal with the media to how they deal with all communication problems. As I wrote more case studies on the subject and worked with managers inside companies, I saw the need for a more integrated function. The reason for this is that most companies were conducting communication activities in a highly decentralized way.

For example, the employee communication function at Hewlett-Packard (HP) in the mid-1980s was in the human resources department, where it had always been, when I wrote a case on how HP dealt with voluntary severance and early retirement programs. As I looked at other companies, I found the same basic structure everywhere. Yet the people in those various human resources departments were doing exactly the same thing internally that a communication specialist in the public relations department was doing for the external audience—sending a specific company message to a specific audience.

The same was true of the investor relations functions, which typically resided exclusively in the finance department in most companies until the 1990s. Why? Because the chief financial officer was the one who knew the most about the company's financial performance and historically had been responsible for developing the annual report. Communication was seen as a vehicle for getting that information out rather than as a function in itself.

Again, as I worked with companies on developing new identities and images, I found marketing people involved because they had traditionally dealt with image in the context of products and services. Yet those marketing experts didn't always know what was being communicated to the press or to securities analysts by their counterparts in other functional areas.

These experiences led me to believe that corporations and other organizations, from universities to churches to law firms, could do a much better job of communicating if they integrated all communication activities under one umbrella. That was the theory at least, but I could find precious little evidence in practice.

Then, in 1990, I was fortunate enough to be given a consulting assignment that allowed me to put into practice what I had been talking about in theory for many years. I received a call from the chairman and chief executive officer of a major corporation after my picture appeared on the front page of the *New York Times* Sunday business section in an article about how professors were teaching business students about dealing with the media.

Ostensibly, the chairman's call was about how his company could get more credit for the great things it was doing. Specifically, he wanted to know if I had a "silver bullet." My silver bullet, as it turned out, was the development of a new corporate communication function for the company.

This company, like most, had communications that were decentralized into a variety of other functional areas, with the predictable result: no integration. The media relations people were saying one thing; the investor relations department was saying another; the marketing team was developing communication strategies for the outside; the human resources department for the inside.

No one except the chairman, who sat at the top of this $30 billion organization, could see the big picture, and none of those intimately involved with the various activities had an inside track on the overall strategy for the firm. Over the next year and a half, the chairman and I came up with the first integrated communication function that had all the different subsets I had tried unsuccessfully to bring together at other companies and even at my own university.

We changed everything—from the company's image with customers to its relationship with securities analysts on Wall Street. Today this company has one totally integrated communication function. This book explains what all the component parts of that function are all about.

WHAT IS THIS BOOK ABOUT?

This book covers all aspects of communication and its development globally with an emphasis on India. It also looks more deeply at corporate communication as a function in the United States as a contrast for managers reading this book and doing business with U.S. companies.

We also look at the business environment in India and how that has shaped the communication function in corporations. This changing environment for business in India as well as the rest of the world has had a huge effect on how companies communicate. Put simply, companies must now find ways to communicate with constituencies they were able to ignore 50 years ago.

The book also emphasizes the importance of strategy in communication—both in terms of how communication serves as an extension of an organization's strategy and how communication can become more strategic rather than intuitive when it is approached in the business setting.

Most of the book, however, deals with the key functions within a corporate communication area. Many assume that communication is simply media relations or what we once called "PR," but instead, corporate communication officers now have responsibility for everything from the annual report to the company's corporate advertising campaign.

WHY IS CORPORATE COMMUNICATION SO IMPORTANT TODAY?

Every functional area at one time or another was the newest and most important. But as we enter the twenty-first century, the importance of communication is obvious to virtually everyone throughout the world. Why?

First, we live in a more sophisticated era in terms of communication. Information travels with lightning speed from one side of the world to another as a result of technological developments such as the Internet and blogs.

Second, the general public is more sophisticated in its approach to organizations than it has been in the past. People tend to be more educated about issues and more skeptical of corporate intentions. Thus companies cannot get by on statements like, "What's good for General Motors is good for everyone," or "If we build a better mousetrap, customers will beat a path to our door." Maybe not, if they don't know who you are.

Third, information comes to us in more beautiful packages than it did before. We now expect to see glossy annual reports from major corporations. We don't want to walk into grimy-looking stores, even for our discount shopping. Gas stations are modern looking and have been "designed" from top to bottom by high-profile New York– or

Mumbai-based design firms. The bar is high for a company's message to stand out in this environment.

Fourth, organizations have become inherently more complex. Companies in earlier times (and the same is true even today for very small organizations) were small enough that they could get by with much less sophisticated communication activities. Often, one person could perform many different functions at one time. But in organizations with thousands of employees, it is much more difficult to keep track of all the different pieces that make up a coherent communication strategy.

This book describes not only what is happening in an era of advanced communication but what companies can do to stay one step ahead of the competition. By creating a coordinated, strategic corporate communication system, organizations will be able to face the new century with the strategies and tools that few companies in the world have at their fingertips.

I am sure that 20 years from now, when another functional area develops that we cannot even imagine right now, much will have been written about strategic communication, and most complex organizations in India will have a corporate communication department with many of the subsets described in this book. Until then, however, I hope you enjoy reading about this exciting field as much as I have enjoyed discovering it.

—Paul A. Argenti
Hanover, New Hampshire
June 2008

The author would like any comments or questions as well as corrections to the text. Please write to Professor Paul A. Argenti, The Tuck School of Business, Dartmouth College, Hanover, NH 03755; or e-mail comments to paul.argenti@dartmouth.edu.

Acknowledgments

Without the help and support of the Tuck School at Dartmouth College I could not have completed this book. Over the last 25 years, I have been given funds to write cases and conduct research as well as the sabbatical time to visit and conduct research in India.

I must also, however, thank my colleagues in India for their generous support and guidance. First, I would like to thank Mr. Vinay Rai, founder and president of the Rai Foundation, former businessman, and philanthropist for his financial support during my sabbatical; I would not have been able to write this book without his generous support. I would also like to thank my trusted advisor and colleague, Nymph Kaul, for her support and guidance, and Mohita Datta and Devjyoti Ghosh for their research support through the Rai Foundation. Finally, I would like to thank Abbey Nova and Courtney Barnes for their help with this manuscript and additional research support. Courtney was particularly integral to helping me rewrite this book.

Many clients helped me test the ideas I have developed over more than 25 years, but I am particularly indebted to Joseph Antonini, former chairman and CEO of Kmart, for allowing me to think creatively about the possibilities for a unified corporate communication function. I also would like to thank Andy Sigler, formerly chairman and CEO of Champion International, and Jim Donahue for allowing me to test new ideas with top managers at their company; Nancy Bekavac, president of Scripps College, for allowing me to work on Scripps's identity program and for her helpful comments on Chapter 4; and Valerie Haertel of Alliance Capital Management for her input and help with Chapter 7. David McCourt, former chairman and CEO of RCN, also allowed me to work more recently on developing a corporate communication function in his company. In addition, I thank my many colleagues at Goldman Sachs, where I was fortunate to work as a consultant for over eight years, and to Peter Verrengia and all my colleagues at Fleishman Hillard for their support over the last four years.

I am indebted as well to the students I have taught at Tuck, Erasmus University, Singapore Management University, Hanoi School of Business, the International University of Japan, the Helsinki School of Economics, Columbia Business School, and Harvard Business School. They have tested these ideas in their fertile minds and given me inspiration for coming up with new ways of thinking about communications.

Chapter 1

The Contemporary Global Business Environment

oday's corporate leaders have witnessed a significant evolution in the business landscape. The environment in which they likely began their careers decades ago has transformed from mainly localized business transactions and relationships to a completely globalized "business without borders" backdrop, where even small organizations must think like multinational conglomerates. Furthermore, what the public expects of corporations today is also different from their expectations 40 or 50 years ago. To attract customers, employees, and investors, companies need to be progressive leaders on a host of global issues and place their vision in a broader social context. Public scrutiny of business is constant and intense, and in the past decade, disillusionment has grown over perceived excesses in stock market operations, questionable accounting practices, willful default on loans, and moral laxity on the part of corporations.

These developments can be attributed to a number of catalysts, but one can be identified as especially influential: the rise of technology. Technology has enabled businesses to forge partnerships, market products, recruit talent, connect employees, and attract consumers all over the world, regardless of where their corporate headquarters are based. This reality has innumerable business implications, but most significant to our discussion are those related to communications that are strategic and that enable viable, profitable business relationships across the globe.

Before we begin our discussion of strategic corporate communication on a global scale, we must first put it into the context of this international business environment. To do so, we focus on the nation that many would consider to be central to globalization's evolution, and that which many international business leaders must now integrate into their strategies and portfolios: India.

India began emerging as a major power when outsourcing—the act of subcontracting a business process to a third-party organization—became a prominent component of business to cut costs and make use of efficient labor resources. Though outsourcing processes to India began in the 1980s when companies such as British Airways, American Express, and General Electric sent various back office operations to Delhi, its substandard infrastructure prevented it from being an international business hub for some time. However, India moved beyond the back office as multinationals realized the potential of its vast domestic market and its skilled but low-cost talent pool. The information technology (IT) boom raised its profile even further.

Today, according to a report by the TPI Index, the Asia-Pacific region's outsourcing contracts alone contributed $12.8 billion to the global outsourcing market in 2007—a 30 percent increase over 2006—and Indian companies were the engine behind the growth, accounting for $4.9 billion.[1] Now a major manufacturing hub, multinationals including Ford, Nokia, Siemens, and Honeywell have substantial operations that produce for domestic and export markets. On January 8, 2008, Ford announced its $500 million investment to expand its manufacturing facilities in the city of Chennai. This announcement came just months after Nokia CEO Olli-Pekka Kallasvuo said this in an interview with *Business Week*:

> We look at the Indian market as versatile, co ple , and interesting, but our business model is the same. In fact, we have expanded in India rapidly and h v
> people. Some of the people here are serving i
> market. We are going to do even more of this—

Indian talent pool for global services. There are lots of opportunities there. We just announced that we are locating the global headquarters of the Nokia Siemens Networks service unit in India. This unit will have a big global responsibility.[2]

But India's business presence is not solely defined by other nations' brands flocking to its shores; Indian companies too are redefining the nation's role in the global marketplace. For example, in January 2008, Tata Motors unveiled its plans to release the Nano—at $2,500, the world's cheapest car—in the fall of 2008. The announcement was met with enthusiasm worldwide, even among Tata competitors.

What do all these factors mean for global business leaders? In short, they must understand the Indian business environment as an emerging power to be functional and profitable, and they must begin to participate in it, whether directly or indirectly, to maintain global prominence—that is, if they aren't already doing so. This chapter introduces the Indian business environment by looking at some of the events that have influenced its operational growth. We begin by looking at a history of public attitudes toward Indian business and their reflection in popular culture. Next we turn to the effects of globalization (and the antiglobalization backlash) on businesses. Finally, we look at how improved corporate communication helps companies compete in the constantly changing environment.

ATTITUDES TOWARD INDIAN BUSINESS THROUGH THE YEARS

On a cold wintry night in December 1984 when the residents of Bhopal, a town in central India, went to their beds, they had no inkling that many of them were doing so for the last time. Not far from them in the factory of Union Carbide (India) Limited, a subsidiary of the American multinational Union Carbide, a chemical reaction would soon slaughter thousands. At around midnight, this chemical reaction culminated in the leakage of deadly methyl isocyanate (MIC) gas from one of the factory tanks.[3] A cloud of gas slowly started descending and enveloping the city in its lethal fold. Thousands died, many more thousands were maimed for life, and to date, Indian citizens are convinced that Carbide got away with genocide.

This gruesome incident reinforced a typically Indian mindset about business: "Foreign companies are a malignant influence. Give them an inch, and soon India will lose its sovereignty to multinational corporations." This mindset is rooted in India's history as a British colony for close to 200 years. The East India Company came to India to trade during the reign of the Mughal Empire in the seventeenth century. By the early nineteenth century, the trading house was in political and military control of large swathes of the country. The first battle of independence (which British historians prefer to remember as the 1857 mutiny) eventually led to the formal coronation of Queen Victoria as the ruler of India. As we all know, India remained a British colony until 1947 when it emerged as one of the first major independent third-world countries. There exist hundreds of research papers, books, and theses that have documented how the East India Company and the subsequent British rule destroyed Indian industry. Many such arguments may be exaggerated, but that doesn't help when it comes to Indian perceptions about multinationals.

The East India Company experience has left deep-rooted scars on the Indian psyche. For instance, political parties, even today, portray multinationals as ruthless exploiters who will not hesitate to snatch political control to serve their corporate interests. When it is pointed out that the era of colonialism is well and truly over, people opposed to multinationals argue that it is now the era of "neo-colonialism," where economic domination has replaced political domination. It is surprising to note that even in a rapidly globalizing twenty-first-century India, many Indians buy this rhetoric about multinational corporations.

If the colonial experience shaped Indian attitudes toward foreign companies, perceptions toward domestic businessmen have been shaped by many historical factors, prime among them being the caste system of India where the dominant castes routinely abused the lower castes. The trader caste has often been seen as allies of the ruling castes, cheating poor Indian consumers and smothering poor Indians in debt. Subsequently, the domestic businessman has been perceived as someone who had sold his soul to the British masters to be able to earn a profit. These perceptions were strongly reinforced during World War II when the British regime had imposed rationing that had led to Indian consumers facing massive shortages of essential items such as sugar.

This attitude of mistrust toward business in India still exists despite the laudable achievements of homegrown industrialists, such as G. D. Birla, J. R. D. Tata, and Vikram Lalbhai, to name just a few. Some of these tycoons not only beat the British at their own game by overcoming all odds rigged against them and in favor of British business, but they also publicly financed and supported the Indian National Congress in its struggle for India's freedom. India got its freedom, but Indian entrepreneurs seem to have been lost in the battle.

The fact is that while a majority of Indians perceived foreign companies as colonizers and exploiters, they also perceived Indian businessmen as greedy profiteers rather than nation builders. This is reflected in the economic policies pursued by India in the years immediately after it gained its independence.

For a good four decades and more, India adopted the socialist approach to economic policy making. Many in India would be familiar with the term "five-year plan"—adopted by the Indian government in 1951. The five-year plans were inspired by similar exercises in the Soviet Union, which had used planning to rapidly industrialize an agrarian society. It was revealed only much later on that the dictatorial Soviet regime had achieved rapid industrialization at a very heavy cost in terms of human life and misery. Nevertheless, the 1950s were heady days for a newly independent India, with dominant economic thought positing that the state must play a key role in triggering and sustaining economic growth in the country. Somehow there seemed to be a virtual consensus on one key issue: barring a minority of thinkers backing free markets and capitalism, most Indians "perceived" that private business would not do a great job of nation building.

The five-year plans and an industrial policy that reserved the "commanding heights" (major industries) of the economy for state-run enterprises ensured an economy that was dramatically different in structure and performance from that of the United States. Yet, despite high hopes that the Indian economy would deliver the kind of growth that is required to reduce poverty, performance at the ground level was not very encouraging. In the three decades between 1950 and 1980, the Indian economy grew annually at an average of 3.5 percent, which was dubbed the "Hindu rate of growth." With high rates of growth in the population, this ensured that there was no significant improvement in the per capita incomes of Indians. Poverty continued to be widespread.

By the late 1960s, disenchantment had become common in India and was reflected in political and social upheavals. Yet business historians now marvel at how public perception toward private business remained negative despite the manifest weaknesses of the state-run sector that bred red tape, inefficiency, poor quality, and corruption. The Indian economy took an even more dramatic turn toward socialism in the late 1960s and early 1970s. You could say that a perception about businesspeople being unethical profiteers was at its peak. In the next section, we see how Bollywood movies reflected these trends and perceptions. Since India's socialist policies were tailor-made to create an economy rife with shortages of all major consumer products, traders and businesspeople were identified as the culprits who exploited the Indian consumer to make ill-gotten profits. A few voices point out that the virtual stranglehold of the state on economic activities might after all be the cause of endemic shortages. But they were in a minority.

Virtually every major private bank and insurance company was nationalized. The coal industry was nationalized. Severe restrictions were imposed on private businesses via repressive monopoly and foreign exchange laws. Astonishingly, a majority of Indian citizens seemed to have fallen for this "hard socialism" because the state communicated its message to Indians more effectively than private business could (with the exception of print media, whose reach was limited because of huge illiteracy levels in India; thus media were controlled and manipulated by the state right up until the satellite revolution of the 1990s). Though formal surveys were not conducted at the time, there can be little doubt that corporate India was perceived as anti "little guy." Many have also argued that the persistent negative perceptions about business and enterprise may have been the result of successful state propaganda.

For different reasons, public perception about American business was on a downswing during the period. Though the United States did not face a state-dominated economy like India's, voter and consumer disenchantment fueled antibusiness sentiments in both countries. Research surveys in the United States confirm the growing negative perceptions about corporate America.

Over a period of 30 years, marketing consultancy Yankelovich asked U.S. citizens the question, "Does business strike a balance between profit and the public interest?" In 1968, 70 percent of the population answered yes. By the time Richard Nixon was president of the United States, the nation was torn by civil unrest, the continuation of the civil rights struggle, and demonstrations against U.S. involvement in the Vietnam War. Disagreement over the role of the United States in Vietnam marked a serious deterioration of public attitudes toward all institutions, including business. For those who were against the war, the executive branch of government came to stand for all that was wrong with the United States.

Because it helped make the war possible, American industry became the target of much public hostility. When Dow Chemical started manufacturing napalm and Agent Orange for defoliating Vietnamese jungles, student protests began on many U.S. university campuses. Young people in the United States started distrusting the institutions involved in the war, regardless of whether they were government agencies or businesses. This represented a dramatic change from the attitudes Americans had during World War II. Those in power failed to see that Vietnam was different because Americans were ambivalent about what the country was fighting for.

Toward the end of the 1960s, a rise in radicalism in the United States marked the beginning of a long deterioration of trust in institutions. The events of the early 1970s also contributed to this shift. For example, the Watergate break-in, orchestrated by Nixon's operatives, only confirmed what most young Americans had believed all along about the Nixon administration. The aftermath of the oil embargo, imposed by Arab nations after the Middle East war in 1973, had even more of an effect on attitudes toward business in the United States. Petroleum, which was cheap and abundant and responsible for improving the American way of life, suddenly became scarce and expensive as Saudi Arabia and other Arab producers punished the United States for supporting Israel in the war. Although the cut-off lasted less than three months, its effects still exist today.

By the mid-1970s, as a result of Watergate, Vietnam, and the oil embargo, the attitudes of Americans toward business reached an all-time low. In answer to the same question, "Does business strike a fair balance between profit and the public interest?" those answering yes in the Yankelovich poll dropped to 15 percent in 1976—when Jimmy Carter took office. This drop of 55 points in just eight years says more about the changing attitudes toward business in the United States than a thousand anecdotes.

An opinion research poll that asked the general public to rate its confidence in a number of institutions showed declines in all areas (see Table 1-1). Although figures do not exist for other institutions, we can imagine similar dips in American attitudes toward the police, the armed forces, and even organized religion, based on how people felt about large institutions in the 1970s.

In India, citizens, consumers, and other stakeholders increasingly sensed that there was something wrong with India's economy, something that needed to be fixed. The emergence of a vocal

Table 1-1 How Much Confidence Do You Have in These Institutions?*

	1966	1971	1989
Large companies	55%	27%	14%
U.S. Congress	42%	19%	10%
Executive branch	41%	23%	27%
Supreme Court	51%	23%	26%

*Answers reflect those answering most positively.
Source: Yankelovich Monitor

and pro free market press around this time in the late 1970s also started influencing public perceptions about business. The introduction of some liberal economic policies resulted in a stronger economic performance during the 1980s, with the GDP growing at an annual average rate of 5 to 6 percent, instead of 3.5 percent noted earlier.

However, it was only in 1991 that a severe balance of payments and an economic crisis forced the government to adopt liberal, market-oriented policies. For students of corporate communication, 1991 is a landmark year that marked a paradigm shift in the way the average Indian looked at business and enterprise. As integration with the global economy gathered momentum, there seemed to be a visible shift in attitudes and perceptions toward business. The amazing success of the Indian information technology sector created new business icons whom the younger generation wanted to emulate. The arrival of satellite TV, glitzy soap operas, and relaxed import controls triggered what is known as the *consumerism revolution* in India. Suddenly, it was no longer sinful to be rich and successful. And these changing attitudes are well documented in Bollywood movies.

BOLLYWOOD: A WINDOW ON DALAL STREET AND CORPORATE INDIA

Throughout history, literature and the arts have both affected and reflected perceptions about institutions. Greek attitudes about government and religion have manifested themselves in theater;

Shakespeare has shaped notions about English history for generations; and in India, cinema and television over the past several decades have reflected some of the public's negative attitudes about business. But in the last decade the perception of business has changed. After all, films are the mirrors of the society.

For many Indians today, fictional or "factional" accounts in films and on television help shape their attitudes; more so than educational institutions. In fact, Indians spend far more time in front of the television set than they do in the classroom. Many people have written about what this has done to Indian society in a broader context over the last 10 years. According to research undertaken by a number of different organizations, the average Indian spends approximately 12 to 15 hours per week in front of the television set.[4] In this book, however, we focus on the relationship between popular culture and business.

Bollywood has, with unerring regularity, been able to glean the inside story of the Indian business scene and its changing status. In the 1950s, in actor-producer Raj Kapoor's films, businessmen are portrayed as petty landlords involved in unscrupulous money-lending, land-grabbing, and other illegal activities. The plot usually ran: Poor boy meets rich girl and they fall in love. Rich girl's dad is the villain—a rich businessman or landlord—who frames the poor boy in a crime. After many tears and tirades against the rich, the poor boy and the rich girl live happily ever after. The evil father of the girl either repents for his misdeeds or is nabbed by the cops in the climax. With businessmen portrayed as evil in movie after movie, India's negative perceptions about business were deeply reinforced.

In the 1970s, superstar actor Amitabh Bachchan portrayed an angry young man challenging the authority of businessmen, who were smugglers, kidnappers, counterfeiters, hoarders, or black marketers. The era of Amitabh movies coincided with what we describe earlier as the era of hard socialism. Shortage and corruption were endemic, and the common person—swayed by state propaganda—was convinced that it was crooked businesspeople and not illogical government policies that caused them misery. By the 1980s, many Indians had begun to see through the phony socialism practiced by politicians and the cozy deals they made with businesspeople. Bollywood movies started reflecting this growing cynicism in India. To the gallery of villains were added corrupt cops, officials, and politicians who connived with rich businessmen to exploit poor Indians. In the movie *Inquilaab*, the hero guns down all the newly elected members of a state cabinet. Their fault? They were all crooked businessmen and corrupt politicians who had hijacked the elections.

In the 1990s however, the moviemaker's perception changed in favor of the business class. Businesspeople were no longer shown as the bad guys in society. Movies such as *Dilwale Dulhaniya le Jayenge* and *Hum Apke Hai Kaun* portrayed rich people as the "good guys." This probably happened only after liberal economic policies unshackled the Indian entrepreneur, and Indians found new icons in people like Sabeer Bhatia of Hotmail and Narayana Murthy of Infosys.

Are these examples instances of life imitating art? More likely, it is the other way around. In India particularly, two seemingly contradictory forces seem to be at work: On the one hand, Indians are increasingly shedding their antibusiness mindset and are beginning to appreciate the fact that entrepreneurs like N. R. Narayana Murthy of Infosys and Azim Premji of Wipro are wealth and job creators who do a better job than the state. Sabeer Bhatia, who cofounded Hotmail and sold it to Microsoft for $400 million,[5] is a hero to the Indian youth. In this, Indians seem to be getting closer to American perceptions about business, where individual success and enterprise are admired and emulated.

On the other hand, the persistence of scandals and seemingly anticonsumer activities of Indian corporations has also mirrored public disenchantment of the kind witnessed in the United States. Some egregious examples that have reinforced negative perceptions among Indian investors, consumers, and average citizens are:

• The controversy generated by Enron setting up a power plant in India

- A series of stock market scandals that have shaken investor confidence
- Revelations that corporate India has defaulted on debt to the tune of Rs. 1,00,000 crore, or approximately $23.6 billion.
- The virtual collapse of the state-run mutual fund, Unit Trust of India, endangering the savings of millions of middle-class Indian households
- Revelations by a public advocacy agency, Center for Science and Environment, that the pesticide levels in soft drinks produced by global brand leaders such as Pepsi and Coke were unacceptably high
- Discovery of worms in packets of chocolates manufactured by the market leader Cadbury

Many more instances can be cited and are discussed in subsequent chapters. For the moment, it is important to realize that public perceptions about business are changing in a dynamic manner in India and around the world. For example, the 2008 Edelman Trust Barometer, which measures the level of trust in various institutions among global business leaders, revealed these findings:

- In Brazil, Canada, Germany, the Netherlands, Spain, Sweden, and the United States, "a person like me" is considered the most credible source of information about a company.
- In France, India, Ireland, Mexico, Poland, South Korea, and the United Kingdom, a financial or industry expert comes in first on the list of credible spokespeople.
- The United States is experiencing the widest divide between business and government in the survey's nine-year history, with 58 percent of respondents saying that they trust business to do what's right, an all-time survey high, compared with only 39 percent for government. The gap between business's and government's credibility is also especially wide in developing nations like India, Mexico, and Poland.[6]

Newly evolving attitudes offer both a great challenge and an opportunity for global business to send out the right message and enlarge the constituency of goodwill that is being built after years of distrust and hostility toward business.

The rapid emergence of new technology and the shrinking of the world into one global marketplace are also creating challenges that global companies can no longer afford to ignore.

THE GLOBAL VILLAGE

Technology has strengthened communication channels around the globe, disintegrating national borders to produce what Canadian philosopher Marshall McLuhan foresaw decades ago—the creation of a world so interwoven by shared knowledge that it becomes a "global village."[7] Namely, interactive digital communication channels including blogs, social media networks (such as MySpace and Facebook), and virtual worlds like Second Life make physical proximity irrelevant to people's ability to communicate with one another. This trend has had a monumental impact on business, particularly over the last decade.

Out of the top 100 economies, 51 are multinational corporations, and the remaining 49 are countries.[8] Thus it may not be surprising that individuals have begun to turn to large companies to provide the direction that was more strongly offered in the past by distinct national cultures, communities, and inspirational narratives. Coupled with this is the heightened level of interest in social responsibility on the part of organizations. In Chapter 4, we discuss the growing importance of corporate social responsibility and its implications for corporate reputation. But generally, the public is looking for companies to demonstrate care for the communities in which they operate, from both an environmental and human perspective.

In his book *The Mind of the CEO*, Jeffrey Garten explains, "As the world gets smaller, CEOs will be unable to escape involvement in some of the most difficult political, economic and social problems of our times. There will be no way to avoid operating in countries with fragile economies, weak democratic structures and mega-cities with severely overburdened infrastructures."[9]

The disintegration of national borders, coupled with the liberalization of trade and finance in today's global village, has also fostered an increase in cross-border corporate mergers and the number of multinational corporations.

Today, companies tend to specialize in their core competencies and outsource what remains or, alternatively, merge to integrate the suppliers into their own organization. Statistics compiled by the Centre for Monitoring Indian Economy (CMIE) reveal that in the fiscal year 2003–2004, there were 1,118 mergers and acquisition (M&A) deals in India, including 72 open offers, aggregating Rs. 35,981 crores, or $8.5 billion. Indian acquirers made more than three-fourths of the open offers announced during the fiscal year. But these accounted for less than half of the total offer amount. The largest deal of 2003–2004 was when the government disinvested Rs. 10,542.40 crores (approximately $2.5 billion) of a 10 percent stake in the Oil and Natural Gas Corporation Ltd. (ONGC).[10]

The Tata group is a perfect case study of this booming cross-border M&A climate. In early February 2008, Tata Chemicals announced a deal to acquire the U.S.-based chemical firm General Chemical Industrial Products for $1 billion. This is just one of the latest overseas acquisition efforts in a spree that began in the late 1990s when Tata Tea acquired Tetley for $431 million. Since then, cross-border acquisitions have included that of the United Kingdom's Corus in 2007, Daewoo of Korea, as well as the Land Rover and Jaguar brands from Ford Motors, which was officially announced on March 26, 2008, for the price of approximately $2.5 billion.[11]

On a global level, according to data from Thomson Financial, 2006 was a record-setting year for mergers and acquisitions. Deals totaled $3.79 trillion worldwide—a 38 percent increase over 2005. For the United States alone, deals totaled $1.56 trillion, 36 percent higher than in 2005.[12] In 2007, 42 Fortune 1,000 companies were acquired—the largest number since 2000.[13]

According to the 10th Annual Global CEO Survey, released in 2007 by PricewaterhouseCoopers, 47 percent of all CEOs interviewed were actively engaged in some degree of M&A activity;

however, this activity presented significant business challenges because of the global nature of the transactions. For example, 67 percent of surveyed CEOs said that their companies' efforts to integrate people, processes, and systems took anywhere from one to more than five years, while experts say the optimal time for integration is 6 to 12 months; 63 percent said their companies' postmerger efforts were "average or below average"; and the top three integration-related issues in need of improvement were communications, leadership and decision making, and process and results measurement.[14]

In addition to these challenges prompted by globalization and multinational mergers and acquisitions, many individuals and communities around the world object to the enormous political clout that large corporations wield today.

Outside India, the antiglobalization movement extends beyond traditional union bodies to include young and old consumers, concerned parents, and vocal student activists alike. Earth First! produced a calendar listing important anticorporate protest dates, announcing the first "End Corporate Dominance Month."[15] Vancouver-based *Adbusters* magazine devotes itself to deriding corporate giants—a practice now officially referred to as culture jamming.[16] Some of the routine tactics that culture-jamming activists have employed include plastering the image of Charles Manson's face over a Levi's jeans billboard, hurling pies at Bill Gates, and dumping garbage bags full of shoes outside Nike Town to protest against Pakistani children manufacturing Nike soccer balls for six cents an hour.[17]

Anticorporate activism has also benefited from technological advances. The 1999 antiglobalization protests at the World Trade Organization's (WTO) annual meeting in Seattle were largely coordinated by extensive Web planning.[18] John Delicath, a University of Cincinnati expert on antiglobalization protests, explains that, "Starting with the protests against the WTO in Seattle, so-called 'anti-globalization' activists have used the Internet to build relationships and create networks for sharing ideas, information and resources."[19] Ironically, just as technology has helped companies grow into multinational behemoths, it has also aided their anticorporate adversaries in mounting coordinated campaigns against them.

The 2004 World Social Forum (WSF) was organized for the first time in the city of Mumbai, which is referred to fondly as India's New York. Representatives from trade unions, community organizations, women's groups, economically and socially backward sects, students, and environmentalists got together to oppose the "neocolonialism" imposed on poor nations by "forces of globalization." Big business could hardly ignore or scoff at this gathering—more than 1 million activists loudly demonstrated against the "baneful" clout of big business. Antiglobalization and anti-big-business protests—a common occurrence in developed countries of the West—had arrived in India.[20]

Continual technological advances have also made it difficult for companies to prevent both positive and negative news from reaching individuals in virtually all corners of the world. As a consequence, media outlets have expanded their reach such that events are no longer confined to local communities; they can create reverberations that are felt worldwide. The fact that the total number of telephone users in India is close to 80 million lends support to this statement.[21]

Business leaders today must therefore be prepared not only to handle the national and international media spotlight but also to proactively counter the advocacy groups looking to use today's media environment to compromise corporations' reputations—and bottom line—globally.

HOW TO COMPETE IN A CHANGING ENVIRONMENT

Beyond the situation-specific changes that affected the Indian business climate—from technological advances to the end of British colonialism—there are sweeping macroeconomic changes affecting the very fabric of corporations and their constituents, thus affecting the ways in which global business leaders can best interact with their Indian counterparts. The shifting sociocultural patterns mentioned in previous sections have altered perceptions and influenced businesses operations, be it effectively or ineffectively. For example, antimultinational sentiments often prevail among Indian consumers of all backgrounds, exacerbating already inflamed branding challenges. As the importance of branding grew exponentially, companies had to reconcile these conflicts in strategic ways. Colgate did just that by associating its brand with tenets of protection—an attribute of great importance to the Indian culture. By aligning itself with the characteristics of the people and underscoring its role as a protector, Colgate was able to overcome complex sociocultural factors stemming from decades of colonization, profoundly different social groups, and vast territorial differences.

Similarly, shifting demographics have prompted new competition in the changing Indian business environment. India is a democratic nation with approximately 1 billion people (approximately 350 million of whom could be defined as belonging to the middle class), 26 different states, 15 national languages, and 6 major religions, making it no small task for corporations to transcend this diversity and compete successfully. In addition, corporations must compete not only with one another, but also with small local shops that cater to traditional Indian needs and mentalities. Thus a number of challenges exist, the largest of which is isolating one message to appeal to an entire diverse population.

One solution to this seemingly impossible task is to appeal to the things nearly all people can agree on. For Indians, no matter what demographic category they belong to, these common preferences include music, film, and sports. In an advertising campaign, automaker Hyundai successfully leveraged these affinities by making use of celebrity endorsements (thus, piggybacking on the popularity of Bollywood films) to raise consumer awareness of its new Santro brand. Not only did Hyundai align itself with a universally accepted lifestyle, but it built a 12 percent market share based on its success.

Similarly, Britannia Industries promoted a new brand of biscuits through the endorsement of two cricket celebrities, Sachin Tendulkar and Saurav Ganguly. This partnership prompted a successful entrée into a competitive and convoluted Indian market.

But, despite success stories like these, even well-respected companies face attacks in this antibusiness environment. For example, even the Tata group had to face widespread protests when it decided to set up a steel plant at Gopalpur in the eastern state of Orissa. A large number of activist organizations accused the Tatas of displacing thousands of people from their homes without adequately compensating them. Some of the organizations also took the legal route and approached the state High Court. The Tatas continued getting bad press coverage, in spite of the fact that in India the group has a most impeccable record for social responsibility. The activists won the battle, and the High Court did not allow the Tatas to evict people from the proposed site of the plant.[22]

In the United States, protests of this kind are more widespread and better organized. For example, when Nike faced allegations of unfair labor practices in Asia, including children working in dangerous conditions for low wages, the company initially denied the charges. The media's portrayal of Nike became increasingly negative, and television footage of Asian children working in sweatshoplike conditions furthered the controversy. While protests against Nike for these alleged practices were relatively contained and did not have a considerable impact on sales, the problem of the company's labor and environmental policies continued to reappear in the press for years.[23] One could question how long this can go on before it does have a measurable effect on the company's profitability.

So how do managers adapt to the challenges of a business environment that is constantly in flux but seems to be moving in the direction of greater scrutiny, less favorable impressions of corporations, and more diverse and complex constituencies? In the next section, we look at some of the ways companies can stay on course while navigating these choppy waters.

Recognize the Changing Environment

First, managers need to recognize that the business environment is constantly evolving. The short-term orientation of today's managers rarely gives them an opportunity to look at the big picture of how this changing environment affects the company's image with a variety of constituencies. Over the long term, this can have damaging results.

McDonald's in the United States took note when, in the late 1980s and early 1990s, environmentally conscious consumers raised concerns over the company's use of nonrecyclable plastic "clamshell" packaging for many of its popular sandwiches. Disapproving customers mailed the containers to the company's headquarters at Oak Brook, Illinois, in addition to sending thousands of hostile letters. So in August 1990, McDonald's forged an agreement with the Environmental Defense Fund (EDF), an environmental research and lobbying group, to form a joint task force and brainstorm ideas to reduce the company's annual solid-waste production.

The decision tapped into the company's awareness of growing consumer concerns. Edward H. Rensi, then president of McDonald's U.S.A., explained that the company had first adamantly insisted that its foam packaging was not detrimental to the environment, only to realize that "our customers just don't feel good about it. So we're changing."[24]

Coca-Cola took note of this rapidly evolving business environment when, in January 2006, the University of Michigan suspended the purchase of its products on campus.[25] The action had nothing to do with pricing or the products themselves; rather, it was taken based on environmental concerns in India and labor issues in Colombia. Among the allegations was a contention that products contained unacceptable levels of insecticides. (PepsiCo's products were also found to contain unacceptable levels of pesticides.)

The global business and communication implications of this revelation and the university's subsequent reaction are manifold: First, the University of Michigan's decision was prompted by one man, Amit Srivastava, who ran a small nonprofit out of his home in California. He mobilized students on campus to petition for the ban—an organizational feat that, just a few years before, would have been unthinkable. Second, these visceral reactions on the part of students applied so much pressure that the company agreed to open its overseas facilities to independent, transparent, third-party environmental and labor audits.[26] Finally, it points to a major evolution in business—that sustainable business practices are becoming core brand values that can inspire change. Coca-Cola's sustainability efforts changed dramatically over the course of a year, and the company appeared on the 2007 Global 100 Most Sustainable Corporations in the World list.

In India, there were widespread protests over the use of child labor in the fireworks factories of Sivakasi in Tamil Nadu. In fact, schoolgoing children were urged not to burst firecrackers on Diwali, the most important festival of the Hindus. The campaign was so successful that hundreds of thousands of schoolchildren signed pledges not to use firecrackers. Sales of firecrackers actually declined in big Indian cities. To tide over this crisis, All India Federation of Fireworks Associations issued many advertisements in newspapers and magazines, trying to counter the blitz of negative publicity. One such advertisement in the *Sunday Express*, March 3, 2004, said: "We are workers' children and not working children. Every child is our customer and no child is our worker. Fireworks are made for children and not by children. If you still have doubts, you are invited to Sivakasi, the Mini Japan of India. See for yourself, interview the District Collector, Deputy Chief Inspector of Factories, Deputy Chief Controller of Explosives, and you can find that not even a single child is employed in any fireworks factory in Sivakasi. Sivakasi means Education and Hard Work. Sivakasi means Fireworks, Matches and Printing. Sivakasi means Social Services and Public Welfare Services." This battle continued with both activists and factory owners trying to use mainstream media to get their point of view across to consumers.[27]

One of the most important challenges facing senior managers is the profoundly unsettling impact of technological change. Andrew Grove, cofounder and CEO of Intel Corporation, explained, "We make a cult of how wonderful it is that the rate of [technological] change is so fast. But ... what happens when the rate of change is so fast that before a technological innovation gets deployed, or halfway through the process of being deployed, [an] innovation sweeps in and creates a destructive interference with the first one?"[28] While many people agree that technology has helped business, they believe that it also leads to greater uncertainty for business leaders and consumers alike.

Unlike many shifts in the market that companies can anticipate by keeping their fingers on the pulse of change, such as evolving consumer tastes, technological innovations can happen swiftly and have profound effects. Companies need to quickly determine what, if anything, they need to do to respond to such changes.

Adapt to the Environment without Compromising Principles

It is necessary that companies adapt to the changing environment without changing what they stand for or compromising their principles. As an example, Starbucks, the Seattle-based coffee company in the United States, adopted guidelines aimed at improving working conditions at its foreign coffee suppliers. Starbucks's guidelines called for overseas suppliers to pay wages and benefits that at least "address the basic needs of workers and their families." For example, the company asked suppliers to allow child labor only when it did not "interfere with mandated education." Global human rights groups applauded these guidelines, saying that they substantially widened the possibilities for corporate codes of conduct.

In another instance, chemical giant Monsanto faced challenges when its foray into genetically engineered crops met with resistance from protesters who labeled its products "Frankenfoods." Protests were not just limited to the company's headquarters in St. Louis; they spread to some of Monsanto's large, visible customers, forcing McDonald's, for one, to announce that they would no longer use the company's genetically modified (GM) potatoes.[29]

Monsanto faced similar protests when it launched GM cotton in India in partnership with Maharashtra Hybrid Seed Company (MAHYCO). Many environmentalists and nongovernment organizations (NGOs) raised objections to the commercial use of Bt cotton, a genetically modified form of the crop due to the insertion of the soil bacterium *Bacillus thuringiensis*. They pointed out that the field trials and results were clouded in secrecy and that the initial field trials were considered illegal by Greenpeace and other activist groups. Environmentalist Vandana Shiva's Research Foundation for Science, Technology and Ecology, Dehradun, filed a public-interest litigation in the Supreme Court against the department of biotechnology, alleging large-scale violations of biosafety guidelines during the field trials of Bt cotton. Members of the Karnataka Rajya Raitha Sangha (KRRS) repeatedly burned genetically engineered cotton crops in the state on the plea that it was harmful to the environment and encouraged monoculture.[30]

Meanwhile, in the United States, the protests against "Frankenfoods" ultimately took their toll on Monsanto's stock price in the late 1990s, despite the company's meeting Wall Street expectations. In response, Monsanto adopted education and outreach as their new approach to handling the "GM backlash." Historically, the company had been perceived as aggressively marketing products that the public did not understand or trust. Now, Monsanto communicated "the new Monsanto pledge," which outlined five key elements, including dialogue, transparency, respect, sharing, and delivering benefits.[31] While the company continued to produce GM foods, it also worked with consumer groups and farmers to foster greater understanding of the role of biotechnology in food production. This was viewed positively by many who had previously opposed Monsanto's approach.

Arie de Geus of the MIT Sloan School of Management analyzed the strengths of what he defined as "living companies"—a group of 30 companies ranging in age from 100 to 700 years scattered throughout North America, Europe, and Japan.[32] One of the primary reasons these companies—including DuPont, W.R. Grace, Sumitomo, and Siemens—managed to endure has been the result of their ability to adapt to the rapidly evolving environment in which they live. De Geus explains, "As wars, depressions, technologies, and politics surged and ebbed, they always seemed to excel at keeping their feelers out, staying attuned to whatever was going on. For information, they sometimes relied on packets carried over vast distances by portage and ship, yet they managed to react in a timely fashion to whatever news they received. They were good at learning and adapting."[33]

Do Not Assume That Problems Will Magically Disappear

If we assume that things will only get worse, we will be better off in today's complex environment. For example, Sony executives let a bad situation turn worse before addressing the fallout. In October 2005, a blogger broke the story that Sony BMG Music Entertainment distributed a copy-protection scheme of CDs that contained rootkit software, which self-installs on computers and allows hackers to access the systems, posing huge security threats. Within hours, the story was percolating throughout the blogosphere, but Sony executives turned a blind eye, and the Sony BMG's president of global digital business, Thomas Hesse, made matters worse with this statement made to National Public Radio (NPR) on November 4: "Most people don't even know what a rootkit is, so why should they care about it?"

Needless to say, the problem didn't disappear over time. Bloggers, traditional media, and consumers grew increasingly incensed by the company's disregard, and class-action lawsuits soon followed. Had the company's executives anticipated the length of the story's appeal and had they addressed the issue at its inception in the blogosphere, they no doubt would have changed their communication strategy.

Sony executives had no way of knowing that the rootkit story would run as long as it did. If they had anticipated the length of the story's appeal, no doubt they would have changed their communication strategy. Most managers assume that the public has a short memory about problems companies get into. In fact, consumers have longer memories than one might think, as witnessed by boycotts of companies such as Coke, Pepsi, Parke-Davis, and so on.

Some companies seem to be getting it right, but most are still getting it wrong. Bata India Ltd., a subsidiary of Bata (BN) BV of the Netherlands, is India's largest manufacturer of leather goods. It allowed itself to get into a battle with labor unions in West Bengal. Ultimately, the union prevailed over the company, which had to sign a three-year wage agreement with the labor union at Batanagar in West Bengal, its largest manufacturing unit in India. Confrontations with trade unions did not help Bata, and frequent closures ensured that the company lost the leader status to new rivals in the market.[34]

USX, the former U.S. Steel Corporation, adopted a different approach. The president of the vast steel operation, Thomas J. Usher, unexpectedly appeared at the offices of the United Steelworkers local to listen to what union leaders had on their minds about the company's largest mill. The president of the local union said that this kind of behavior was unusual: "Other heads of U.S. Steel would never have dreamed of being in the same room with the union people. He is bringing in a breath of fresh air."

This book focuses on approaches such as USX's, although no one can say for sure how well the company will fare in the years to come. Recognizing that the union's interests are essentially the same as management's is a stretch for managers mired in old-fashioned thinking. President John Kennedy once referred to autocratic managers at U.S. Steel as "a bunch of SOBs," who would never have been able to step up to the changes in the environment the way Mr. Usher did.

Keep Corporate Communication Connected to Strategy

Corporate communication must be closely linked to a company's overall vision and strategy. Since few managers recognize the importance of the communication function, they are reluctant to hire the quality staff necessary to bring success in today's global business environment. As a result, communication people are often kept out of the loop.

Successful companies connect communication with strategy through structure, such as having the head of corporate communication report directly to the CEO. The advantage of this kind of reporting relationship is that the communications professional can get the company's strategy directly from those at the top of the organization. For example, to combat sociocultural and demographic complexities, companies like Unilever, GlaxoSmithKline, and Citibank have appointed Indian CEOs for their Indian operations to tailor products more effectively to suit different markets. This ensures that all of the company's communications will be more strategic and focused (see Chapter 3 for more on structure).

In Chapter 10, we take a look at how Johnson & Johnson handled the Tylenol cyanide crisis of the early 1980s. Part of what helped the company so successfully deal with this dire situation was the existence of the J&J credo, a companywide code of ethics that spells out J&J's promises to its many constituencies. This helped guide the company's actions during an episode that could have irreparably damaged the Tylenol brand and possibly J&J itself.

Companies' corporate communication teams play a pivotal role in defining a corporate mission—the cornerstone of a company's overarching strategy—and communicating that mission to internal and external constituents. Given today's rapidly changing environment, a clear-cut corporate mission not only keeps employees aligned with what the company is striving to be but can also act as a source of stability for consumers weary of the constant change surrounding them.

CONCLUSION

The business environment is prone to constant change. The terrorist attacks in New York and Washington, D.C., in September 2001 and the attack on Indian Parliament in December 2001, as well as terrorist strikes in other parts of India, have added another dimension of uncertainty to an already fragile business environment. Everyone involved in business today, whether at a large corporation with a national union to deal with or a small business looking to make its mark in the international arena, needs to communicate strategically. The way organizations adapt and modify their behavior, as manifested through their communications, will determine the success of global business in the twenty-first century.

Chapter 2

Strategic Communication for Multinational Corporations

I n Chapter 1, we examine the changing environment for global business over the last century in the context of India's role as an emerging business leader. In this chapter, we explore how these changes have affected corporate communication and why the changing environment requires a different approach to the function.

Let us begin this chapter with understanding the basic theory behind all communication, whether individual or organizational in nature. Much of this theory comes from Aristotle, the ancient Greek philosopher. In modern times, communication experts have adapted these theories to individuals, as they communicate in writing and speech.

Interestingly, when examined closely, these same basic theories apply in the corporate communication context too—that is, in the way organizations communicate with various groups of people. Communication, more than any other field in business, has implications for everyone within an organization—from the peon to the CEO. Overall, most Indian managers have learned to think strategically about their business, but few think strategically about what they spend most of their time doing—communicating.

This chapter discusses how communication theory developed and, further, how that theory can be used to work out communication strategies in organizations. The discussion then turns from the application of communication theory to making the critical link between corporate communication and the firm's overall corporate strategy.

EVOLVING COMMUNICATION THEORY

Most theories associated with communication are based on notions that can be traced back thousands of years. In ancient Greece, the subject we now refer to as communication was known as rhetoric, that is, the use of language to persuade the listener to do something. The Greeks had a high regard for the art of rhetoric.

Aristotle, who studied under Plato and taught in Athens from 367–347 BC, is most often associated with the development of rhetoric. In Aristotle's major work, *The Art of Rhetoric*, we can find the roots of modern communication theory.[1] Early in this seminal text, Aristotle defines the composition of every speech:

> Every speech is composed of three parts: the speaker, the subject of which he treats, and the person to whom it is addressed, I mean the hearer, to whom the end or object of the speech refers.

Working out a meaningful and focused communication strategy is critical at all times—whether an organization is trying to develop a coherent identity for itself through image advertising, to communicate effectively with employees about VRS (voluntary retirement scheme), to convince shareholders that the company is still worth investing in, or simply to get customers to buy more of its products.

This strategy depends on thinking carefully about the same three parts that Aristotle used to describe the components of speech:

1. Instead of a speaker, the first component in a corporate communication strategy is the organization.
2. The second component, in place of Aristotle's "person . . . to whom the end or object of the speech refers," is the constituency.
3. The final component, which Aristotle describes as "the subject of which he treats," is referred to as *messages*.

The corporate communication strategy framework, seen in Figure 2-1, synthesizes ideas from Aristotle and communications

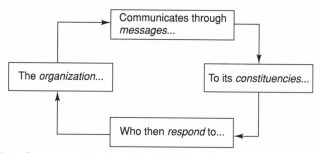

Figure 2-1 Corporate Communication Strategy Framework

theorist Mary Munter to form a useful framework for analyzing corporate communication.[2]

As we look at the interaction among the three variables, we see that each is connected to the other. As U.S. communication theorist Annette Shelby states, "The unique interrelationships of these variables determine which messages will be effective and which will not."[3] In addition, the framework is circular rather than linear, which reflects the reality that communication of any kind is an ongoing process rather than a system with a beginning and an end.

CORPORATE COMMUNICATION STRATEGIES AT WORK

Let's further develop each of these variables and apply them to real situations and see how they operate in practice.

Setting an Effective Organization Strategy

The first part of an effective corporate communication strategy concerns the organization itself. The three subsets of an organization strategy include: (1) determining what the objectives are for the particular communication, (2) deciding what resources are available for achieving those objectives, and (3) diagnosing the organization's reputation.

Determining Objectives

Like an individual, an organization has many different reasons for deciding to communicate. For example, a company might want to announce to employees a change in its benefits package for the upcoming year. Let's suppose that the organization has decided to withdraw a perquisite like employee's annual leave travel allowance, popularly referred to as LTA in India, as the result of a profit squeeze. In this case, the company instead of retrenching personnel has decided to bring down its operating cost by cutting down on the perquisites package of its employees in order to be able to ride out tough times. Here we note that the company's communication objective is more than just announcing the revised package; it must also convince employees that it has a good reason for taking something away from them. Thus the objective here is to inform the employees of the current situation and how this is a more acceptable option than loss of jobs. Effective communication would ensure that the employees accept that this short-term bitter medicine may have long-term benefits that will improve the condition of the organization and the employees, who would accrue the benefits, in turn. It would also prevent a far worse alternative: the loss of jobs. This approach to communication aims at making employees willing partners in the belt-tightening process, rather than suspicious, hostile, and unmotivated workers.

In contrast are the problems of communication with the U.S. cereal manufacturer that enters the Indian market—a scenario that is not uncommon among any multinational company entering the market for the first time. Expecting a waltz through the breakfast market, the multinational does not think it relevant to study India's cultural ethos and instead spends time and other resources on just pushing its product via advertising. The company expects Indians to embrace this new breakfast habit and does not tackle the cultural barriers.

These barriers include, for example, the price barrier, since the U.S. product is much more expensive than its nearest Indian cereal competitor; then there is the habits barrier, which stems from the fact that it is tough to break into the "hot and fresh" breakfast norm of an Indian household by offering a cold cereal alternative. The company's objective, then, is to create a demand among Indian consumers for something that fits in with neither their spending nor their consumption pattern. The company does not give a thought to the multicultural complexity and its ramifications. Instead, it assumes that India too has the near-homogenous lifestyle of American society—where most of the households have a cold cereal breakfast, rush to their respective workplaces or study centers, and commute back home for an evening of microwavable dinners.

Most households in India, however, have a different and more leisurely lifestyle. Here, hot and fresh breakfast items are still the norm, ranging from puris and parathas in the north to idlis and dosas in the south. Not surprisingly, the U.S. company's presentation of the cereal as a lifestyle product fails to displace the traditional breakfast habits, even in urban India.

We can also look into the lessons learned by the U.S. multinational in the aftermath of product failure and the rectification exercise it undertook. The company takes stock of the situation and nails its unsuccessful communication exercise. In the next phase of advertising, it promotes the cereal as a nutritionally superior breakfast item and not just a convenience or lifestyle product. Focusing on a smart strategy of presenting the product as a health-giving and intelligence-boosting cereal for growing children, the company seems to have found the right selling proposition for concerned mothers, who in India are more than willing to put in extra money and effort in a bid for their children to secure higher school grades. Stress on studies is almost a national paranoia, and the company looks like it has found the right niche. In the ongoing example, consumers in India would easily identify the U.S. cereal manufacturer as Kellogg's India and its saga of ups and downs in the Indian marketplace.[4]

In contrast, corporate behemoth McDonald's does not make assumptions on the nature of its constituency; instead, it acknowledges that consumption habits do not translate across cultural lines and adapts its product accordingly. Since the opening of its first restaurant in India in October 1996, McDonald's has offered a range of local, regional, and national food items while aligning the customized options with its trademark fast-food brand offerings: Chicken Maharaja Mac, Chicken McCurry Pan, and McAloo Tikki, for example. Also understanding the importance of vegetarian practices, McDonald's outlets across the country ensure that separate cooking equipment is used for vegetarian and nonvegetarian products, and crew members who prepare vegetarian items wear green aprons to help identify them. In observance of traditional tastes and practices, no beef or pork items are served. This is a prime example of an organization's messages meeting its needs as well as those of its constituencies through successful marketing and brand identification.

Notice that in all these cases, the response from the constituency in question is what is most important. That is the basis for defining an objective: what does the organization want each constituency to do as a result of the communication? Management communication expert Mary Munter writes in *Guide to Managerial Communication* that managerial communication is successful only if you get the desired response from your audience.[5] To get that response, you have to think strategically about your communication, including setting measurable objectives.

Determining What Resources Are Available

Determining how to communicate about something like the VRS or introducing a new product into a market depends heavily on what resources are available to the organization, including money, human resources, and time.

Money

Let's go back to our example of the company that has decided to withdraw the LTA perquisite of its employees. The company must decide whether it is better to simply announce the program as clearly as possible to its employees—say, through the company newsletter, via e-mail, or on the company's intranet—or to hire a benefits consultant with experience in helping other companies sell scaled-back benefits to employees. The first option looks less expensive in the short term than the second. However, if the employees revolt because they feel they are losing something for no good reason, the company might end up spending far more than it would have if it had hired the more experienced consultant in the first place.

Unfortunately, most companies often err on the side of short-term, inexpensive solutions to communication problems because they do not look at the problem from the perspective of the constituency in question. This is similar to a problem individuals often have in communicating: they look at their own needs rather than those of their audience and end up having difficulty achieving their communication objective.

Human Resources

Human resources are also an important factor in determining the success or failure of a company in achieving its communication objectives. Typically, too few are assigned to deal with communication tasks, and those involved are often inexperienced or unqualified.

Imagine a company that has just gone public and has decided to create an investor relations function to deal with shareholder relations and communication with securities analysts. It could assign one person to do all these things, or it could decide that it really needs three. The best approach varies with the size of the company and its shareholder base. Let's look at the case of a well-known, multi-billion-dollar U.S. company that turned this function over to one person with weak communication skills rather than devote two or three experts to deal with the different constituencies involved. In this case, it was not a question of whether the company could afford to pay more people to do the job correctly; it was lack of understanding about how important corporate communication really is and the limitations put on the human resources needed to accomplish a specific task.

This Fortune 500 company changed its approach after analysts started to downgrade its stock on the New York Stock Exchange despite healthy prospects for the company's future. The CEO discovered that analysts felt that the investor relations person at the company was not interested in giving them sufficient information to rate the company's stock. This led them to believe that something was wrong. The investor relations person, on the other hand, was actually trying to do two or three jobs at the same time and simply could not keep up with the demands of the job. After this incident, the company hired two more professionals to handle the job properly, creating a more effective and efficient investor relations function. Its stock price shot back to where it should have been all along.

In the United States, the Department of Labor rated public relations as one of the top 10 growth industries, projecting a rate of increase of almost 50 percent through the year 2005, and therefore, companies are increasingly investing both money and human resources in corporate communications.[6] These trends are global in their reach and can be safely extrapolated to reach the Indian majors in years to come.

Time

Like human resources and money, time is also a critical factor in determining an organization's corporate communication strategy. Let's look at two approaches for dealing with the same problem involving the allocation of time.

In spite of their efforts, several Japanese, U.S., and European giants could not get a stable foothold in the slippery markets of India. The U.S. cereal maker mentioned earlier failed to shift the Indian breakfast habits to cornflakes and milk. Instead, it was forced to add biscuits to its menu while Indians continued to eat idlis, parathas, and puris. What was missing here was a quick response and time sensitivity. Not realizing the importance of being alert and responsive in uncharted waters, it moved like a giant with a slow turnaround time.

However, three Korean corporates—Hyundai Motor Company, Samsung, and LG Electronics Corporation—proved themselves equal to the challenges of the Indian market. Hyundai, South Korea's top automobile manufacturer, in 1996 set up a wholly owned subsidiary, Hyundai Motor India Limited, with a state-of-the-art plant near Chennai. The company sold over 350,000 cars in a record time of 50 months since the commencement of its commercial production, to become the second biggest manufacturer in India.[7]

In the consumer durables market, Samsung and LG have secured leading market shares, displacing old and trusted brands like Onida, Sony, Usha Lexus, Godrej, and Videocon. Business analysts attribute the rapid rise of their market shares to the companies' speedy and flexible market strategizing and implementation. For example, Samsung recognized that the Internet was a quick and reasonably priced channel for marketing and support activities. So in 1998, within three years of setting its operations in India, the Korean company launched an e-enterprise as a business facilitator and posted all its communication and business processes on the Internet. As a result of this, all communication—internally and to consumers—became much faster and easier, and instant online stock updates reduced delivery times to the consumers. The Indian customer was delighted with these new marketing and communication initiatives, and thus consumer satisfaction for Samsung products multiplied. This readily translated into increased sales.

LG got the Foreign Investment Promotion Board's clearance to set up shop in January 1997, and it started operations that May. The products hit the market later that year. "It was the fastest nationwide launch by a company," says an LG official. The Korean multinational, credited with launching the latest and the best in consumer goods in India, added another weapon in its arsenal—that is, being agile and fast on its feet.

"The trick is to stay ahead in thinking," says Ganesh Mahalingam, general manager marketing, LG Electronics India. "Because we are successful, people think we must be doing something right and follow us. So we have to keep changing our benchmark every quarter."[8] This increased awareness of managing time—an important business resource—is proving advantageous for the Korean multinationals.

The communication program of the U.S. cereal maker mentioned earlier failed to bridge the cultural differences between American and Indian lifestyles, and to top it off, the company took an unduly long time in readjusting its business strategies. Even in the repositioned avatar, the product has a long way to go before it dislodges traditional dishes from the Indian breakfast table. In stark contrast to this business blunder of overlooking cultural perceptions (especially of U.S. products), McDonald's allocated resources up front to adapt to the Indian marketplace, and the company has since profited as a result.

The allocation of time, like the allocation of all resources, should be determined by what it will really take to achieve the company's objective rather than to seek a short-term answer. In some cases, this might mean allocating more resources than the organization would like. But almost always, the organization is better off allocating the resources up front. Correcting mistakes in corporate communication can be a costly proposition.

For example, on July 23, 1995, a Mumbai tabloid featured an ad for Tuff shoes that had Indian models Madhu Sapre and Milind Soman posing in the nude with a python wrapped around them, just about covering their vitals.[9] The controversy about and protests against this ad dragged on for a long time. The ad agencies defended their creative rights while the nation pooh-poohed the couple's audacity. A heated debate engulfed the advertising and corporate world, but the brand lost its momentum as the company failed to rectify or capitalize on the ensuing scenario. Both time and opportunity were wasted.

DIAGNOSING THE ORGANIZATION'S REPUTATION

In addition to setting objectives for a communication and deciding what resources are available to accomplish that objective, organizations must also determine what kind of image credibility they have with the constituencies in question. An organization's overall reputation with constituencies is based on several factors. In Chapter 4, we get into this in greater detail when we talk about image, identity, and reputation, but it is also a critical factor in the development of all communication strategies, whether specifically related to image or not.

Image credibility is based on a constituency's perception of the organization rather than the reality of the organization itself. As an example, think of an Indian university that is trying to generate positive publicity in the international press. This might prove to be difficult if the university is not well known outside its own country. Its image credibility in this situation would be low because international press representatives would have limited experience with the institution compared to an institution that already has an international reputation, like Harvard in the United States or Oxford in the United Kingdom. Thus, no matter what kind of resources the university puts behind this effort, it will be an uphill battle.

Worse than limited image credibility is credibility that is lacking or damaged. In 1992, Indian chocolate manufacturers reeled from the blow of the Environmental Research Laboratory's (ERL) finding of unacceptably high content of nickel in chocolates manufactured in the country. Some mainline publications, like *The Times* of India, focused on the harmful presence of nickel in Indian chocolates. Immediate concern followed the oft-repeated question, "Is nickel carcinogenic?" Popular chocolates positioned as a gift now attracted immense public ire. The chocolate manufacturers, led by Cadbury India, unveiled a series of confidence-restoring campaigns. Cadbury ran advertisements in almost all major publications: "How could we ever do anything to harm you?"[10] The chairman tried to salvage the situation by stating that there was no minimum prescribed level of nickel content laid down by food and drug authorities of any country. To add to this, Cadbury went all out with a full-fledged communication campaign disclaiming the ERL findings. The focused advertising campaign cited "44 years of trust" as the reason why the company's products could never be harmful. The chocolate sales did take a dip in those controversial days, but Cadbury survived to see a brighter tomorrow because of its proactive crisis-management approach and image-building communication that projected the company as a concerned and responsive corporate citizen.

A more recent example of corporate reputations among global companies is that of Mattel. The fall of 2006 kick-started a string of product recalls by toy maker Mattel resulting from problems that included choking hazards and excessive levels of lead paint in many of its products. While all of the affected toys were manufactured in China in 2006 and 2007, the company's credibility took repeated hits with the news of each recall, from that of magnetic toys with faulty designs in November 2006 to Fisher-Price brand toys with high levels of lead paint in August 2007 to lead-paint-laden Barbie accessories in September 2007.

Once the most credible of U.S. toy makers, Mattel found its credibility with investors and customers to be damaged because of the widespread recalls. During the height of the high-profile recalls, the stock value fell as much as 25 percent, hitting a 2007 low in September. However, Mattel executives took aggressive action to help upend the credibility crisis, opting for complete transparency and leveraging digital communications channels to deliver messages to constituents. For example, in August 2007 CEO Bob Eckert candidly addressed constituents with his concern and his commitment to safety via a streaming Web video that was posted on Mattel's Web site. The communications team also launched an advertising campaign with the headline "Because your children are our children, too," and spokespeople constantly reiterated the company's investigation of the safety breaches and communicated openly with the media.

Sometimes, damaged image credibility can result from circumstances beyond an organization's control rather than from any specific actions or missteps taken by the company itself. Mattel fits this description to some degree, as its Chinese manufacturers were the root of the problem; their glaring safety oversights instigated the rash of recalls. While Mattel's executives should have ensured more stringent safety requirements and monitoring standards, there are really two credibility crises at play: the handling of the product recall by Mattel, and the overall reputation crisis of China, whose credibility took additional hits in the summer of 2007 after a pet food recall that stemmed from products made in China.

Thus, we can see that an organization's reputation is an important factor in setting a coherent communication strategy. For simple tasks, this is not a problem. But in other cases, the image credibility an organization has built with a specific constituency can make a huge difference in determining the success or failure the organization has in achieving its objectives.

Take the first KFC outlet in the southern Indian city of Bangalore. It was temporarily closed for two months in 1996 after food inspectors charged that the chicken had illegally high levels of monosodium glutamate—a toxic chemical used as a flavor enhancer in processed foods. The second outlet also suffered a similar fate when the visiting city officials found the chemical sodium aluminum phosphate—a toxic and carcinogenic food additive that imparts a crunchy texture to the covering of flour—in the coating mix imported from the United States. A follow-up inspection turned up a pair of flies buzzing around the Colonel's kitchen, and so the restaurant was closed 23 days after it opened. Various public-interest groups and activists took up cudgels against KFC's multinational antecedents and targeted it as serving substandard and unhealthy products in the developing countries. The multinationals were accused of having dual and discriminatory standards by providing poor-quality goods when dealing with less affluent economies such as India's but showing greater respect by providing superior products and service when dealing with economically better-off western counterparts.

KFC's closing has to be viewed against the deeper perspective of ongoing multinational distrust in India (as discussed in Chapter 1) where multinational corporations (MNCs) were perceived to be operating as profiteers and buccaneers while exerting little effort to become responsible corporate citizens. The MNC culture was viewed as being detrimental to third-world countries, which roused the ire of nationalists and consumer interest groups.

While these corporate examples represent lacking or damaged credibility, Indian technology conglomerate Infosys managed to build and maintain its credibility and image on the reputations of its chief executives, namely, Chairman and Chief Mentor N. R. Narayana Murthy. His widely noted sincerity and humility helped make Infosys a trusted corporate powerhouse as well as a symbol of India's technological dexterity and growing global business leadership. Infosys's corporate reputation is consistently ranked by TNS India as being among the top-five companies (along with the Tata Group, as discussed in Chapter 4) thanks in part to its valued management. It is a case where information and products are less image defining than the character behind it.

N. R. Narayana Murthy

The three considerations for creating an effective organization strategy—setting objectives, deciding on the proper allocation of resources, and diagnosing the organization's reputation—are the building blocks upon which all other steps in communication strategy depend. A second set of issues the organization can turn to is an assessment of the constituencies involved.

ANALYSIS OF CONSTITUENCIES

Analyzing constituencies is similar to analyzing your audience when you want to plan a speech or write a memo. The analysis determines (1) who your organization's constituencies are, (2) what each thinks about the organization, and (3) what each knows about the communication in question. We look at each of these in turn.

Who Are Your Organization's Constituencies?

The answer to who your organization's constituencies are is sometimes obvious, but more often than not, it will take careful consideration to analyze who the relevant constituencies are for a particular corporate message. Do not be fooled into thinking that it is always obvious who the main constituency is. Usually, constituencies come from a group that is primary to the organization, but a secondary group can also be the focus for a particular communication (see Table 2-1).

Companies have different sets of constituencies depending on the nature, size, and reach (i.e., global or domestic, local versus regional or national) of their businesses. While a company could list its constituencies on a piece of paper (as in Table 2-1), it should resist thinking of its constituencies as too fixed or too separate. An organization's primary constituency (or constituencies) can change over time. In a time of crisis, for example, it may be wise for a company to focus more intently on its relations with the media—which it may normally consider a secondary constituency—in order to manage its reputation and attempt to minimize negative press. Additionally, constituencies should not be thought about in

Table 2-1   Constituencies of an Organization

Primary

- Employees
- Customers
- Shareholders
- Communities

Secondary

- Media
- Suppliers
- Government
  - Local
  - Regional
  - National
- Creditors

"silos," or groups defined by a single common interest (investors, media, etc.) and thus thought of separately from other audiences, because the lines between them can blur.

When employees are also shareholders in a company, for instance, they belong simultaneously to two constituency groups. An employee stock option plan or ESOP, for example, is mainly used as a motivation tool. By vesting stock options with its employees, a company is vesting a part of its ownership with its employees. This gives the employees a sense of belonging to the organization and motivates them to perform. The employees would also make efforts to enhance the company's performance so that the market price of a share would increase, and this in turn would benefit them. Further, the lock-in period ensures employee retention. Stock options work best in companies that require a high level of intellectual capital, such as in software and financial services. In India, employees of companies like Infosys Technologies, Satyam Computers, Wipro, and Bharti have benefited from ESOPs.

Also recognize that constituencies interact with one another, especially in the age of digital communications platforms, such as social media networks and blogs, and an organization must sometimes work through one to reach another. For instance, if a department store is focused on revitalizing a customer service focus to establish more loyalty (and sales) from its customer constituency, it must reinforce this mission with employees before customers will see results. An example of this can be seen in the typical employee-customer-profit chain model created by big chain stores that track success from management behavior through employee attitudes to customer satisfaction and ultimately financial performance.

An ideal example can be seen in the high-flying success of the Indian chain of retail stores, Shopper's Stop. This outward-looking company was the first to professionalize Indian retailing in an industry dominated by family-owned mom-and-pop stores. Shopper's Stop pioneered the luxury, multiproduct chain of department stores in major metropolises of the country, employing only qualified graduates and professionals. B. S. Nagesh—the CEO of Shopper's Stop—credits its success to the fact that it is a very open and a flat organization.[11] Every employee, from the CEO to the shop-floor assistant, is called a customer-care associate. This drives home with clarity that the desired focus of every employee is the customer. Shopper's Stop has defined its strategy as making shopping a pleasurable experience and to convert shoppers into actual buyers. To further retain customers and tempt them to come back for repeat purchases, the company has a customer loyalty program called First Citizen Club, which has over 70,000 members and generates nearly 40 percent of the company's sales.[12]

Constituencies can have competing interests and different perceptions of a company. For example, cutting employee benefits may be welcomed by shareholders but in all likelihood won't be popular with employees. Finally, keep in mind that communications intended for one constituency often reach others.

One marketing vice president's individual communication experience brings this point to life. The executive vice president to whom he reported had decided to cut the group's administrative support staff because of the increased use of voice mail technology to handle communications while professionals were away from their desks. This vice president detailed his plan for cutting the support staff by almost two-thirds in a memo to the vice president in charge of human resources. The plan involved laying off five assistants in the department over a period of six months; a number of them had been with the firm for several years.

As usual, the marketing VP typed up his thoughts in rough form on his PC and e-mailed the message to his assistant, asking her to format the letter and print the final draft on his letterhead. Although his assistant was not one of the five affected by the layoffs, she could not help but empathize with her colleagues of many years, and within an hour the marketing VP had a revolt on his hands.

Now, obviously, he didn't intend his assistant to be a part of his constituency, nor did he stop to think about her reaction to the change when he asked her to format and print the letter to the HR VP. Nonetheless, she became a conduit to a more important constituency—the employees who would actually be affected by the plan.

This simple example is instructive to organizations seeking to communicate at a more macro level as well. Just as we cannot always control the flow of information to one constituency alone on an individual level, at the corporate level, the same set of problems arises.

What Is the Constituency's Attitude toward the Organization?

In addition to analyzing who the constituencies for a particular communication really are, organizations also need to assess what each constituency thinks about the organization itself.

We know from personal experience that it is easier to communicate with people who know and like us than it is with those who do not. The same is true for organizations. If a company has built goodwill with the constituency in question, it will find it much easier to reach its objective.

The classic example of good corporate communication is Seagram and some other alcohol manufacturers in India. Barred from advertising in the national media, the industry has shown an ideal example of corporate social responsibility (CSR).[13] The industry, including top liquor manufacturers like United Breweries, Bacardi-Martini India Ltd., UDB, and Seagram, on its own has shown restraint and in fact promoted the Society for Alcohol Related Social Policy Initiative (SASPI).[14] This public-awareness platform educates people on making a choice between drinking and not drinking and when and how much to drink. McDowell's and Seagram have undertaken campaigns for responsible drinking. The campaign highlights the dangers of drinking and driving and gathers goodwill from its primary and secondary constituencies, which include parents of youngsters, wives, and employers likely to be affected by the consequences of irresponsible drinking.

What Does the Constituency Know about the Topic?

In addition to the constituency's attitudes toward the company, we must also consider the constituency's attitude toward the communication itself. If constituencies are predisposed to do what your organization wants, then they are more likely to help the organization reach its objective. If they are not, however, the organization will have great difficulty in trying to achieve its goals.

Consumers are often wary of new or unknown products. The U.S. cereal maker mentioned earlier was a victim of such bias as it tried to convince Indians to buy a product that was well known and liked in the United States but which was quite alien to a majority of Indians. In the United States, Kellogg is seen as one of the highest-quality manufacturers of cereals of different types. Given its long history and the fact that consuming its cereal has become an accepted habit, the company assumed that the product would speak for itself in the Indian market. Since there was not much competition for this premium brand, managers in charge of the Indian operation assumed that the introduction of the cereal would be a huge success. However, most of the people who heard about the product did not perceive it as value for money, and when they tasted it in its cold form, they did not quite like it.

Companies that try to sell an idea to the public are always in danger of failing because of the lack of information or the negative feelings consumers may have from previous experiences and entrenched perceptions or stereotypes, as well. This is especially true for global business leaders who are entering emerging global economies such as India for the first time.

Based on previous experiences, Indian consumers had decided a long time back that Chinese products were low tech, unreliable, and therefore not worth it—even at rock-bottom prices. However, Chinese white goods giant Haier launched its extensive range of consumer durables in the festive season of November 2003 and was determined to shake off the nation's dismal reputation among Indian buyers. Haier—the world's fifth-largest white goods company—has invested some $6 million in distribution, advertising, and brand building since launch and has showcased its technological prowess, selling its products through over 1,000 dealers across the country. The company launched a huge array of goods—refrigerators, televisions, washing machines, microwaves, air conditioners, clothes dryers, and even dishwashers.

Haier is determined to avoid making the mistake its Chinese rivals like TCL or Konka made in the Indian market by positioning itself as a price cutter. Instead, it is targeting the premium segment of each market, taking on rivals like the Korean chaebols, or conglomerates Samsung and LG, and even the Japanese company Sony in battle. The struggle for market share has begun, and it will be a while before it can be determined whether Haier can shake off its low-end and unreliable image from the Indian consumers' mind and carve a respectable market share for itself.[15]

American Eagle Outfitters' (AEO) problems with conservative Hindus in the United States show us another example of what can happen when constituents do not know enough about the topic under discussion. It is a story with a message—crisis and problems come uninvited and largely unforeseen, but it is the way of assessing and managing the situation, and using the powerful tool of communication that can effectively mitigate the potential image crisis.

In April 2003, AEO introduced a new range of summer flip-flops in its retail stores across the United States and Canada. The product had images of the sacred Hindu deity Ganesha on its insole, and this caused major outrage among members of the Indian community of North America, as they accused AEO of blatantly ignoring Hindu sentiments. Soon the issue caught the attention of Hindu activists, who were monitoring an increasing number of cases of insensitivity of U.S. businesses toward Hindu religious sentiments.[16]

Protests were launched and action groups were formed by the Internet activist enterprise IndiaCause.com, and a fiery electronic campaign was set in motion by American Hindus Against Defamation on its Web site www.hindunet.org. Faced with mounting pressure and community anger, the manufacturer, which had

750 stores in North America, withdrew its controversial product and issued a written apology in order to maintain the goodwill and customer relations with the Hindu community. IndiaCause, in turn, thanked visitors to its Web site and activists "for their activism" and commended the AEO management for its "positive and immediate response."

Clearly, then, after a company has set objectives for its corporate communication, it must thoroughly analyze all the constituencies involved. This means understanding who each constituency is, finding out what each thinks about the organization, and determining what it already knows and feels about the communication in question. Once this is accomplished, the organization is ready to move to the final phase in setting a communication strategy: determining how to deliver the message.

DELIVERING MESSAGES APPROPRIATELY

Delivering messages appropriately involves a two-step analysis for companies. They must decide how they want to deliver the message (choose a communication channel) and what approach to take in structuring the message itself.

Choose a Communication Channel

Determining the proper communication channel is more difficult for organizations than it is for people. An individual's channel choices are usually limited to writing or speaking, with some variation in terms of group or individual interaction. For organizations, however, there are several channels available for delivering their message.

Table 2-2 shows that there are now more communication channels than ever before for an organization's internal and external communications. For example, a company looking to reveal a change in top management may decide to announce it through a press release, which gets the message out to a broad set of constituencies. In addition, it might also announce the change in a

Table 2-2   Communication Channels

Old Channels

- Writing
- Speaking

New Channels

- Blogs
- E-mail
- Voice mail
- Videoteleconferencing

---

memo and e-mail it to its employees, as well as post it on the company's intranet.

Even this simple example, however, has multiple channel possibilities. Should the press release go to newspapers, magazines, or electronic media? If the company operates globally, should it get the message out on an international newswire, such as Reuters? Should it transmit the message through its home page on the Web? Should the message go to employees through video communications since many companies today have satellite hookups for far-flung operations? Then there is the whole question of timing: Should the employees hear about it first? Should the story be given to one reporter before all others, on an exclusive basis?

When a PC and computer equipment manufacturer spun off from its parent company and faced plummeting sales and a grim business outlook in 2001, the CEO had to communicate some difficult news to investors as well as to employees. As he prepared to release a report of a large quarterly loss to financial analysts, the CEO decided that he wanted employees to hear the news from him rather than from the media. So he got on the company's public announcement system and delivered the news to the employees himself. Included in the message was straight talk about further job cuts that would have to take place and also sincere thanks and praise to all the employees who had worked hard to carry out cost-cutting measures and had done whatever they could to help the company.[17] The CEO won praise from the employees for his candid, direct approach in communicating with them about issues that would affect them, and while the news was not good, they appreciated hearing it from the company's CEO before hearing it from a business network news anchor.

At the other end of the spectrum is AOL executives' approach to announcing layoffs without considering the potential effect of digital communications channels to reach constituents regardless of their physical location. In October 2007, AOL announced layoffs of 2,000 employees. CEO Randy Falco sent e-mail announcements to affected employees' corporate accounts on the eve of October 15. The following day, he issued an explanatory letter beginning with "Dear AOL colleague" to put the news into context. However, he wasn't the first to deliver the bad news to the affected employees; rumors of impending layoffs percolated throughout the blogosphere for weeks leading up to the official announcement. With the real-time, 24/7 news cycle that is increasingly dominated by social media platforms, the company didn't address rumors and "declined to comment." Thus despite Falco's "personal" note to employees, blog commentary suggests that AOL staffers caught wind of the impending layoffs well in advance of the official announcement. It's just one example of the necessary actions companies must take to protect sensitive information and to deliver it to the intended audience before it leaks in cyberspace.[18]

Yet another example of poorly communicated layoffs: In January 2008, Nokia laid off more than 2,300 employees from its Bochum, Germany, production site in order to outsource to Romania and other low-cost regions. However, instead of hearing the news personally from managers, most employees heard of the layoffs via the radio.[19]

Each time a corporate communication strategy is developed, the question of which channels to use and when to use them should be explored carefully. Before this step, the company needs to think about the best way to structure the message and what to include in the message itself.

Structure Messages Carefully

According to most experts in communication, the two most effective message structures are direct and indirect. Direct structure reveals your main point first and then explains the reason; indirect structure explains the reason first and then reveals your main point.

When should a company choose to be direct, and when indirect? Normally, organizations should be as direct as possible with as many constituencies as possible because indirect communication is confusing and harder to understand.

Take the example of Home Trade, in 2001, when it introduced its e-brokering outfit through a countrywide campaign in India. The portal splurged on a Rs. 17 crore (approximately $4 million) celebrity-based campaign, which instead of bolstering the company's image ended up in an ignominy of confusion and lost opportunities. High-profile celebrities—Shah Rukh Khan,[20] Sachin Tendulkar,[21] and Hrithik Roshan[22]—endorsed the high-wattage campaign promoting the financial dot-com company.[23] Like many of the other dot-com companies of that era, it went bust. In this case, however, much of the blame for the bankruptcy can be shared by the company's poor and often misleading communication and image-messaging. Instead of coming out with direct product/service advertising, the company adopted a more indirect approach by showing high-profile celebrities endorsing Home Trade, without actually spelling out what Home Trade was all about. Although this was a creative success, the campaign unfortunately did not garner any sales. This indirect advertising campaign with an indeterminate punch line, "Life means more," and directionless, though glossy, visuals completely confused Indian consumers. The question clueless investors asked was, "Is it a home furnishing company?" or more often asked was, "Does it sell homes?" These investors probably got the impression that the three endorsing superstars wanted to furnish their homes or buy homes with the company's merchandise/service. The company's name, the lifestyle advertising, the punch line, all seemed to point in that direction, which was far from the truth. For the record, Home Trade was a financial portal offering e-brokering services and selling financial instruments online and through franchisees.

In short, there was high brand recall of Home Trade, but the campaign did not substantiate the product benefit, and the nebulous communications left everyone confused.

The company had to change tracks completely. The mistake proved to be too costly, and predictably, Home Trade had to close down, burdened with ever-growing debts and a very poor product takeoff. The embittered agencies and consultants in queue still continue to wait for their payments.

A third option in terms of message structure is simply to have no message. Traditionally, the response from companies when confronted by questions is "No comment." Today, this approach just does not work with a public hungry for the next sound byte and the media looking for an "angle" on the story. Usually, saying that the company cannot talk about the situation until "all the facts are in" is better than just saying "No comment" or nothing at all. But lawyers who are thinking about the legal ramifications of saying anything often influence managers, particularly in the United States. Deciding to be direct often means taking the court of public opinion into consideration, which, to some companies, is often far more important than a court of law.

CONSTITUENCY RESPONSES

After communicating with a constituency, you must assess the results of your communication and determine whether the communication has had the desired result. For example, did sales rise in response to an advertising campaign? After determining the results, you must determine how you will react. Has your reputation changed? Do you need to change your communication channel? These questions reveal the circular nature of the corporate communication framework.

The three variables discussed earlier are involved in creating a coherent corporate communication strategy: defining the organization's overall strategy for the communication, analyzing the

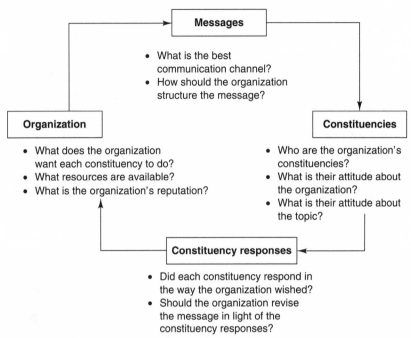

Figure 2-2 Expanded Corporate Communication Strategy Framework

relevant constituencies, and delivering messages appropriately. In addition, the organization needs to analyze constituency responses to determine whether the communication has been successful. Figure 2-2 summarizes this more complete version of the corporate communication strategy model introduced earlier.

CONCLUSION

By creating a coherent communication strategy based on the time-tested theories presented in this chapter, an organization reinvents its way of handling communications. Just as important for the firm, however, is its ability to link its overall strategy to its communication efforts.

In the last 20 years of the twentieth century, the field of strategy blossomed with intriguing ideas from academics like Michael Porter,[24] Prahalad and Hamel,[25] Porras and Collins,[26] Adrian Slywotzky,[27] and Richard D'Aveni.[28] Their ideas drove strategy at large corporations and small businesses alike. None of them, however, focused on how to implement their ideas through the use of an effective corporate communication strategy.

For example, Prahalad and Hamel's article "Strategic Intent"[29] is based on the idea of generating an intense, single focus for an organization like President Kennedy's desire to send a man to the moon in the 1960s or British Airways' quest to become the "World's Favourite Airline." To be effective once it has been developed, however, this sort of strategy must be communicated to everyone in the organization; for global companies with employees scattered around the world, this becomes increasingly challenging. Managers should develop a method for communicating this kind of plan using the corporate communication strategy framework presented in this chapter.

In addition, as discussed in Chapter 1, firms are facing increased scrutiny from external forces (such as the nongovernmental organization [NGO] Greenpeace on the environmental front) and key constituencies (such as the farmers/consumer interest groups/ swadeshi [advocates of the Indian independence movement] groups that fought over the opening of the KFC fast-food chain and bringing in of genetically modified seeds by Monsanto group). By linking corporate strategy to corporate communication, managers can mitigate the potential loss in reputation (see Chapter 4) that can result from a weak or negative response from the organization to these external groups.

The extent to which an organization is affected by external forces is also determined by what industry the firm is in, where it does business, and how public its operations are. In addition to staying competitive, the question of how the firm is perceived externally must be considered. Just as the company's awareness about competitive forces protects it from competitors, its awareness of external forces also protects it from attacks.

The fact that Johnson & Johnson (J&J) consistently ranks at or toward the top of a number of highly publicized reputation surveys is not surprising when you consider the care the company takes to ensure a strong connection between vision and communication. This was evidenced during the Tylenol crisis, when the company lived up to the values codified in the J&J credo (see Chapter 10) in the caring manner in which it attended to the needs of its constituencies.

When developing an overall strategy, firms need to consider their corporate communication effort as manifested in the company's vision and mission statement. By doing so at the inception of an overall strategy, the firm avoids repercussions later. Since all organizations operate at the behest of the public will, this egalitarian approach to communications will be appreciated by a society that has come to depend on its organizations more than ever before.

Chapter 3

An Overview of the Corporate Communication Function

Chapters 1 and 2 paint a broad picture of the Indian business environment, as well as the global business environment, and provide a framework for communicating strategically. Against this backdrop, we turn now to a discussion of the corporate communication (corp comm) function itself. A growing number of companies recognize the value of corp comm and are adapting their budgets and internal structures accordingly. In India, the importance of corp comm is better understood by the larger companies, which deploy journalists to provide steady progress through the rough and tumble realities of the real world. This vital function strives to communicate about the company to make sure its constituents understand that it is a dynamic, positive, and responsible corporate citizen.

This chapter traces the evolution of corporate communication in the United States and abroad, with specific focus on India, and the developments in recent years that have led to a heightened recognition of the field. We first examine the roots of corp comm and then discuss the most appropriate structure for the function within an organization, including reporting relationships. We also showcase each corp comm subfunction that is explored in greater detail later in this book.

FROM PR TO CORP COMM

Public relations (PR), the predecessor to the corporate communication function, grew out of necessity. Although corporations had no specific strategy for communications, they often had to respond to external constituencies whether they wanted to or not. As new laws forced companies to communicate in many situations they had not previously confronted, the constant need for a response meant that dedicated resources were required to manage the flow of communications.

The Indian PR Story

This PR function, which was tactical in most companies, was almost always called either public relations or public affairs. In India, PR evolved into the function of corporate communication in a unique way. In the initial four decades after independence, India's business growth remained mired in "license raj," which meant that all companies had to procure permits or licenses from government departments for setting up, expanding, or diversifying business. The license raj was ostensibly set up to optimize the utilization of capital in the country through targeted investments. In reality, it shackled enterprise and encouraged red tape and bribery, since bureaucrats and politicians in government were vested with sweeping discretionary powers. As a consequence, companies hired PR professionals whose main task was to lobby with government officials by dining, wining, and bribing to get a new license for operating a business venture or renewing an existing one. Companies started recruiting PR executives with powerful connections to network with state officials; they were aptly called liaison executives. However, the political climate changed in 1991, and economic reforms were set in motion with liberalization and deregulation. Those multinationals that had reached a plateau of sales in the mature Western economies and were waiting in the wings took this opportunity to launch their varied businesses in India. In consonance, this era also saw the advent of PR companies and their offering of strategic communications advice and a medley of services to promote brands. Brands competed, and so did PR companies.

The public relations industry in India grew manifold in these years to what it is now—a multicrore (multi-million-dollar) industry providing strategic and integrated communications solutions to businesses in India. Thus PR slowly evolved toward the holistic function of corporate communication, employing media, marketing, management tools, and professionals. Today, some of these firms have developed into specialist firms, offering communication packages for specific sectors like the information technology (IT) sector, health care, biotechnology, and the financial services sector.

ANCHOR OF THE INDIAN STORY: DILIP CHERIAN

Dilip Cherian, consulting partner, Perfect Relations, and a doyen of the corporate communication industry in India, elucidates on the visionary and functional difference between public relations and corporate communication.

"In the Indian context, I'd say that about 70 percent of the companies don't see the differences between the two, partially it comes from their need basket—they don't need to differentiate between the two. Partly it comes from their competence problem—they don't have the competence to fine-tune their inputs toward nurturing and building a long-term image, investing their brand with enduring values that will stand the vagaries of time. We see that public relations is all about dealing with your public, a large part of this function broadly put, ends up in practicing media relations. While corporate communication also, in significant proportion, deals with media relations, the fundamental difference is that when a corporate communicates, it has to understand that it communicates more by what it chooses not to do than by what it does. They are silent on some issues, or they do not respond to some queries—that is an aspect of communication which impacts the image of a corporate."

This point can perhaps be best illustrated by some primarily profit-driven companies that do not practice corporate social responsibility (CSR) and focus solely on sales promotion activities. By choosing to ignore the socioeconomic concerns of the country or by remaining silent in times of geopolitical upheavals like the Kargil War of 1999

(India-Pakistan war for securing border areas near Kargil), the company communicates a certain image.

For example, during the Kargil War, when patriotic sentiments in India were at an all-time high, companies had extended corporate sponsorship to armed forces welfare projects such as rehabilitation of maimed soldiers and education and employment for dependents of martyred soldiers. Or they had contributed to the prime minister's relief fund. Indian Oil Corporation and Bharat Petroleum had provided many LPG/Petrol dealerships to the dependents, Reliance provided educational support, and scores of other such instances heartened Indian citizens and bolstered long-term goodwill for these companies. However, at the same time, some of the corporations turned a blind eye to the nation's need of the hour and are now destined to carry the cross of being perceived as unreliable profiteers by the Indian citizens. This is a clear case of poor understanding of the power of corporate communication and losing out on the opportunity to build an enduring image of being an exemplary corporate citizen.

Dilip Cherian sums up the differences: "Corporate communication is essentially about three or four important things: first is investor relations; second is employee value, meaning giving employees a sense of value or worth so that the client-company is able to draw in employees from higher values at lower cost. Third, which most people don't understand in corporate communication, is that a lot of corporate communication is about buying insurance, treating it as a bulwark against future problems. Public relations is a here-and-now approach while corporate communication is about putting a series of guarantees to prevent trouble tomorrow. The fourth thing probably would be a sense of longer-term vision, which is not the focus of public relations. Concerns like, why are we headed in a certain direction, is that the desired path, what is our vision, what are we doing today to achieve our long-term goals—these concerns guide the growth path of corporate communication of enlightened companies."

Cherian has further delved into the reasons for the slow transformation of PR into corp comm: "A lot of Indian companies don't have either the mind space or the spend speed for making a strong

(continued)

corporate communication base. It's a huge investment which may or may not give immediate returns. There are some corporate managers who see the value, but 60 percent of the Indian companies do not allow spending in this area. We see there is some similarity with the American corporation, which is quarterly results driven and lets the company spend for what it gets in the next quarter, but the American corporations come from a much longer history of understanding the need for corporate communication.

"Unfortunately in India, shortsighted corporate players think how much can they spend and get back as a proportion of sales and sometimes not even as a proportion of sales but as a proportion of profits. Mostly, the corporate communication budget may be an abysmal 1 percent to 2 percent of the profit."

The Evolution of the Corporate Communication Profession

In the 1980s, when the PR role was beginning to be understood as a distinct work function in India, it was not unusual to find public relations officials handling speechwriting, annual reports, and the company newsletter. Given that the majority of work in this area involved dealing with the print media (television was not truly a factor until the early 1990s), many companies hired former journalists to handle this job. The former journalist-turned-PR professional brought the organization the first dedicated expert in the area of communication.

Until recently, the top managers in large multinational companies came from backgrounds such as engineering, accounting, finance, production, or at best (in terms of understanding the company's communication need) sales or marketing. Their understanding of how to communicate depended on the abilities they might have gained by chance or through reading of specialized books or attending a one-year postgraduate diploma course in communications (very few Indian universities, even today, offer a three-year degree course in communication) rather than years of experience. And given their more quantitative rather than verbal orientation, these old-style managers were delighted to have an expert communicator on board who could take the heat for them and offer guidance in times of trouble.

PR professionals were often seen as capable of turning bad situations into good ones, creating excellent relations with their former colleagues in journalism, and helping the chief executive officer become a superb communicator. In some cases, this was true, but for the most part, the journalists were not the answer to all the company's communications problems. When situations turned from bad to worse, they were the obvious ones to blame—easy scapegoats for irresponsible managers.

The First Spin Doctors

In addition to the internal PR staff, outside agencies often helped companies that either could not afford a full-time person or that needed an extra pair of hands in a crisis. The legends of the public relations field—such as Dilip Cherian, Sam Balsara, Rajiv Desai, and Anil Nayar in India, and Ivy Lee, Edward Bernays, Howard Rubenstein, and John Graham outside of India—helped the public relations function develop from its journalistic roots into a more refined and respected profession.

For many years, PR agencies dominated the communications field, billing companies hefty fees for services they could not handle in-house. Few large companies were willing to operate without such a firm for fear that they might be missing an opportunity to solve their communications problems painlessly by using these outside "spin doctors."

Some of the top global PR firms today such as Perfect Relations, Rediffusion-DY&R, Madison PR, Good Relations, and IPAN in India and Fleishman-Hillard and Edelman in the United States still provide some of the best advice available on a number of communications-related issues. But outside agencies cannot handle all the day-to-day activities required for the smooth flow of communications from organization to constituencies. Therefore, they often work alongside in-house communication professionals on strategic or project-based communications activities.

A New Function for a New Environment

As individual corporations and entire industries were increasingly scrutinized and had to answer to a much more sophisticated set of journalists, the old-style public relations function was no longer capable of handling the flak. The aforementioned global powerhouse PR firms became integral pieces of the business communications landscape, and corporations altered their internal communication strategies and functions. The focus now shifted to structuring these new public relations departments effectively to fit the function into the existing corporate infrastructure.

In more recent years, the corporate communication function has continued to evolve to meet the demands of the ever-changing business and regulatory environments. Many changes were sparked by scandals within U.S. companies, but their repercussions could be felt in organizations around the world. For example, at the outset of the millennium, a string of financial scandals at corporations including WorldCom and Enron resulted in the Sarbanes-Oxley Act of 2002, which made full disclosure, transparency, and corporate responsibility the expected norm for companies large and small. The need to maintain this level of transparency has elevated the corporate communication function within companies to a new strategic level. Messages, activities, and products—from investor conferences and annual reports to philanthropic activities and corporate advertising—are now analyzed by regulators, investors, and the public at large with unprecedented scrutiny. And the proliferation of online communication vehicles, including Web portals, instant messaging, and Weblogs, or "blogs," has accelerated the flow of information and the public's access to it to record speeds.

Under this higher-resolution microscope, the clarity, alignment, and integration of communications to all constituencies have the ability to make or break a corporate reputation.

Turning our attention back to the Indian story, we see that, while the evolution of its typical communication function occurred for different reasons, the modern-day result is congruent with changes worldwide. Postliberalization of the 1990s, when prospective multinational corporations (MNCs) came to India lured by the vast untapped markets, the business environment required more than the simple internal PR function supplemented by the outside consultant. The rise in importance and power of special-interest groups, such as the CSE (Centre for Science Environment) and environmentally oriented organizations such as Greenpeace, forced companies to increase their communications activities. During the pesticide controversy—Pepsi and Coca-Cola were accused by the environmental watchdog CSE of using highly contaminated underground water—the entire aerated drinks industry came under a stormy cloud. The effects of an unprecedented boycott by consumers in August 2003 are still making the cold drinks reel. Many consumer groups felt that the U.S. cola giants were not taking enough care to ensure international safety norms and at the same time making "obscene" profits by vending unsafe toxic drinks. Perhaps for the first time in India in terms of corp comms, two bitter rivals got their act together and started churning their PR wings in sync and in overdrive. Their objective was the same—to communicate that the Indian consumer is top priority for these multinationals (see Chapter 6 for more details).

In October 2003, Cadbury India, barely recovered from the nickel controversy (discussed in Chapter 2), got yet another jolt when consumer complaints started trickling in about finding worms in their chocolate. The megabrand's image took a brutal beating, sales dipped by 20 percent, and public confidence was shaken. In response, the company launched Project Vishwas—Vishwas is a Hindi word meaning *confidence* or *trust*. This aptly named communication program set about its task of regaining the consumer's confidence, using publicity tools and increasing visibility through COPs (contact opportunity programs), press, talking to all concerned groups to pick up the shattered pieces of its brand.

It was a tough uphill battle. To further bolster its image of being trustworthy, Cadbury appointed the services of the venerable public icon Amitabh Bachchan. The embroiled company's managing director, Bharat Puri, publicized the new three-step program, which was being introduced to ensure the freshness and quality of Cadbury products. He gave his assurance that the program was moving in the right direction, "It is a result of our discussions with consumers, retail partners and the Food and Drugs Administration in Maharashtra. We are confident of the quality of products leaving our factory. Our focus now is on ensuring that all parts of the storage chain handle and store Cadbury's products better."[1]

The worm fiasco underlines the critical importance of corporate communication in all business operations, whether they are local or international in scope. A visionary company needs to keep its communications machinery well-oiled all the time and not wait for emergencies to crop up.

SHOULD COMMUNICATIONS BE CENTRALIZED OR DECENTRALIZED?

One of the first problems organizations confronted in structuring their communication efforts was whether to keep all communications focused by centralizing the activity under one senior officer at headquarters or decentralizing the activities and allowing individual business units to handle communications. The more centralized model provided an easier way for companies to achieve consistency in and control over all communication activities. The decentralized model, however, gave individual business units more flexibility in adapting the function to their own needs.

The same structural challenges persist today for all business leaders, and the answer to the centralization/decentralization debate often depends on a company's size, the geographic dispersion of its offices, and the diversity of its products and services. For organizations as large and diversified as Tata Industries, for example, the question is moot: there is no way such a sprawling organization involved in activities as diverse as automobiles and IT services could remain completely centralized in all of its communication activities.

The same is true for Johnson & Johnson (J&J) in the United States: with over 100,000 employees in 190 operating entities and 35 businesses in 50 different countries, complete centralization of communications would be difficult, if not impossible. Instead, William Nielsen, former vice president of corporate communication at J&J, describes the function as "a partnership of professionals in communication."[2] J&J even avoids centralizing its external communications counsel with a single public relations firm. Instead, the company uses both small firms on a project basis as well as large, global agencies with resources around the world, amounting to a total of over 20 different agencies worldwide to support various elements of its business.

Global events and economic trends also affect decisions about the structure of an organization's communication function. In the United States, the shock of the September 11 attacks in 2001 taught companies the importance of expecting the unexpected in terms of crises. This provided a new impetus for decentralizing communication structures in many companies. However, in India, where the majority of the companies are still discovering the power of corporate communication, it remains a centralized function at corporate headquarters. Industry analysts predict that corporate communication in India will eventually follow the same structuring that now appears in the West.

The catalysts for the decentralization of communications can be varied: they could be spin-offs of positive growth factors like major expansion and diversification, or fallouts of negative factors like security threats or economic downturns. Consider a major international airline that imposed significant staff reductions on its corporate communication department because of across-the-board cost cuts. As a result, the director of communications explained that the department became more selective about what it committed itself to, saying, "We don't do everything for everybody anymore." Instead, other departments throughout the company established communication positions, doing some of the activities formerly handled by the centralized corporate communication department.[3]

In instances of scaled-back budgets, delegating tasks is doubly important because economic uncertainty can also force the communication department to handle activities it would generally outsource to a full-time PR agency.

While decentralization allows for more flexibility in tough economic times, the advantages of centralization are more obvious. The central oversight focuses corporate communication to relay a consistent image and message. Scope for communication inconsistencies is less, and gaffes are far fewer. In decentralized structures, a company's communication professionals must be vigilant about ensuring quality, consistency, and coordination of messages across the board.[4] Companies often require formal mechanisms of checks and balances to ensure that this coordination takes place.

Perhaps, then, finding a middle ground between a completely centralized and a wholly decentralized structure is preferable for large companies whether in India or in other parts of the world. For example, a strong, centralized, functional area can be supplemented by a network of decentralized "operatives" that adapt the function to the special needs of the independent business units.

In India, with the growth of corporate communication, we will see that this function is best organized as an evolved "matrix" based on customers, products, and geography. Different combinations can be worked out to ensure maximum efficacy of this critical function. In case of a big team, it could be physically located within the businesses it supports, while the head of the team could be located at headquarters. This would promote interactivity between corporate staff and senior management. Importantly, the corporate communications people would be fully in the information loop, which would substantially decrease the time lag between the action-reaction cycles. So firefighting could be begun immediately. This combination of centralized communication management with "operatives" dispersed throughout the various businesses is already practiced in big U.S. conglomerates, and it promises to be a successful working model in India.

To Whom Should the Function Report?

Surveys conducted over the last decade have consistently shown that a high percentage of the average CEO's time is spent communicating. Research conducted at the Tuck School of Business suggests that on average Fortune 500 company CEOs in the United States spend between 50 and 80 percent of their time on communication activities.

CEOs generally devote their time to communicating their company's strategic plan, mission, operating initiatives, and community involvement both internally and externally. Because of investors' increasing demands for companies to deliver short-term results, a substantial portion of the CEO's time is devoted to capital markets and communicating with up to four dozen analysts and investors.

All this implies that the CEO is often the person most involved in both developing the overall strategy for communications and delivering the messages to constituencies. Ideally, the corporate communication function will have a direct line to the CEO (see Figure 3-1 and Table 3-1 for samples of corporate communication reporting structure and Table 3-2 for a sample of senior communication executive titles). A PR corporate survey in the United States revealed that more than half the respondents said their company's head of corporate communication reported directly to the CEO, president, or chair. Even if reporting lines on paper do not go directly to the CEO, it is vital that the head of corporate communication have access to the highest levels of senior management.

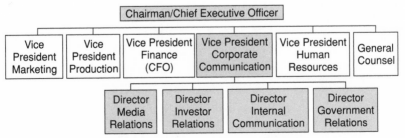

Figure 3-1 Ideal Structure for the Corp Comm Function

Table 3-1   Where Corporate Communication Reports[5]

Communication Head Reports to:	Total (% of Companies)
Chairperson/CEO/president	51
Head of marketing	22
Other	14
Chief financial officer	4
Chief operating officer	4
General counsel	3
Head of human resources	2

Note: Figures obtained from a U.S. survey.

Without this connection, the communication function will be less effective and far less powerful.

To keep the number of direct reports to the CEO down to a handful of senior executives (often the biggest stumbling block to getting the corporate communication function "plugged in" at the top), many companies have corporate communication report to a strategic planning function. Given the importance of tying communications to the overall strategy of the firm, this might benefit the growing corporate communication function. In fact, new research confirms that the corporate communication functions in the world's most highly regarded companies have prominent organizational status. This research report, titled "The Rising CCO," was conducted by Weber Shandwick, Spencer Stuart, and KRC Research and released in January 2008. Nearly one half (48 percent) of surveyed chief communication officers (CCOs)

Table 3-2   Title of Senior Communication Executive[6]

Title	Total (% of Companies)
Senior vice president	9
Vice president	37
Director	34
Manager	15
Other	5

Note: Figures obtained from a U.S. survey.

report directly to the CEO and are visible to their boards (these executives had a median seven interactions with their board during the past year).[7]

In some cases, however, the function still reports to the catch-all executive vice president in charge of administration. This person also has responsibility for areas such as personnel, security, and buildings and grounds. This structure can present tremendous problems for the communications function—especially if the executive vice president has little knowledge about or lack of interest in communications.

When Union Carbide Corporation was dealing with the aftermath of its Bhopal plant accident in India, the company transferred its communications responsibilities to the vice president of strategic planning. In a letter to its executives, the chairman and CEO of the company, Robert Kennedy, said:

> The Corporation's strategic direction is a key element of our communication to shareholders, employees and the public at large.... It is therefore more important than ever to be open and consistent in our communications to all of these groups, to keep them informed of our progress as we implement strategy, and to make sure that we address the special concerns and interests of all the groups and constituencies with a stake in Union Carbide's future.... To ensure the closest possible alignment of our communications with management directed at strategic planning developments, the management of those functions is being consolidated under...[the] Vice President of Strategic Planning and Public Affairs.[8]

Gerald Swerling, head of the graduate public relations program at the University of Southern California Annenberg School of Communication, observed that the increased recognition of communications and public relations by senior management over the last decade has caused an increasing number of CEOs to "demand that there be PR professionals at the strategic planning table for new products and initiatives."[9] In turn, employees begin to perceive communications rightfully as a critical management tool when senior management places value on the function.[10] Let us now take a look at what that function should include.

THE FUNCTIONS WITHIN THE FUNCTION

A PR corporate survey in the United States revealed that over half of the heads of corporate communication departments tend to oversee communications functions that include media relations, crisis management, employee communications, reputation management, community relations, and product/brand communications.[11] In India, this portfolio of functions is unified under a single designation and is a composite task of the corporate communication department. Interestingly, a PR person in an Indian corporate system may well be an equivalent of a liaison officer whose job is exclusively to deal with government functionaries or state setups to promote the company's interest. And this person may just be reporting to the CEO and have no further interaction with the

Table 3-3   Functions Included in Corporate Communication Departments[12]

Department	Total (% of Companies)
Media relations	98
Crisis management	79
Employee/internal communications	72
Special events	70
Reputation management	68
Community relations	62
Product/brand communications	60
Marketing	44
Annual/quarterly report	42
Public affairs/government relations	36
Product/brand advertising	35
Issues advertising	28
Financial/investor relations	25

Note: Figures obtained from a U.S. survey.

communications people. However, as the license raj declines and the Indian economy is showing robust signs of opening up, the need for such PR people is decreasing.

While not every company can include all the subfunctions listed in Table 3-3 under one umbrella, to operate most effectively, a majority of these functions must be included in the overall communication function.

The best approach to building a corporate communication function is to begin with the most global and strategic issues and then move into the narrower aspects of the function. We begin this section with a discussion of identity and image, and then move on to the various subfunctions of corporate communication.

Identity and Image

Difficult to classify as a separate subfunction, an organization's identity and image strategy is the most critical part of any corporate communication function. (In the next chapter, we explore these constructs in greater detail.) What is the difference between image and identity, and how do they shape the operations of a corporate communication department?

Image is the corporation as seen through the eyes of its constituencies. An organization can have different images with different constituencies. For example, cigarette companies might be reprehensible to many Indian consumers who think that smoking is injurious to health or whose religion does not permit smoking, but a delight to International Trade Commission (ITC) shareholders reaping the profits from international sales of tobacco products. Conversely, customers might have been perfectly happy with what textile manufacturer Bombay Dyeing had to offer in its many stores throughout the country, but security analysts were reluctant to recommend the parent company's stock knowing that the scrip, or credit used in place of currency, is on the decline right now.

Determining what the organization's image is with different constituencies is usually less obvious than in the preceding examples— particularly given the increasingly blurred lines separating one constituency from another, as discussed in Chapter 2. In order to establish the corporation's image with different constituencies, the corporate communication department should conduct research to understand and monitor each constituency's evolving needs and attitudes. Obviously, the organization cannot please everyone, but by monitoring what constituencies are thinking about, it can make a conscious effort not to create hostility toward a particular group. A similar monitoring system can also be used on a regular basis to gauge the impact and success of the company's communications activities.[13]

Unlike its image, however, the organization's identity should not vary from one constituency to another. *Identity* consists of a company's defining attributes, such as its people, products, and services. An organization has some kind of identity whether it wants one or not, based in part on the visual components it presents to the world. People all over the world know Coca-Cola's red can and white script lettering; they also know McDonald's golden arches, whether they're in Mumbai or New York City.

Since identity building and maintenance require a variety of skills, including the ability to conduct marketing research, to design attractive brochures, and to enforce identity standards and cohesion, they should be spread around several different functions in the absence of a single, centralized corporate communication function. For example, the marketing research needed to determine a firm's image with various constituencies might be a minor by-product of the overall marketing research effort currently underway at a company to determine customer attitudes toward particular products and services rather than toward the firm as a whole.

Determining how a firm wants to be perceived with different constituencies and how it chooses to identify itself are the cornerstone functions of corporate communication. If the firm is making serious changes in its identity, this subfunction can easily be a full-time job for a team of corporate communicators for a period of time.

For some companies, outside agencies specializing in identity and image are involved in the makeover if the company alters significant components of its identity. These changes can range from the merely cosmetic—to keep the "look" of the company up-to-date—to the more momentous—such as a name change or a new logo.

Corporate Advertising and Advocacy

A company's image can also be enhanced or altered through corporate advertising. This subfunction of corporate communication is different from its product advertising or marketing communication function in two ways (Chapter 6 covers more on corporate advertising).

First, unlike product advertising, corporate advertising does not necessarily try to sell a company's product or service. Instead, it tries to sell the company itself—often to a completely different constituency from its normal customers. For example, the mega-company of modern times and a unique example is the pan-Indian company Sahara India Pariwar. The general audience may not be able to clearly spell out the company's products beyond airlines or guess which particular activity makes it a stupendous Rs. 32,000 crore, or $7.6 billion, company. But by projecting an image of being synonymous with the world's largest family, having more than 900,000 employees and no trade union, it has assiduously sculpted an ever-patriotic image. Sahara's communications are mostly swathed in the tricolors of the Indian flag, and the company associates itself with events of high interest to the Indian populace like sponsoring the country's cricket team, funding relief plans for families of the Kargil martyrs, and the like. Also, it remains high profile in political functions and hosting celebrities. These activities are not part of a product-specific sales campaign but are strategic in promoting Sahara India's interests with various constituencies such as government functionaries, public and financial institutions, investors, and so on.

When upscale discount retailer Sahara Mall, Gurgaon, ran an extensive corporate advertising campaign in 2003–2004 featuring products ranging from satin lingerie to grocery items, accompanied only by the product name and discounted price, the goal was not to sell more of these products but rather to showcase the company's diverse merchandise from basic to fancy and its potential to be the discount retailer of even trendy products.[14] In much the same way, the aerospace firms that advertise extensively in publications such as *The Economic Times* are not trying to sell their Boeings or Airbuses to the government controlled airlines, but rather are trying to influence public opinion and facilitate approval for sanctions in the mega–Public Sector Undertaking's (PSU) budget.

Even though product advertising is the purview of the marketing department in most large companies, corporate advertising is often run from the CEO's office or through corporate communication departments. In the 2000s, this is the fastest-growing segment of the advertising industry, as senior officers try to present a coherent company image for opinion leaders in the financial community.

An important subset of corporate advertising is issue advertising. This type of advertising attempts to do even more than influence opinions about the company; it also tries to influence the attitudes of a company's constituencies about specific issues that affect the company. Sometimes, government pressure might compel a company to take on an unrelated activity in the name of corporate social responsibility (CSR). Another approach is for a company to involve itself in socially relevant projects in which it feels it can make a difference. The approaches are indicative of the directions for CSR in India. The plastics industry is a rare example of an industry that is spending money to control the manufacture and use of non-degradable plastic bags while preventing their litter. Seagram's campaign for responsible drinking is a classic example of product promotion with social responsibility in India. Godfrey Phillips—the cigarette monolith—has instituted the much-advertised Red & White Bravery Awards in an effort to put a more caring face on a company many hold in contempt for its role in producing addictive, carcinogenic tobacco products. ITC—another cigarette giant—has revived private degraded lands by planting vegetation that augments the otherwise limited raw materials for their paper factory. Its success prompted the state government to ask the company to duplicate its efforts with public wastelands.

As we will see in Chapter 6, issue advertising is risky. By taking a stand on a particular issue, the company is automatically creating a negative image with one or several constituencies. But many companies take this risk nonetheless, facing the consequences of adding their opinions to debates that they consider important.

Media Relations

While the old-style public relations function that focused almost exclusively on dealing with media relations may be a thing of the past in the United States, the subfunction we now refer to as *media relations* is still central to the corporate communication effort in India. Most of the average companies' corporate communication staff typically resides within this subfunction, and the person in charge of the corporate communication department as a whole must be capable of dealing with the media and serving in the role of spokesperson for the firm. Although the media relations subfunction started off as a "flakking" service for managers in response to requests from news organizations, today the best corporate communication departments actively set the discussion agenda of the firm in the media (see Chapter 7). Unlike other subfunctions, there is little debate about whether media relations should come under the purview of corporate communication or other corporate functions.

Technology has helped companies communicate through the hundreds of media services available from virtually anywhere in the world. Satellite up-links are available at most corporate headquarters, such as Infosys or TCS, and companies can put their press releases out to wire services electronically or through the Internet without making a single phone call. Despite these advances, the relationship between business and media remains largely adversarial, although positive relationships are much more common today between sources and reporters than they were in the past. Since the media and businesses rely on one another to a certain extent, most companies try to make the best of these relationships.

Marketing Communications

The marketing communication department coordinates and manages publicity relating to new or existing products and also deals with activities relating to customers. It also may manage corporate advertising.

Product publicity almost always includes sponsorship of events for major corporations, such as golf tournaments, cricket matches, knowledge quizzes, film and TV award functions, fashion events, achievement awards, special exhibitions, and car rallies. In addition, celebrities are often involved in these activities; this requires coordination within the company. Given how important such events and sponsorship agreements can be in shaping a company's image, corporate communication experts are often involved in setting the events agenda.

Customer relations activities have increasingly become a part of corporate communication because pressure groups among consumers try to exert their influence on an organization. This consumer influence has become all the more powerful as a result of digital platforms that enable coordination and communication among individuals around the world. Now rather than simply making sure that the customer is happy with the product or service, as in the past, companies must get involved in quasi-political activities with constituencies claiming to represent a firm's customers.

For example, in August 2002, the environment watchdogs in the ecologically fragile mountain lands of Himachal Pradesh pursued a conservation agenda against the cola multinationals—Coca-Cola and Pepsi—for defacing the Himalayan boulders with brightly painted advertisements. Exemplary fines were imposed by the

Supreme Court. The multinationals, after their initial dismissal of the issue as a franchisee misdemeanor, were compelled to accept direct responsibility and promise more vigilance on public-interest issues.

Fair and Lovely—a frequently advertised fairness cream (a cream that makes skin lighter)—raised a maelstrom of criticism from women's organizations for being "unfair" to women. The advertisements were targeted by the public-interest groups for two reasons: First, they showed fair-skinned women getting jobs and handling assignments easily, while dark-skinned women had problems getting jobs and handling assignments. Second, the TV advertisement was full of references to longing for a son, and thus the brand campaign was accused of being "an affront to a woman's dignity and blatantly promoting preference for a son." Public-interest vigilantes forced the company to put a stop to its advertising campaign and redo its message. As a consequence, Fair and Lovely had to relaunch its advertising where it suitably profiled a woman of substance spurning a prospective greedy bridegroom who demanded a dowry (a common social custom in Indian society). The brand promoted the new face of Indian women— independent and intelligent—and could now be perceived in the venerated category of being a social reformist. However, the brand has to still proactively deal with activist groups assailing the very essence of the product—a promise for a fairer and hence "lovelier" skin.

More informed consumers—able to examine the messages and advertising thrown at them with a discerning eye—mean that marketing communication teams must ensure that product and brand promotions are sending the right messages.

Internal Communication

As companies focus on retaining a contented workforce given changing values and demographics in India, they have to think strategically about how they communicate with employees through internal communication (see Chapter 5 for more on this subfunction, also referred to as *employee communication*). While strong internal communications have always generated a more engaged, productive, and loyal workforce, the meteoric globalization of the work environment and the concurrent rise of public-interest issues, environmental concerns, and work ethics of several respected global firms in recent years has further necessitated strong communication channels between management and employees.

Additionally, difficult economic times, layoffs, and uncertainty require open, honest communication from senior management to all employees, and the sensitive nature of some of these messages further reinforces the need for the involvement of seasoned communication professionals alongside their human resources counterparts.

The example of the AOL layoff's news reaching employees before it was communicated to them officially by management, as described in Chapter 2, illustrates the delicacy of modern internal communications. Alternatively, the Polaris example shows with clarity how effective and timely internal communication can avert damaging fallout resulting from an external crisis. Polaris Software, an Indian financial technology company and an IT services provider, faced an unforeseen distressing situation in December 2002. The Polaris Software CEO, Arun Jain, and senior vice president, Rajiv Malhotra, were detained by the Indonesian police for 11 days over a commercial dispute that Polaris had with Bank Artha Graha of Jakarta. The news shook up the corporate world and made the headlines of every Indian newspaper. Polaris understood that the damaging news would affect all its constituencies. But it also knew that it was of paramount importance to maintain employee morale through this crisis since it would affect everything from productivity to harmful rumor mongering to the exodus of employees. So the company focused efforts on providing transparent and open communication channels to all its employees, or "associates" as they are called at Polaris. The software corporation saw to it that the associates received regular, detailed communication on the status of the crisis and the role played by the company in it. The empathy that such communication created among the workforce was remarkable and inspired confidence. It also ensured that the associates stuck together and that business operations did not suffer during the crisis.[15]

Polaris reflected the adage "communication begins from the top." Even CEO Arun Jain took some time from his cell at the Jakarta police detention center to share his thoughts on a piece of paper and send it to the Chennai office. This was sent to every associate as a morale booster. The effect of this communication was truly inspirational, and the associates could hold their heads high, assured that they were working with a company that had high integrity and strong business ethics. The employees/associates reciprocated by ensuring that none of the other clients' work was affected and deliveries on other projects were on schedule.

Finally, let us also understand the point that, because of the blurring of constituency lines, companies must recognize that employees now may also represent investors and members of community advocacy groups, which makes thoughtful communications even more critical.

Investor Relations

Investor relations (IR) has emerged as the fastest-growing subset of the corporate communication function and an area of intense interest in all companies (see Chapter 8 for more on investor relations). Traditionally, investor relations was handled by the finance or treasury department, often reporting to the company's chief financial officer, but the focus in recent years has moved away from "just the numbers" to the way the numbers are actually communicated to various constituencies.

IR professionals deal primarily with securities analysts who are often a direct source for the financial press, which this subfunction cultivates in conjunction with experts from the media relations area. IR professionals also interact heavily with both individual and institutional investors. They are also highly involved in the financial statements and annual reports that every public firm must produce.

Given the quantitative messages that are the cornerstone of the IR subfunction, as well as the need for IR professionals to choose their words carefully to avoid any semblance of transferring inside information, this subfunction must be a coordinated effort between communications professionals and the chief financial officer, controller, or vice president of finance.

Philanthropy and Corporate Social Responsibility

Many companies in the United States have a separate subfunction in the human resources area to deal with community relations and a foundation close to the chairperson that deals with philanthropy. But the two should be tied closely together, as companies take on more responsibilities in the communities in which they operate. (For more on corporate social responsibility and philanthropy, see Chapter 4.)

In India's case, following the Kargil War, the bar for expectations regarding corporate citizenship was raised considerably. There is heightened awareness among Indians, and they expect companies to address social issues, especially during a period of emotional and financial turmoil, with an equal number wanting to know about specific corporate efforts in both local and national communities.[16] Similarly, the Gujarat earthquake refocused the outlook and objective of corporate communication and forced it to have something beyond a narrow short-term vision. Ambani, directors for the foundation of the International Federation of Red Cross and Red Crescent Societies, urged business corporations to "go beyond financial equity to building social equity in India and US." Thus, given the importance of the constituency involved and the importance this has in shaping the image of the firm, this subfunction also needs to be housed within the corporate communication function.

Corporate philanthropy has also become increasingly important as companies are expected to do more than just give back to the community. As a result, firms now feel a greater obligation to donate funds to organizations that could benefit the firm's employees, customers, or shareholders. Examples of this include donations to universities that might be conducting research in the industry and organizations representing minority interests. Plus, global standards for sustainability reporting, as defined by the Global Reporting Initiative, are making huge strides in developing an international framework for corporate responsibility practices.

Government Relations

The government relations function, also referred to as public affairs, is more important in some industries than in others, but virtually every company can benefit by having ties to legislators on both a local and national level (see Chapter 9 for more on government relations). Many companies have established offices in their country's political capital to keep a finger on the pulse of regulations and bills that might affect the company. Because of their critical importance in heavily regulated industries, such as public utilities, government relations efforts in such companies are often staffed internally and supplemented by outside government relations specialists.

In their lobbying and government affairs efforts, firms can either "go it alone" or they can join industry associations and deal with important issues as a group. Either way, staying connected to what is happening in New Delhi and Washington through a well-staffed and savvy government relations team is important to virtually all businesses given the far reach of government regulations within industries from pharmaceuticals to computer software.

Crisis Management

While crisis communications are not really a separate function requiring a dedicated department, this area should be coordinated by the corporate communication function, and communication professionals should be involved in crisis planning and crisis management. Ideally, planning for such eventualities should include a wider group of managers from all over the organization (see Chapter 10 for more on crises).

Company lawyers typically need to be involved in crises, but the fact that they often operate with a different agenda from their communication counterparts, not always considering how actions can be perceived by specific constituencies or the public at large, poses problems to both the organization and the corporate communication function.

A recent study on the subject of communication versus legal strategies stated: "... legal dominance is shortsighted and potentially costly ... organizations [must] reconcile the often contradictory counsel of public relations and legal professionals and take a more collaborative approach to crisis communication."[17]

By working collaboratively with in-house counsel and, more importantly, with senior management, corporate communication professionals can make the difference between good and poor crisis management. We will see examples of both in Chapter 10.

CONCLUSION

The success of a company's communication strategy is largely contingent on how closely it is linked to the strategy of the business as a whole.[18] In addition to thoughtful design and careful planning of a firm's strategy, a company must have a strong corporate communication function to support its mission and vision.

While the investor relations function could be in the treasury department of a company, the internal communication function within the human resources department, and the customer relations function within the marketing department, all these activities require communication strategies that are connected to the central mission of the firm.

Corporate communication professionals must be willing to perform a wide variety of subfunctions within a function. Their roles will continue to broaden and become diversified as information flows from a variety of sources worldwide, which will require that communications be strategic and purposeful. The greater number of multinational firms and the increasing demand for senior management to travel to and speak at international venues is now placing additional pressure on the communication function to communicate successfully with more diverse, foreign audiences.[19]

Corporate communicators must not only have a firm grasp of rapidly evolving technology, but they must also have a grasp on prevalent cultural issues, political trends, and shifting demographics in order to keep in tune with a company's diverse constituencies. In this way, the corporate communication function must add context to and actively support the activities of the entire corporation.

Chapter 4

The Growing Importance of Corporate Reputation

Chapter 3 covers the various components of the corporate communication function. This chapter examines the first and most critical part of that function: a corporation's identity, image, and reputation. The chapter also addresses how a close alignment between a company's identity and image generates a strong reputation for Indian and multinational corporations.

Looking at an example of image at the personal level might be a good place to start. Everyone chooses certain kinds of clothing, drives particular cars, or styles their hair a certain way—to express their individuality. The cities and towns in which we live, the music we prefer, and the restaurants we frequent all add up to an impression, or identity, that others can easily see. In India, the clothing and food habits of southern Indians are quite different from those of northern Indians. For instance, a Punjabi family (in the north) would prefer parathas for breakfast, while a Tamilian family (south) would prefer idli or dosa.

Consider the following scenario from India: a gray-haired man pulls up to a five-star hotel in a Mercedes E220. He's dressed in a blue Reid & Taylor suit and is wearing an Omega watch. He steps out of the car, and the parking valet drives the Mercedes further on. The next moment, a middle-aged man in a Maruti 800, commonly known in India as one of the smallest and most widely owned cars in production, pulls up. He is dressed in blue jeans and a plaid button-down shirt; he's wearing a Timex digital watch. Even for people with little understanding of Indian culture, these quick glimpses of the two men speak volumes (whether those impressions are right or wrong is another issue).

The same is true for corporations: walk into a firm's office and it takes just a few moments to capture those all-important first impressions and learn a great deal about the company. This effort to understand is relatively easy at the personal level but is significantly more difficult at the organizational level. One reason for this complexity is that many potential identity options exist. Take, for instance, the following example from the hotel industry.

A U.S. executive and his wife decide to treat themselves to one of life's great pleasures: a weekend in a suite at the Oriental Hotel in Bangkok. During their stay, their daily copies of the Asian editions of the *Wall Street Journal* and *Herald Tribune* are ironed for them to eliminate creases; the hotel staff, omnipresent, runs down the hallway to open their door lest they should actually have to use their room keys; laundry arrives beautifully gift wrapped with an orchid attached to each package; every night, the pillows are adorned with a poem about sleep; and, outside the lobby, Mercedes limos are lined up, ready to take the couple anywhere at any time of the day or night.

A few weeks later, the couple returns to the United States, and the wife is giving a presentation to a group of fellow executives at a Midwestern resort. A *USA Today* appears on the outside doorknob squeezed into a plastic bag; the staff, invisible if not for the cleaning carts left unattended in the hallway, is unable to bring room service in under 45 minutes; her pillow is "adorned" with a room-service menu for the following morning and a piece of hard candy; the vehicle waiting to whisk guests to various destinations is a Dodge minivan; and for flowers, the resort provides silk varietals in a glass-enclosed case that plays the song "Feelings" when the top is lifted.

Both hotels have strong identities, and the choices each has made about its businesses are at the heart of what identity and image are all about. These choices contribute to and shape the image of these hotels and, more generally, convey the identity and image of any institution.

Just what are identity, image, and reputation? How do organizations distinguish themselves in the minds of customers, shareholders, employees, and other relevant constituencies? And, above all, how does an organization manage something so seemingly ephemeral as reputation?

WHAT ARE IDENTITY AND IMAGE?

A company's identity is the visual manifestation of the company's reality as conveyed through the organization's name, logo, motto, products, services, buildings, stationery, uniforms, and all other tangible pieces of evidence created by the organization and communicated to a variety of constituencies. Constituencies then form perceptions based on the messages that companies send in tangible form. If these images accurately reflect an organization's reality, the identity program is a success. If the perceptions differ dramatically from the reality (and this often happens when companies do not take the time to analyze whether a match actually exists), then either the strategy is ineffective or the corporation's self-understanding needs modification.

As discussed in Chapter 3, image is a reflection of an organization's identity. Put another way, it is the organization as seen from the viewpoint of its constituencies. Depending on which constituency is involved, an organization can have many different images. Thus, to understand identity and image is to know what the organization is really about and where it is headed. This is often hard for anyone but the CEO or president to grasp. What, for example, is the reality of an organization as large as Reliance, as diversified as Tatas and Birlas, or as flat and nonhierarchical as Infosys?

Certainly the products and services, the people, buildings, names, and symbols are a part of this reality. While there are inevitably differences in how the elements are perceived by different constituencies, it is this cluster of facts, this collection of tangible and intangible things, which provides the organization with a starting point for creating an identity.

Organizations can get a better sense of their image (as conveyed through visual identity) by conducting research with constituents. This research should be both qualitative and quantitative in nature and should try to determine how consistent the identity is across constituencies. As an example, a U.S. consulting firm, Arthur D. Little (ADL), found through research that its image was not clear to a variety of constituencies. Was the organization a consulting firm? A think tank? Was it involved in engineering? Defense? By asking people what they thought about the organization, ADL was able to find out perceptions of its image and discovered how unclear it was.

Although image can vary among constituencies, identity needs to be consistent. One constituency, for example, might see ADL as a consulting firm that is too involved in the defense sector in the United States and therefore might have a negative image of the company; another constituency might be delighted with the extensive work the consulting firm has done to help the defense industry become stronger over the last 20 years and might then have a positive image of the firm. But at least they both have the firm's identity right. It is involved in defense work and is a consulting firm. That could be either positive or negative, depending on whom you ask, but at least it's accurate.

The logo that Dartmouth's Tuck School of Business adopted several years ago was a carefully crafted visual designed to reflect what faculty and officers felt was the reality of the school: it is the oldest graduate school of business in the United States (founded in 1900), it is prestigious (a part of the Ivy League; Tuck is a part of a great college—Dartmouth), and it is elite (usually ranked among the top 10). The symbol conveys all these meanings, but they can add up to very different images, depending on whom you ask.

For example, some potential students might think that old and Ivy League mean stodgy or conservative; others might think that prestige is great and that this is the best place to go for graduate business training. Whatever their decision about the school, the logo should accurately reflect what the place is all about. Constituents can then decide whether that is an image they like or not.

Similarly, Rai University, India's largest private university (as rated by Just Careers), which prides itself on being an educational institution of excellence offering a holistic approach to learning and combining high-tech with traditional knowledge systems has accordingly evolved a visual identity to reflect its values.[1]

The logo for the university has been designed to reflect this carefully chosen image and philosophy for higher education. The chosen color, orange, demonstrates vibrancy and energy, and this is reinforced with a shining sun as the focal point. The emblem also has myriad stick figures across it depicting students from different social strata, different talents bound together under the banner of Rai University. The sign-off further fills in the picture as it encapsulates the image with the words, "evolving thinking minds." It is hoped, in this case, that the constituents would have the image, as portrayed, clearly etched in their minds as they decide where they wish to study. However, perceptions may differ from person to person, and some potential students may think that innovation in education is risky and that it is better to persevere with the more conventional government university system. There would be others still who would want to move with the times and study in a multidisciplinary learning environment which is more a global practice.

DIFFERENTIATING ORGANIZATIONS THROUGH IDENTITY AND IMAGE

Given how every industry now faces global competition and companies are trying to manage with limited resources, an organization's identity and image might be the only difference that people can use to distinguish one company from the next. Is there really any difference between getting a connection of your mobile phone from T-Mobile, Airtel, or Vodafone? Given that the same distributor often sells the SIM (subscriber identity module) of these companies around the world, the answer would seem to be no. Yet consumers make distinctions about such homogeneous products all the time based on what the company's image is all about rather than on the products these companies are selling.

As products become much the same all over the world, consumers are increasingly making distinctions based on notions other than the product, thereby making image and identity even more powerful differentiators. We now turn to a more in-depth discussion of, first, identity and, then, image. We then conclude with a discussion of how these come together to create an organization's reputation.

SHAPING IDENTITY

Because identity building is the only part of reputation management an organization can control completely, we first discuss some of the things that contribute positively to corporate identity—an inspirational corporate vision, careful corporate branding (with a focus on names and logos), and consistent self-presentation.

A Vision That Inspires

Most central to corporate identity is the vision that encompasses the company's core values, philosophies, standards, and goals. Corporate vision is a common thread that all employees, and ideally all other constituencies, can relate to. Thinking about this vision in terms of a narrative or story of sorts can help ensure the overall coherence and continuity of a company's vision and the collective messages it sends to its constituencies.[2]

Cees B. M. van Riel, a professor at Erasmus University in the Netherlands, links the importance of narratives to successful corporate reputations. He explains that "communication will be more effective if organizations rely on a ... sustainable corporate story as a source of inspiration for all internal and external communication programs. Stories are hard to imitate, and they promote consistency in all corporate messages."[3] To get information about a company, external constituencies rely on articles in publications, television advertisements, discussions about the company with other people (e.g., family, friends, and colleagues), and direct interaction with company employees. The most appealing of stories, literary and corporate, often involve an underdog—an unsung hero who audiences can admire and rally behind. Going against the grain can instill a sense of noble purpose in the actions of a hero—or an entrepreneur—who hopes to do things differently. Consider Sunil Mittal, founder of Bharti Telecommunications that controls the Airtel brand. His bravado in holding out against Reliance Infocom and Tata Teleservices, companies that are much larger and have deeper pockets, had "hero appeal" that did wonders for Bharti's brand.

Names and Logos

Just as our society demands top-10 lists and rejects the full story in favor of "sound bites," it also prizes brands as identification tags that can allow us to quickly and effortlessly gauge everything around us. Given this phenomenon, a company's value can be significantly influenced by the success of its corporate branding strategy. Coca-Cola, for example, has a value that far exceeds its total tangible assets because of its strong brand. It is consistently rated as the number-one brand both globally and in India.[4]

Top-10 Global Brands

1. Coca-Cola
2. Microsoft
3. IBM
4. General Electric
5. Nokia
6. Toyota
7. Intel
8. McDonald's
9. Disney
10. Mercedes Benz

Top-10 Brands in India[5]

1. Gold Flake Cigarettes
2. Pepsi
3. Thums Up
4. Wills Navy Cut Cigarettes
5. Scissors Cigarettes
6. Britannia Biscuits
7. Coca-Cola
8. Parle Biscuits
9. Nirma Detergents
10. Colgate

Source: AC Nielsen retail audit for all categories except carbonated soft drinks and cigarettes.
Source for carbonated soft drinks: company figures.
Source for cigarettes: industry estimates, company figures.

Over the years, these brands have created a modern and value-for-money image in consumers' minds and therefore enjoy high brand equity or goodwill.

Branding and strategic brand management are critical components of identity management programs. While it is beyond the scope of this book to fully explore corporate branding, this chapter focuses on a subset of corporate branding—names and logos—to help illustrate the conscious actions organizations can take to shape their identity and differentiate themselves in the marketplace.

Companies often institute name changes either to signal identity changes or to make their identities better reflect their realities. For example, after the takeover of BSES—Brihanmumbai Suburban Electric Supply—by Reliance, the company was renamed Reliance Energy Ltd. In this case, Reliance wanted its positive and vibrant image to counteract the stodgy and lackadaisical connotations. The newly renamed company showed enterprise by setting up two wholly owned subsidiaries for power transmission and trading businesses. According to Anil Ambani, chairman and managing director, BSES would focus its strategy on integrated services. The integrated services would include generation, transmission, distribution, trading, and bundling of services in the power sector. Thus, Reliance Energy Transmission would supply power to its networks across the country, while Reliance Energy Trading traded in electricity, both physically and in derivatives.[6]

A clear example of a name change to effect an image change can be seen in the case of Matsushita Electric Industrial. In January 2008, the company's president, Fumio Ohtsubo, announced that the 88-year-old Japanese electronics manufacturer would officially shed the name of its founder and adopt that of its most universally well-known brand, Panasonic. Executives at the company took great care to ensure that all constituents would be amenable to the change, even going so far as to ask journalists via e-mailed questionnaires what it would take for them to consistently refer to the company as Panasonic.[7]

Another example that illustrates the importance of properly communicating about name changes (and the risks inherent in not doing so) is that of Nissan in Japan. To consolidate the company's brands worldwide, an edict from Nissan's company headquarters in the early 1980s eliminated the well-known Datsun brand name from the U.S. market in favor of the company name Nissan. This name change took over five years to complete because dealers refused to pay for new signs and resisted the change in general. In addition, the name change confused customers. Just about everyone in the late 1960s and early 1970s knew Datsun 240Z and the company's line of small cars that helped Americans get through the first oil crisis.

After the name change, however, some customers thought that Nissan was a subsidiary of Toyota, its arch rival. Almost a decade later, Nissan was still less known in the United States than the old Datsun name. As this example illustrates, while organizations can differentiate themselves based on identity through names and logos, they also risk losing whatever identity they have built up through changes in the use of names and logos that are not communicated to the public properly.

Logos are another important component of corporate identity—perhaps even more important than names because of their visual nature (which can allow them to communicate even more about a company than its name) and their increasing prevalence across many types of media. When upscale discount retailer Target placed an ad in the *New York Times* in 1999 depicting only its "bull's-eye" logo and inviting readers to call a toll-free number if they knew what the symbol meant, phone lines were tied up immediately and were forced to shut down because of the staggering response.[8]

One of the most recognizable logos in the world today (besides perhaps Coca-Cola's) is Nike's "swoosh." Designed for Nike founder Phil Knight by Portland State graduate Carolyn Davidson in 1972 for $35, some experts believe that the swoosh is better known today than McDonald's golden arches. Golfing sensation Tiger Woods wears the swoosh on his hat and clothes. Teams in hockey's Canada Cup and national soccer teams have also worn the swoosh in competition. With Nike as their sponsor, 700 winter athletes at the 2002 Winter Olympics in Salt Lake City sported the swoosh outside the competition.[9]

On the India front, another recognizable logo is that of Air India's "Maharaja." This logo first made its appearance on Air India in 1946 when Bobby Kooka as AI's commercial director and Umesh Rao, an artist with J. Walter Thompson, Mumbai, created it. The maharaja began merely as a rich Indian icon, symbolizing graciousness and high living. It went on to become the most recognizable of icons among globetrotters.[10]

Logos can simply be symbols like the Nike swoosh, or they can be symbols that represent names, like the Target "bull's-eye" or Arm & Hammer's arm and

A young woman in Hanoi, Vietnam, sports a counterfeit version of the Nike swoosh on her hat.

hammer. Logos can be stylized depictions of names or parts of names (like the golden arches that are the M in McDonald's), or stylized names with added mottos or symbols. Accenture's logo, for example, is the company name with a greater-than symbol above the *t* that is meant to connote the firm's goal of pointing the way forward and exceeding clients' expectations.[11]

Firms that specialize in identity management and design should be involved in the process of logo creation. Later in this chapter, we take a closer look at the processes behind creating new names and logos as part of an overall identity program.

PUTTING IT ALL TOGETHER: CONSISTENCY IS KEY

An organization's vision should be presented consistently across all its identity elements, from logos and mottos to employee behavior. Overnight package-delivery pioneer FedEx is a good example of this. In the 1990s, the company had noticed that customers routinely referred to it as FedEx rather than its official name, the multisyllable Federal Express. Additionally, office workers were beginning to use FedEx as a verb; few people said they would "UPS a package" or "Airborne Express a letter." Instead, it was "let's FedEx this." The company thus decided to use the abbreviation already used by thousands of customers (and competitors' customers) as its official name. On June 23, 1994, Federal Express changed its name to FedEx and paired the name with a distinctive new motto: "The World on Time." A launch advertisement in 1994 read: "We're changing our look to FedEx. Isn't that what you call us anyway?" (see Figure 4-1).

By officially making the company name synonymous with punctual overnight delivery (the world on time), FedEx demonstrated that it was in touch with what its customers wanted and made an open commitment to reinforce the same message throughout its organization. The new motto and logo, FedEx's clean and pressed uniforms, immaculate transport vehicles and service centers, and the employee mantra, "Service without excuse," all echoed a consistent commitment.[12]

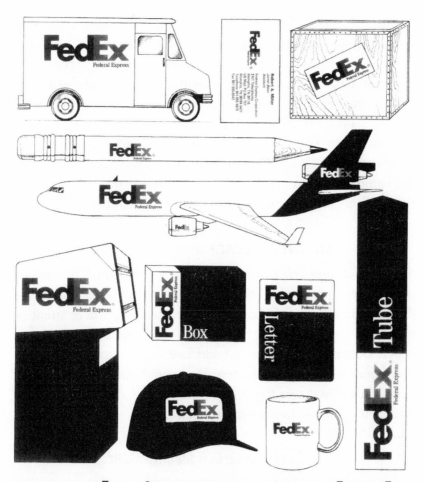

Figure 4-1
Source: USA Today, *July 6, 1994, p. 7A. © 1994 Federal Express Corporation. All rights reserved.*

Michael Glenn—senior vice president, worldwide marketing, customer service, and corporate communications for FedEx—explained that by embracing its one-word association, "FedEx and its name have changed their environment from morally neutral to morally charged."[13] Putting its promise of delivering "the world on time" on every package, truck, and plane, FedEx's new motto ensured that every pickup, delivery, and customer interaction would reinforce that promise. Its new name and logo reflected that the company was in touch with its customers, and FedEx's advertising of this new identity reinforced that its customers mattered.

IDENTITY MANAGEMENT IN ACTION

The dual nature of identity and image—embodied in physical objects yet inextricably tied to perceptions—creates a special dilemma for decision makers. In a business world where attention is focused on quantifiable results, the emphasis is on qualitative issues. Devising a program that addresses these elusive but significant concerns requires balancing thoughtful analysis with action. Here is a method that has been successfully used by many organizations to manage the identity process.

Step 1: Conduct an Identity Audit

To begin with, an organization needs to assess the current reality. How does the general public currently view the organization? What do its various symbols represent to different constituencies? Does its identity accurately reflect what is happening, or is it simply a leftover from the past?

To avoid superficial input and objectively respond to these questions, consultants from hundreds of "identity firms" conduct in-depth interviews with top managers and people working in areas most affected by any planned changes. They review company literature, advertising, stationery, products and services, and facilities. They also research perceptions among the most important constituencies, including employees, analysts, and customers. The idea is to be thorough, to uncover relationships and inconsistencies, and then to use the audit as a basis for potential identity changes.

In this process, executives should look for red flags. We saw how FedEx took action after learning that its customer constituency was no longer using its official name. Typical problems include symbols or names that conjure up images of earlier days at the company or just generally incorrect impressions. Once decision makers have the facts, they can move to create a new identity or institute a communication program to share the correct and most up-to-date profile of the company.

While the identity audit may seem like a fairly straightforward and simple process, it usually is not. Often, the symbols that exist and the impressions they create are not how the organization sees itself in the present at all. Companies trying to change their image are particularly difficult to audit because the vision that top executives have of what the company will be is very different from what the reality currently is. Often, executives disregard research that tells them how constituents' perceptions about the organization differ from their own. Such cognitive dissonance is the first challenge in managing identity for executives. The reality of the organization must be far enough along in the change process so that the new image the company is trying to adopt will actually make sense, some day at least, to those who will encounter this company in the years ahead.

Consider this recent rebranding exercise: In the spring of 2006, the Swedish-based umbrella organization The Observer Group officially announced the rebranding of its entire organization to centralize all its brands, products, and services under one brand name and identity. It was a massive undertaking, as there were at least 10 subbrands and names across the company that different constituencies associated with different things. The rebranding initiative required communication to all constituencies, from media to investors, and involved the implementation of new logos and imagery.

To effectively unroll the rebranding, the organization's management formed an executive committee that included marketing and communication heads from all involved subbrands. This committee was responsible for identifying the values that would shape the new brand, and for maintaining consistent messaging as the new brand name—Cision—was unveiled to employees, investors, and consumers.[14]

Another recent rebranding exercise by Asian Paints, India's largest paint manufacturer, took the market watchers by surprise when the company made a difficult decision in casting off its popular mascot Gattu. The mischievous boy with paint can and brush—Gattu—was born in 1954. Designed by India's well-known cartoonist R. K. Laxman, Gattu served as an endearing anchor for all Asian Paints communication for over four decades. However, after years of a sedentary existence, the company needed to go ahead with an image-rebuilding exercise. The task at hand was to identify the desired image for the company, communicate it to the various constituencies, and manage it.

In 2002, Asian Paints went ahead with the well-thought-out rebranding strategy, wherein the marketing directive was to give the company and all its products a vibrant image, which would be contemporary, urban, upmarket, and consistent. First of all, the decision was made to promote all brands under the umbrella brand Asian Paints, instead of promoting individual brands like Apex Emulsions, Touch Wood, Royale Interior Emulsions, and Apcolite. Second, the company launched some innovative steps to directly communicate with potential consumers and promote the image of an active, concerned, and responsive company. Asian Paints launched India's first paint helpline, where paint-related information was made available to callers; additionally, the consumer could outsource painting jobs directly to the company. Also, knowing the consumers' prime concern with selecting exactly the right shade, a series of retail shops branded Asian Paints Color World were set up, which served as a one-stop color shop of Asian Paints. These unique paint shops generated shades with the help of computer software that managed 1,511 shade combinations. This was another first in India, where the tradition was low involvement, because the consumer who did not show much interest in choosing the brand of paints used was sought to be converted to a high involvement by promoting direct communication. The advertising campaign reiterated the message with a housewife proclaiming with joy at finding just the right shade, "Mera wala cream." Last, even the logo underwent redesigning and the new-look company logo was stylized in all lowercase letters, as in "asian paints," using high-energy shades of yellow and red, with the vertical line of the p converted into a brushstroke, to incorporate a mnemonic for quick identification. In line with the new imaging strategy, the brand got a facelift, new packaging, a contemporary logo, vibrant corporate colors, and one-stop paint solutions.[15]

Step 2: Set Identity Objectives

Clear goals are essential to the identity process. These goals should be set by senior management and must explain how each constituency should react to specific identity proposals. For instance, "As a result of this name change, analysts will recognize our organization as more than just a one-product company," or, "By putting a new logo on the outside of our stores, customers will be more aware of dramatic transformations that are going on inside." Most important, however, is that emphasis be placed on constituency response rather than on company action.

This is where problems often arise. Most managers, particularly senior managers, are focused more on the internal than the external. Thus, they have great difficulty in getting the kind of perspective necessary to see things from the viewpoint of constituents. Consultants can certainly help, but the organization as a whole must be motivated to change and be willing to accept the truth about itself, even if it hurts.

In addition, change for change's sake or to meet some kind of standardization worldwide (which was true in the case of Nissan) is not the kind of objective that is likely to be met with success. Usually, such arbitrary changes are the result of a CEO's wanting to leave his or her mark on the organization rather than wanting to take necessary steps in the evolution of the company's image.

In India, the launching of the cellular service "Idea" is a good example of a carefully coordinated image building at work to communicate the benefits of a new, improved service. To understand this unique case of putting old wine in a new bottle, one will have to delve into the genesis of this brand. The new name Idea was fashioned in such a way that it was an amalgamation of three existing service providers: the Birlas, Tatas, and AT&T. These three telecom companies forged an alliance in April 2001, deciding to combine their strengths, improve service, and augment the combined market. Then came the critical issue of getting the right brand name and image, which would be central to getting the entire campaign together. The company used research results, suggestions from advertising agencies, and even had contests among its employees to come up with suggestions for brand names. More than 700 brand names were considered, and Idea was chosen because it came closest to the brand vision—that is, innovation.

Thus, brand Idea was launched after much brainstorming; it was a hard task to converge on a single identity that would reflect the individual brand values and brand personalities.

The message to the advertising agency Lowe for designing the advertising campaign was to communicate that Idea was a better network than its competitors and a brand full of ideas. The new image had to reflect the core values of being innovative, imaginative, international, and consumer-friendly. For Idea Cellular, the Rs. 600 crore ($140.5 million) merged offspring of Birla, AT&T, and Tata Cellular, where each player held roughly one-third of the Rs. 2,000 crore (approximately $142 million) equity, the objective was to use this opportunity to display its pan-Indian face to its approximately 900,000 subscribers.

The whole communication package, which was launched in June 2002 and which included print media and television spots, had focused on the catch phrase: "An Idea can change your life." Even the logo colors were chosen on the basis of their relevance to the brand vision, such as yellow for energy, blue for youth and innovation, and black for solidarity and stability. The brand logo resembled a SIM card with the brand name.

The campaign signified that Birla, Tata, and AT&T now had a relevant entity, replacing the playful acronym Batata, which the client was keen to shed.

To ensure that customers took to the new transition comfortably, the communication rollout plan was charted in detail for all the markets. Before the launch of this campaign, the company announced the change in newspapers and print ads so that there would be no hitch in the transition. This helped reassure customers that the new brand would actually be an enhanced product.[16]

In the United States, a positive example of clear objectives leading to a necessary change is Kentucky Fried Chicken's desire to change its image and menu in the mid-1990s as a result of changes in the dietary habits of Americans. The strong corporate identity of this company worldwide (one of its biggest restaurants is in Tiananmen Square in Beijing, and it can be found in the remote corners of Japan) conjures up images of Colonel Sanders' white beard, buckets of fried chicken, salty biscuits, and gravy.

To an earlier generation, these were all positive images closely connected with home and hearth. Today, however, health-conscious Americans are more likely to think of potential risks associated with high cholesterol levels, the enhancement of flavor when sodium is used, and gobs of fat in every bucket of the Colonel's chicken. Thus, the company tried to reposition itself with health-conscious Americans by offering broiled chicken and chicken salad sandwiches. The company's goal was to change the old image and adopt a more health-conscious position.

To do so, executives decided to change the name of the 5,000 restaurants gradually to just "KFC." The obvious point was to eliminate the word "fried." Although most identity experts would agree that it is very difficult to create an identity for a restaurant based on initials alone, KFC tactfully used the photograph of the well-known Colonel to go along with the change. The communication objective for this particular change made a great deal of sense and put KFC in a better position in the eyes of a more nutrition-minded set of customers.

A similar example can be found in the cooking oil market in India. It is known that Indian consumers have traditionally used a lot of oil in their diet, paying little attention to the negative side effects associated with excess cholesterol and the danger of heart attacks. By the early 1990s, urban consumers were getting more health conscious as the increasing incidence of heart attacks raised awareness about a healthy diet. One of the market leaders, Marico Industries Ltd., spotted this trend early and decided to reposition the brand identity of Saffola, its bestselling cooking oil. All communication to consumers and other constituencies had the concept of a healthy diet ingrained in the message. Nowadays, consumers clearly identify Saffola as a brand that protects health-conscious individuals from the risks associated with high cholesterol levels and heart attacks. The company has now extended the concept of good health and a healthy diet to all its products.

Step 3: Develop Designs and Names

Once the identity audit is complete and clear objectives are established, the next phase in the identity process is to develop the actual design. If a name change is necessary, consultants must search for possibilities. This is a step that simply cannot happen without the help of consultants. Because so many names are already in use, companies need to avoid any possibility of trademark and name infringement. But options for change can still number in the hundreds. Usually, certain names stand out as more appropriate than others. The criteria for selection depend on several variables.

For example, if the company is undergoing a global expansion, the addition of the word *international* might be the best choice. If a firm has a lot of equity built into one product, changing the name of the corporation to that of the standout product might be the answer, as had happened when Consolidated Foods changed its name to Sara Lee. We saw how Federal Express changed its name to reflect what its constituencies were already calling it, and how Andersen Consulting chose a new name (Accenture) that would give it an identity distinct from its former parent by shedding any vestiges of the Andersen name.

Companies should also ensure that logos continue to reflect the company's reality and should actually consider modifications if they do not. Café Coffee Day is a good example of this. The popular Indian coffee café chain currently owns and operates 179 cafés in all major cities in India. It is a part of India's largest coffee conglomerate named Coffee Day, a Rs. 200 crore (approximately $46.8 million), ISO 9002–certified company. Coffee Day's most unique aspect is that it has approximately 125 years of coffee-growing history and over 5,000 acres of self-owned coffee plantations in South India. It is positioned as being a  prize-winning (winner of prestigious awards at India barista championships in 2002) brand, offering a world-class coffee experience in its cafés and is an affordable lifestyle statement. The tagline, "A lot can happen over coffee," reflects an inherent energy, which is also reinforced by the choice of colors in its logo.[17] The red color of the logo shows vitality and vibrancy, and the green stroke signifies freshness. The café in Café Coffee Day's logo is transcribed in a liquidy font type, a reflection again of its product's attributes. As we see, in the eyes and mind of the consumer, the logo is an important interpretation of the identity the brand seeks to establish.

The process of designing a new look or logo is an artistic one, but despite contracting with professionals to develop designs, many company executives get very involved in the process, often relying on their own instincts rather than on the work of someone else who would have spent his or her entire career thinking about design solutions. One CEO of a multi-billion-dollar company in the United States used a napkin to design what he thought would be the perfect logo for his company. After several weeks of design exploration by a reputable design firm, he kept coming back to that same napkin design. Until the designer finally presented an exploration that resembled the CEO's design on the napkin, each of the suggestions was rejected. The CEO was happy when he saw his own idea come back to him. Although it was not the best design, it was adopted and is still in use today.

Obviously, there has to be a balance between the professional opinion of a designer and a manager's own instincts. Both need to be a part of the final decision whether it is a name change or a new logo being created. In some cases, designers and identity consultants are perfectionists or idealistic, presenting ideas that are unrealistic or too avant-garde for typically conservative large corporations. In the end, strong leadership skills and decision making must be exerted to effect the change, no matter what it is, in order for it to succeed.

Step 4: Develop Prototypes

Once the final design is selected and approved by everyone involved, consultants start developing models using the new symbols or name. For products, prototype packaging shows how the brand image may be used in advertising. If a retail operation is involved, a model of the store might be built. In other situations, the identity is applied to everything, including ties, T-shirts, business cards, and stationery to see how it works in practice.

During this process, it is common for managers to get cold feet. As the reality of the change sinks in, criticism starts mounting from those employees who have not been involved in the process and from others because they do not have a good sense of the evolution and meaning of the design. At times, negative reactions from constituencies can be so strong that proposals have to be abandoned and work has to be started all over again.

To prevent this problem, a diversity of people and viewpoints should be taken into account during the entire identity process. The one caveat is to avoid accommodating different ideas and end up diluting concepts. A company should not accept an identity that is simply the lowest common denominator. Two ways to deal with the task are either to let a strong leader champion the new design or to set up a strong committee to work on the program. In either approach, everyone has to be informed and involved in the project from the beginning. The more people involved in the process from its inception, the less work that will have to be done to sell the idea after much hard work has already been put in.

When Infosys presented its annual report in 2004, the Indian-born software giant had effectively communicated to the marketplace that it was confident of its new global image. Making a distinct departure from its previous style of austere communication, Infosys had splashed the first eight pages of its annual report with impressive graphics and copy that underlined its growth as a top contender in the global software business. The *Annual Report '04* was a designer brochure with a carefully coordinated, glossy format, and the first chapter was suitably titled "New Game, New Rules." With Infosys crossing the $1 billion mark in revenues for the financial year 2003–2004, the new report effectively communicated the new image chosen for the company—savvier, more aggressive, and more global in its outlook and orientation.[18]

Step 5: Launch and Communicate

Given the time involved and the number of people included in the process, news about future changes can easily be leaked to the public. Sometimes, such publicity is a positive event, as it can create excitement and a sense of anticipation. In spite of this, such chance occurrences are no substitute for a formal introduction of the company's new identity. To make the announcement dramatic, public relations staff should be creative in inviting reporters to the press conference without giving away the purpose. To announce their name change, one company sent six-foot pencils and a huge calendar with the date of the press conference marked on it.

At the press conference itself, the design should be clearly displayed in a variety of contexts, and senior executives must carefully explain the strategy behind the program. As additional communication tools, corporations might want to use advertising (for example, see Figure 4-1), Webcasts, or video news releases and satellite links (see Chapter 7). Whatever the choice, we must realize that presenting an identity, particularly for the first time, is a complex process, as constituencies might easily tend to interpret the change as merely cosmetic rather than strategic.

Sometimes, companies might also adopt a new strategy for their launch. For example, Hindustan Lever Limited (HLL) evolved a new strategy to push its most popular detergent Rin into the low-cost washing powder market segment. In a month-long program in the state of Uttar Pradesh (UP), Rin challenge centers were set up in 44 towns, where consumers were invited to live demonstrations of Rin washing powder. Consumers could bring their own dirty clothes and watch a challenge test in which Rin was pitted against other low-cost washing powders. "If the other detergents give us better results, we will provide one year's supply of Rin to the consumers," said Manish Aggrawal of HLL.[19]

Parle Products launched its first national level promotion for Parle-G, its brand of glucose biscuits, and with a slogan, "Make my dream come true," the Parle-G contest was kicked off in March 2002.[20]

Dash! the children's watch from Titan, introduced a unique creative contest for children between ages 6 and 14. The contest on cartoonnetworkindia.com was held to invite and encourage children to use their creativity and imagination to design a watch.

The advertisement promised to launch the prize-winning design as a new watch in the summer of 2002 collection and to give the winner the first watch of this collection. Furthermore, it was announced that the top five winners would receive a Dash! watch and that every participant would be awarded certificates.[21]

Step 6: Implement the Program

The final stage, which is implementation, can take years in large companies and a minimum of several months for small firms. Resistance is inevitable, but what is frequently shocking is the extent of ownership constituencies have in the old identity.

Usually, the best approach to ensure that there is consistency across all uses of a new identity program is to develop identity standards. A standards manual shows staff and managers how to use the new identity consistently and correctly. Beyond this, someone in the organization needs to monitor the program and make judgments about when flexibility is to be allowed and when it should not be. Over time, changes will need to be made in some standards, for instance, when a modern typeface chosen by a designer is not available for use everywhere.

Implementing an identity program is a communication process that involves lots of interpersonal skills and a coordinated approach to dealing with many constituencies. In addition to communicating its new identity program within the organization, Accenture, for example, had to train more than 100 other firms, including ad agencies, printers, and Web designers, on how to use its new logo.[22]

IMAGE: IN THE EYE OF THE BEHOLDER

We just explored some of the means by which a company can manage its identity. An organization's image is a function of how constituencies perceive the organization based upon all the messages it sends out through names and logos and through self-presentations, including expressions of its corporate vision.

Before constituencies even begin to interact with an organization, they often have certain perceptions about that organization based on what they have read about it, what interactions others have had that they have been told about, and what visual symbols they recognize. Even if you have never eaten a veggie burger at McDonald's, you may have certain perceptions about the company and its products.

After interacting with an organization, the constituencies may have a different image of it from the one they had before the interaction. If this happens, the goal is to have an image that is better, not worse. One bad experience with a Reliance mobile phone operator can destroy a customer's relationship for a lifetime. One aloof salesperson at Shopper's Stop in Mumbai could turn a shopper off the store forever. This is why organizations today are very much concerned about customer interaction and consider the quality of each and every interaction as important. The credibility that a company acquires through the repeated application of consistently excellent behavior will establish its image in the minds of constituents in a much more profound way than a one-shot corporate advertising campaign.

Organizations should seek to understand their image not only with customers but also with other key constituencies such as investors, employees, and the community (keeping in mind, as discussed in Chapter 2, that some of these may overlap). Often, a company's image as perceived by a given constituency is driven not only by its own unique corporate identity but also by the image of the industry or the group to which it belongs. Internet companies had to contend with this from the late 1990s into the new millennium. Before the bursting of the dot-com bubble in 2000, virtually all e-based companies rose together on a tide of investor optimism with a collectively vibrant, cutting-edge image. Similarly, when that tide turned and investors wanted tangible products, real business plans, and seasoned management, all these companies suffered, and so did their collective image.

A similar example of this is the image management Tata Consultancy Services (TCS) had to undergo in 2003, when the trend of outsourcing U.S. business to India, especially in the IT sector, had caused a huge social, economic, and political backlash. Many Americans began resenting companies that were threatening their jobs and well-being. TCS underwent immense scrutiny that was almost solely based on its position in the outsourcing industry. Because of its sheer size, TCS was the immediate focus and the major target of any attack on outsourcing.

Although the concept of outsourcing had been around for years, the early part of the twenty-first century had seen a monumental increase in the practice for a number of reasons: First, the dot-com bust accelerated the economic reasons for corporations to find ways to cut costs, and the price of labor in India—where, according to a March 6, 2006, article in *Newsweek*, the average annual income of those employed in India is a mere $737—was the most efficient way of doing so. Second, India has a wealth of educated workers who are well-versed in the language of technology; what's more is that investment banks and pharmaceutical companies are increasingly heading eastward to take advantage of Indian outsourcers.

When the backlash had reached its height, TCS was faced with the challenge of combating the negative image brought about by outsourcing as a business concept. One way the corporate behemoth responded was through education; Phiroz Vandrevala, executive vice president, spoke publicly to educate the government and customers on his company's point of view. Furthermore, media relations efforts responded to vitriolic attacks on the company's activities. One major coup in favor of its practices was the coverage of former first lady Hillary Rodham Clinton's defense of TCS, free trade, and outsourcing. She brought the consultancy's services to New York State where she is a U.S. Senator. When the media began attacking her for taking away jobs from locals, she responded by defending competition and stating that TCS actually brings jobs to Americans.

Although the antioutsourcing sentiment still festers in the United States, it has begun to fizzle out. Recent coverage has acknowledged that outsourcing's assumed detrimental effects on the U.S. economy were not actually as severe as anticipated; thus, TCS's image has begun to rebound as well, though not without extensive efforts taken by its management team.

Turning to the employee constituency, a company's image as viewed by its employees is particularly important because of the vital role employees play in creating a rapport with other constituencies of the company. Starbucks has built one of the strongest brands and reputations by creating a powerful story and unified culture that begins inside and works its way out. CEO Howard Schultz had explained the philosophy: "We built the Starbucks brand first with our people, not with consumers, the opposite approach from that of the crackers-and-cereal companies, because we believed this was the best way to meet and extend the expectations of employees who were zealous about good coffee."[23] The enthusiasm of Starbucks' baristas is meant to be contagious and personally connects them with their customers. Every barista is meant to play such a key role in generating customer loyalty that Starbucks refers to each one as a "partner," the official name for a Starbucks employee.[24]

As former CEO of Procter & Gamble Ed Artz once observed, "Consumers now want to know about the company, not just the products."[25] The day-to-day behavior of employees, from Starbucks' baristas to its executives, can rank just as high as product or service quality as the source of a strong corporate image that is aligned with the company's identity.

BUILDING A SOLID REPUTATION

The foundation of a solid reputation exists when an organization's identity and its image are aligned. Charles Fombrun, New York University professor emeritus and author of the book *Reputation,* says that "in companies where reputation is valued, managers take great pains to build, sustain, and defend that reputation by following practices that (1) shape a unique identity and (2) project a coherent and consistent set of images to the public."[26] (Figure 4-2 gives a visual representation of the relationship between identity/ image and reputation.)

A company's reputation differs from its image in that the former is built up over time and is not simply a perception at a given point in time. Reputation also differs from identity in that it is a product of both internal and external constituencies, whereas identity is constructed by internal constituencies (the company itself).[27] Additionally, as depicted in Figure 4-2, reputation is built based upon the perceptions of all of an organization's constituencies.

Why Reputation Matters

The importance of reputation is evidenced by several prominent surveys and rankings that seek to identify the best and the worst: *Fortune*'s "most admired" list, *BusinessWeek* and Interbrand's "best global brands" ranking, and the Reputation Institute–Harris Interactive's "reputation quotient (RQ) gold study," featured in the *Wall Street Journal*, are just a few.

Such highly publicized rankings have gained so much attention that some corporate PR executives' bonuses have actually been based on *Fortune*'s list of America's most admired companies.[28]

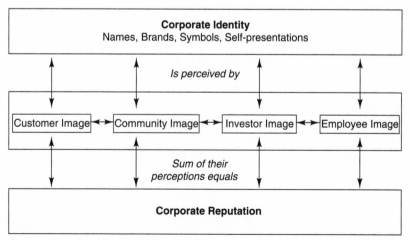

Figure 4-2   Reputation Framework

According to the *PR Week*–Burson-Marsteller 2007 CEO survey, media scorecards are extremely influential: Surveyed CEOs ranked their influence, with *Fortune*'s "100 best companies to work for" topping the list, followed by *Fortune*'s "most admired companies," the *Wall Street Journal*'s "shareholder scoreboard," and the *Financial Times*'s "best places to work." The variety of influence represented here, from employees ("best places to work") to shareholders ("shareholders scoreboard"), suggests the power that constituencies have in a corporation's reputation.[29]

According to the 2006 Hill & Knowlton Corporate Reputation Watch, more than 90 percent of analysts agree that if a company fails to look after reputational aspects of its performance, then it will ultimately suffer financially.[30]

Let us next see what exactly motivates this level of interest. A strong reputation has important strategic implications for a firm because, as Fombrun notes, "It calls attention to a company's attractive features and widens the options available to its managers, for instance, whether to charge higher or lower prices for products and services or to implement innovative programs."[31] As a result, the intangible entity of reputation is undoubtedly a source of competitive advantage. Companies with strong, positive reputations can attract and retain the best talent, as well as loyal customers and business partners, all of whom contribute positively to growth and commercial success. In four out of the five years during 1994–1999, an investor who owned stock in one of *Fortune*'s "most admired companies" would have earned returns that beat the S&P 500.[32]

Recently, some astute companies in India have realized the importance of gaining investors' confidence and have sought a mutually beneficial relationship. The investor-savvy companies have promoted transparency and frequency in communication with this vital constituency. This has contributed to the rapid rise of the stock market in India, and these companies have given manifold returns to the investors, which is discussed in Chapter 8. To focus specifically on the climate in India, let us have a look at India's top-10 investor-friendly companies.

The aim of the latest round of CAMPUSTRACK (III), the third round of a syndicated study conducted by ORG-MARG, was to find out the preferences and perceptions of the latest batch of graduates from Indian B schools across the country and the factors these graduates used to evaluate prospective employers. This study, which was spread across the top-20 business schools of India, had profiled the talent pool and had identified trends in the selection of career preferences over the years. The management graduates were asked to associate recruiting companies with a host of both positive and negative image attributes such as job content, work environment, growth prospects, and likely compensation. Their responses indicate a marked preference for multinational companies. Constructed using 48 corporations, the CRI (campus recruiter index) represents companies that are likely recruiters as mentioned by management graduates, management institutes, media, and employers. The CRI, which helps measure the goodwill of management graduates toward these corporations, shows that companies with a foreign parentage are preferred, the only exceptions to this being ICICI and Infosys.[33]

India's top-10 most investor-friendly companies (*Business Today*, March 14, 2004) are:

1. TVS Motor Co.
2. Bajaj Auto
3. IOC
4. ONGC
5. Ranbaxy Laboratories
6. LIC Housing Finance
7. J & K Bank
8. GAIL
9. HDFC
10. Jindal Steel & Power

The following lists the top-10 companies based on the campus recruiter index (ORG-MARG press release, 2002):

1. Hindustan Lever
2. Infosys Technologies
3. McKinsey
4. Procter & Gamble
5. Citibank
6. ICICI
7. HSBC
8. Nestlé
9. Lehman Brothers
10. Boston Consulting Group

The following lists the bottom-10 companies based on the campus recruiter index (ORG-MARG press release, 2002):

1. Satyam Computers
2. Godrej
3. Polaris Technologies
4. Titan
5. Kotak Mahindra

6. TELCO
7. State Bank of India
8. Dabur
9. Bajaj Auto
10. TISCO

An example of how reputation can also help companies to weather crises is given next. Strong reputations have helped Coke and Pepsi survive the pesticide crisis in 2003. Recently both cola majors saw a dip in their profits after a report put forward by the nonprofit Center for Science and Environment had stated that the pesticide content in the two soft drinks was far higher than that permitted by law.[34]

Change in a company's business environment can have implications for the reputation of that company. The proliferation of media and information, the demand for increased transparency, and the increasing attention paid to social responsibility all indicate the need for organizations to apply greater focus on building and maintaining strong reputations. As noted, public confidence in business is low, and public scrutiny of business is high. When the U.S. energy giant Enron collapsed in 2001, it dragged its auditor, Arthur Andersen, down with it in an accounting scandal that not only irreparably damaged both firms' reputations (and indeed their chances for survival), but also heightened public mistrust of large corporations in general—particularly those adopting complex accounting methods—and of the entire accounting profession.

Against this backdrop, organizations are increasingly appreciating the importance of a strong reputation. But how does an organization know where it stands? Since reputation depends on the perceptions of constituencies, organizations must first find out what those perceptions are. Only then can they examine whether they correspond to the company's identity and values. And only when these are in alignment will a strong reputation result.

MEASURING AND MANAGING REPUTATION

In assessing its reputation, an organization must examine the perceptions of all of its constituencies. As mentioned earlier, many PR firms have developed diagnostics for helping companies conduct this research. Although one size does not fit all when it comes to measurement programs, all organizations require constituency research.

Employees can be a good starting point because they want to understand the company's vision and values and involve themselves in every customer interaction with those ideas in mind. When an organization does not practice the values it promotes, it is likely to run into trouble. As an example, IBM had long espoused the value of lifetime employment. In the early 1990s, however, the company went through severe downsizing in the United States, and employees throughout the company were heard jokingly saying, "IBM means 'I've been misled.'" Clearly, employees did not feel that IBM was being true to its own values, and this disillusionment had caused IBM's reputation to suffer.[35] However, the company took this to heart and made a subsequent turnaround. One initiative it instituted, dubbed the "ValueJam," drew more than 57,000 employees online to post ideas on how IBM's values could be applied to improve its operations, workforce policies, and relationships.[36]

Customer perceptions of an organization must also align with its identity, vision, and values. In the late 1990s, Burberry, the U.K. retailer that originally focused on rain gear, had learned what can happen to a corporation's reputation when customers are in the dark about what a company is actually all about and how this situation can be overcome by taking aggressive steps.

When Rose Marie Bravo became the CEO of Burberry in 1997, the company was facing a number of challenges. Profits were plummeting, and while some of this could be explained by the Asian economic crisis of the mid-1990s (by 1996 Asian consumers—at home and abroad—generated two-thirds of the company's revenues, causing the downturn to dramatically affect Burberry's sales),[37] internal factors were also at work. For one, prior to Bravo's arrival, instead of maintaining a cohesive Burberry brand across the globe, the company allowed each country's management team to develop the brand as was desired in the local markets. As a result, when customers thought of the name Burberry, what came to mind depended on their geographic location. In the United States, it meant $900 raincoats and $200 scarves; in Korea, it meant whiskey; and in Switzerland, it meant watches. Before her arrival, Bravo had explained that "[Burberry] had a disparate network of licensees marketing Burberry around the globe. It wasn't a coherent business. Each country was representing its own version of Burberry. Demand slowed. The business needed a cleanup. The brand was overexposed and overdistributed."[38]

Not only was the company having trouble deciding what it was selling, but it was also struggling to position its products properly. Burberry's inability to decide whether it was targeting upper- or lower-end consumers in Asia, for example, led to its products being sold in bulk to discount retailers, thus undermining the image the exclusive, high-end Burberry boutiques were trying to generate in that same market. Bravo realized that Burberry had to sharpen its focus and concentrate on high-end retailing alone in order to send a consistent message to consumers. Additionally, she realized that as a high-end men's raincoat retailer, primarily supplying clothing preferred by older males, the company was not catering to women, a key consumer constituency, as effectively as it should.

Given that the Burberry store portfolio needed to reflect the high-end focus of the brand, Bravo upgraded the flagship store in London and doubled the size of the New York store. Even more importantly, Burberry began to rein in its detached network of franchises to provide the company greater control over the consistency of its product and identity. The most visible turning point was a print advertising campaign featuring supermodel Kate Moss in a Burberry plaid bikini. These ads pushed Burberry's sales up dramatically, and the average age of its customer down considerably by putting a fresh, playful face on a venerable fashion brand that, although esteemed for its nearly 150-year heritage, was looked upon by younger constituencies as stodgy and by many women as "not for me."

These initiatives, from store renovations to a more unified product focus across all franchises to the elimination of discount retailing, created a cohesive image that helped firmly establish Burberry as a luxury brand, greatly enhancing its reputation around the world.

CORPORATE PHILANTHROPY AND SOCIAL RESPONSIBILITY

When thinking about its own reputation, every organization today needs to consider corporate philanthropy and social responsibility. The *2007 Cone Cause Evolution & Environmental Survey* results revealed that 83 percent of Americans say that companies have a responsibility to help support causes; 92 percent have a more positive image of a company that supports a cause they care about; and 87 percent are more likely to switch from one product to another (price and quality being equal) if the other product is associated with a good cause—an increase from 66 percent since 1993.[39] Many Americans consider philanthropy and social responsibility when deciding where to purchase goods and services.

But corporate philanthropy is not without its perils. As seen in Chapter 1, people's trust in business is low, and even genuine efforts to publicly "do good" can be perceived as self-serving, particularly in the case of "strategic giving," where the charitable activity relates directly to the business the company is in. Alternatively, when companies are too silent about what they are doing for the community or the environment, they face criticism for being apathetic or greedy.

Philip Morris, the U.S. cigarette manufacturing unit of Altria, provides a good example of the former. The company's advertising campaign touting its charitable activities met with skepticism from the public, many of whom viewed the ads as an attempt by Philip Morris to undo its negative image as a big tobacco company rather than as a manifestation of true concern for the community. Despite continued spending on promoting its philanthropic activities, the company still ranked 56 out of 60 in the Harris Interactive–Reputation Institute 2006 RQ gold survey.[40]

Undeterred by the ban on advertising on cigarettes and tobacco products, Godfrey Phillips India annually presents the Red and White Bravery Awards to seven individuals for their valor and compassion. According to senior officials of the company, the objective of these awards is to inculcate and foster the culture of selfless action among people. In this way, it had hoped to undo its negative image in India.[41]

September 11, 2001, provided another fertile ground for communications programs to project companies' social responsibility. Procter & Gamble donated more than $2.5 million in cash and products to relief efforts, but because it did not publicize these activities, the company was accused in the Harris Interactive–Wall Street Journal 2001 RQ gold survey for doing "absolutely nothing to help"![42] P&G had taken a consciously low-profile approach to avoid being seen as "capitalizing on disaster," which backfired.

So how can companies reconcile the public's desire for them to be good for the community and the environment with its equally strong skepticism about corporate motives? Why do some companies' efforts to make their good deeds known meet with approval while the good deeds of others are met with disdain? First, corporate philanthropy and social responsibility programs should be consistent with a company's vision to be perceived as credible and not simply as a "check the box" activity or an attempt to save a tarnished image.

Second, the means by which a company demonstrates that it cares for the community should be carefully considered, using the communication framework provided in Chapter 2. A company will be in a better position to structure the right kinds of programs and choose the right channels to communicate to its constituencies if it understands the concerns of each of its constituencies, what is important to them, and what they think about the company already. For instance, it may decide to describe its community outreach or environmental activities in its annual report or on its Web site rather than through advertising. It may decide that sponsoring a program that allows and encourages employees to volunteer their time in the community will be more effective than just giving money to a local charity.

India has seen some major disasters in recent times, and the lack of preparedness and inadequacy for dealing with such calamities is well known.

For dealing with these disasters, the Confederation of Indian Industry (CII) took the initiative of establishing a disaster management committee in May 2001 at the national level. The CII disaster management committee hopes to facilitate the promotion of disaster prevention, preparedness, and mitigation at all levels of government, the corporate sector, and the community. It also aims to explore the possibility of raising volunteer forces to deal with disasters that result from human and natural causes, as is commonly done in more developed countries.[43]

India offers many examples of companies displaying high standards of social responsibility.

Tata Steel is the only Indian company to have pledged to put the Global Compact principles on human rights, labor, and environment into practice and was conferred the Global Business Coalition Award for Business Excellence in the Community for HIV/AIDS in 2003.[44] The Tata Group pioneered labor welfare measures such as the eight-hour working day in 1915, established a welfare department in 1917, and had ensured maternity benefits in 1928, even before the law had enforced these.

Over the years, Tata Steel's involvement with the community has undergone a significant change. It has moved away from charity toward empowerment and partnership. The many facets of Tata Steel's corporate social responsibility include medical and health services in the rural and semiurban areas, sports, women's health and education, water harvesting and tribal development, relief and rehabilitation, and income generation.

India's largest private-sector company, Reliance, implicitly believes that corporate responsibility extends beyond the scope of a company's facilities and offices and that true corporate citizenship must include a common cause for the betterment of society. In keeping with this belief system, Reliance encourages, funds, and develops numerous education, health, and human capital initiatives. Many of these initiatives are now recognized in India and abroad as model approaches. These initiatives are undertaken through various organizations, including corporations and trusts. Reliance's commitment to corporate social responsibility has a firm footing resulting from the formation of the Dhirubhai Ambani Foundation (DAF), which initiates community welfare and development projects, especially in health care and education.[45]

Another example is of the Nirma Memorial Trust, which builds Ashrams and guesthouses for pilgrims and elderly women in Gujarat. The Nirma Foundation, set up in 1979, contributes toward the running of schools, colleges, temples, and 38 social institutions within and outside the state.

Café Coffee Day extends its financial support to Child Rights and You (CRY) in a unique gesture with the aim of educating 55 children every year.

Many constituencies are beginning to notice how the changing business environment is influencing corporate philanthropy and social responsibility. A company that has a good understanding of its own constituencies and what is important to them and which gives thought to how to include such programs in its corporate vision will be well positioned to create programs that will enhance its reputation.

CONCLUSION

Most managers who have not thought about corporate reputation tend to underestimate its value. This is partly the result of the lack of understanding about what corporate identity, image, and reputation are all about and what they can do for an organization. But skeptics should understand that an inappropriate or outdated identity can be as damaging to a firm as weak financial performance can be. Individuals seek consistency, and if perceptions about a corporation fail to mesh with reality, constituencies tend to shift their business interests elsewhere.

Executives, therefore, need to be fully aware of the tremendous impact that identity, image, and reputation can have on their businesses and must learn how to manage this critical resource. In the long run, an organization with a clear corporate identity that represents its true mission and is aligned with the images held by all of its constituencies will be rewarded with a strong reputation. Reputational success, in turn, matures into pride and commitment—among employees, consumers, and the general public—which are irreplaceable assets in an intensely competitive global business environment.

Chapter 5

Internal Communication: The Emerging Need in Global Organizations

For years, managers have focused on customer care. With the emergence of information technology (IT) and ITES (IT-enabled services) as high-growth sectors around the globe, a new urgency has developed to protect and promote employee concerns through communication and innovative human resources (HR) practices. This increasing need for effective internal communication has come about because of a high attrition rate in these new sectors. While the ITES (popularly termed business process outsourcing—BPO) industry is generating jobs for emerging economies (the National Association of Software and Service Companies, NASSCOM, predicts 1.1 million job openings needing to be filled in India by the end of 2008), employee turnover is as high as 30 to 35 percent in this industry. The unique work pressures of the BPO sector—irregular work hours and night shifts, monotonous job profiles, demanding and consistent performance levels—all contribute to an alarmingly high attrition rate.

Another point worth mentioning is that the IT and ITES sectors also have to deal with the relative youth of their employees and having to keep them engaged in a creative and stress-free environment; these sectors have also realized that their core strength and assets are their people and the resulting importance of looking after the interests of this key constituency. In fact, recently, antipoaching agreements were signed in both sectors—by software and BPO majors—promising to stop poaching from each other's resource pool.

Over the years, multinational corporations have taken their employees for granted, investing little thought and effort in employee concerns apart from routine HR practices involving promotions and salary increases.

More recently, they have begun to treat their employees as they would treat their customers, recognizing that employees have more to do with the success of a business than virtually any other constituency. The enlightened internal communication practices, which arose out of pressing need in the IT and ITES sectors, have slowly started to spread among other Indian industry sectors as well.

In this chapter, we examine how organizations can strengthen relationships with employees through internal communication. We start by looking at how the changing business environment has created the need for a stronger internal communication function. We then explore ways to organize internal communication through planning and staffing and how to implement a strong program using various communication channels. Finally, we discuss management's role in internal communications.

THE INDIAN SCENE—PORTFOLIO OF INTERNAL COMMUNICATIONS IN THE HANDS OF HR

Unlike in the United States and other Western economies, in India the job of internal communication still rests in the hands of the human resources department. In general, the strategic management of external constituencies is the job responsibility of corporate communication, while that of the internal constituency is the responsibility of the HR department. Further, the execution of internal communication activities may be partly supported by corporate communication people, but the burden of the job function lies directly with HR. This is a reflection of the changing role of HR—from a recruiting entity to a business partner, internal consultant, and operational as well as an administrative expert. The coming of the twenty-first century has seen a dramatic change in perception of HR by

(*continued*)

corporate leaders. From being viewed as simply a support function, HR today is viewed as a key player in driving corporate success and internal and external constituency satisfaction. In today's knowledge-driven economy, HR plays a strategic role in bringing the right kind of people into the organization, retaining them, nurturing them, and helping make them effective and intelligent brand ambassadors.

INTERNAL COMMUNICATION AND THE CHANGING ENVIRONMENT

As discussed in Chapter 1, the business environment has changed dramatically over the last half century. Today's employees are different in terms of values and needs from their counterparts in earlier decades.

Most of today's employees are well educated, have higher expectations of what they will get out of their careers than their parents did, and want to understand more about the companies they work for. Dilip Mohapatra succinctly sums up the emerging trends on the Tata Consultancy Services (TCS) portal: "The new age economy, with its attendant paradigm shifts in relation to the capital, in terms of its acquisition, utilization, development and retention, has placed a heavy demand on HR professionals.... The new age workforce comprises mostly knowledge workers, who are techno-savvy, aware of market realities, are materially focused and have a higher propensity to switch jobs. They prefer to experiment and explore new opportunities, are high risk takers with higher aspirations and expectations and generally have a totally different mind-set about job and careers."[1]

The workplace of today is also different—tighter staffing, longer hours, greater workloads, and more emphasis on performance are the norm. Additionally, layoffs are a constant threat as companies look to cut costs. Lifetime employment has become a thing of the past. In the United States, a Gallup poll conducted in February 2002 revealed that 51 percent of respondents personally knew of someone who had been laid off or fired within the recent past.[2]

Communicating to employees about layoffs, mergers, and acquisitions and whether or not they are directly affected is something many companies have had to deal with recently. Many corporations looked for creative alternatives to firing people during the most recent round of job cuts (80 of *Fortune*'s 100 Best Companies to Work For in 2001 avoided layoffs altogether).[3] But when alternatives run out, the way layoffs are handled is as important to the employees who remain at a company as it is to those who are let go.

Ned Barnholt of Agilent Technologies made sure that employees heard about impending job cuts from him before he announced the news on the company's quarterly conference call with investors. When it came to carrying out the initial round of 4,000 job cuts, Barnholt sent managers through a series of daylong training sessions where they role-played and learned about the right and wrong ways to communicate when firing someone. Additionally, Barnholt did not authorize "across-the-board" cuts; instead, he made his managers evaluate every program and every position individually, and only then were employees let go by their direct managers. The forms used to evaluate employees were posted on the company's intranet so that employees could see the criteria used to assess them. A company that had cut 27 percent of its staff, by the end of 2001 was thus able to land at number 31 in *Fortune*'s list of 100 Best Companies to Work For.[4]

In India, when the ICICI board approved the merger between ICICI Ltd. and ICICI Bank in 2001, the HR team put together a video presentation overnight for its 500 branches. The video featured Managing Director and Chief Executive Officer K. V. Kamath's remarks to investors and to the media.[5] Acknowledging that employee concerns were a priority with the company, ICICI posted the detailed report online, presented the highlights as a video, and followed up with personal interactions. At ICICI Bank, preempting news about the company in the media and informing employees of critical developments even 15 minutes before the news was released to outsiders was considered of strategic importance.

The business environment today has become increasingly complex and highly competitive. This puts greater pressure on employees and also calls for a more concerted effort in the area of internal communication. David Stum of the Loyalty Institute comments, "The American worker knows quite well that change is never-ending. How it's handled is what can lead the worker to be secure or insecure."[6]

Rod Olham of Bell South's small business services division offered these "truths" about today's employees at a speech given at the Tuck School of Business at Dartmouth, October 1994.

Ten Truths about Skeptical Employees[7]

1. They are smarter than senior managers believe.
2. They think senior managers are smarter than they actually are.
3. They hate it when they are made to feel stupid.
4. They have short attention spans.
5. They have long memories.
6. They are desperate for direction.
7. They want to be able to think on their own.
8. They want the company to succeed.
9. They do not want to leave.
10. They want to believe in the company.

Part of the problem at many companies is that senior managers simply do not involve lower-level employees in most decisions. This tends to make employees feel alienated and unwilling to accept changes within the company. In a poll conducted by Gemini Consulting and Yankelovich Partners in the United States, more than half the employees surveyed did not know their company's mission statement, 84 percent did not consider it fundamental to their work, and 44 percent did not feel connected to their employers.[8] More than anything else, good internal communication can connect employees to a company's strategy and vision.

This communication must be a two-way process. Managers need to recognize that, if they provide information to employees and also listen to them, those employees will be enthusiastic about their work, connected to the company's vision, and better able to further the goals of the organization.

One company that exemplifies this enlightened attitude toward employee relations is Philips India. Philips's Project Honeycomb[9]— so named because someone compared the company to a honeycomb, which depends on the teamwork of bees—comprises five projects, all aimed at making employees feel they are a part of a single company. The program was developed based on the feedback from young brand managers. *Let's Chat* is a multimedia program coproduced by the representatives of key departments. Every three months, this program includes three 70-minute sessions via streaming video. The first *Let's Chat* in August 2002 evoked 250 advance questions, and a Gallup internal poll revealed that close to 80 percent of respondents felt it was a useful initiative.

"The power of *Let's Chat* lies in employees seeing their management share a platform that cuts across boundaries . . . and investing a full day every quarter to connect with our people," says Chief Executive Officer K. Ramachandran. "The mission was to make a brand ambassador of each of our employees—and their families— and get people involved and charged up."

This behemoth company, with sales of Rs. 1,600 crore (approximately $377 million) has six businesses across 40 locations, and an employee in the bulbs division would have a very different perspective of the company from an employee in the software business. An extended, diverse, and complex network of Philips's workplaces across the country makes such a participative activity of crucial importance to promote empathy and team spirit.

Peter Senge notes that focusing on management development forces managers to pay more attention to their roles, skills, and tools for leadership.[10] He quotes an ancient Chinese visionary:

> The wicked leader is he who the people despise, the good leader is he who the people revere, the great leader is he who the people say, "We did it ourselves."
>
> —Lao Tsu

Internal communication is, in essence, about creating an atmosphere of respect for all employees within an organization.

Communication from management should come directly from one manager to the next, and from supervisor to employee. But as companies grow larger and more complex, this often becomes difficult; hence the need for an internal communication function.

Organizing the Internal Communication Effort

The best way to assess the effectiveness of a company's internal communication efforts is by determining what employees' attitudes are about the firm. This can be done through a communication audit. Based on audit results, communication professionals can design the right program for the organization.

For example, in the United States, both Starbucks Coffee Co. and Kinko's Inc. hired outside consultants to conduct internal communication audits to identify the strengths and weaknesses in the existing communication practices of these companies. Results of detailed questionnaires uncovered precisely how employees viewed internal communications and helped management develop possible solutions to communication problems. In addition, Kinko's used in-person interviews and videoconferencing to conduct nationwide employee focus groups and uncover the sentiments of employees from region to region.[11]

In India, too, employee satisfaction surveys are catching on as an important tool for directing internal communication activities. ICICI Infotech conducts employee satisfaction surveys twice a year.[12] "We believe that employee satisfaction surveys are a valuable tool for assessing job satisfaction, overall workplace productivity, and work culture. It gives an insight into employee perceptions and attitude towards the job as well as the organization," says Manoj Mandavgane, general manager of HR at ICICI Infotech.

Similarly, Patni Computer Systems (PCS) annually conducts employee expectation surveys[13] in its endeavor to understand the needs of its employees. Each of its 4,654 members is considered a key employee, regardless of his or her title, and the company believes that it is important to know their employees' expectations in order to make the "employee satisfaction survey" meaningful.

Once management knows how employees feel about the communications they are receiving internally and whether they understand the messages, it can implement an internal communication infrastructure to meet employee needs. If an infrastructure is already in place, it can be adjusted or enhanced as necessary based on the audit results.

Goals for Effective Internal Communications

Now that we have seen how the changing environment affects the internal communication effort and the importance of collecting employee feedback through a communication audit, we need to explore how companies can organize the internal communication function so that it supports the overall mission of the firm. Let us begin by first describing what the goals for an effective internal communication function should be.

A Conference Board study of over 200 companies in a wide variety of industries reveals what top managers see as the key goals for effective internal communications.[14] In order of importance, these goals are to

1. Improve morale and foster goodwill between employees and management.
2. Inform employees about internal changes such as a reorganization or staff promotions.
3. Explain compensation and benefit plans such as a new health-care plan or an employee assistance program.
4. Increase employee understanding of the company and its products, organization, ethics, culture, and external environment.
5. Change the behavior of employees so that they become more productive, quality-oriented, and entrepreneurial.
6. Increase employee understanding of major health/social issues or trends affecting them such as child care or AIDS.
7. Encourage employee participation in community activities.

In addition to these specific goals, a more overarching aim of internal communication is the creation of an atmosphere in which employees know that they are important assets to the firm. This can happen only if management believes that it is true and if professionals handle the communication effort.

TO WHOM SHOULD INTERNAL COMMUNICATIONS REPORT?

In the United States, as is the case in many countries around the world, including India, internal communication staff members have traditionally reported to the human resources area, since this function has dealt with all matters related to employee welfare. But recent surveys show that over 80 percent of corporations in the United States now place the responsibility for internal communications in the corporate communication area.[15] Often however, both areas have some involvement with internal communications.

Ideally, both the corporate communication and human resources departments of large companies have someone in charge of internal communication. If the person in the corporate communication department reports to the vice president in charge of that area and the person in the human resources department reports to his or her respective vice president, both should have a dotted-line relationship with the vice president in the other area. This will help ensure that the goals of each of the departments are fully met and that the lines of communication are kept open between these two critical functional areas.

At Continental Airlines, responsibility for communicating messages from senior management is shared between human resources and corporate communication.[16] New York–based health-care company Pfizer Inc. renamed its corporate personnel division "employee resources," merging the tasks of organizational structure, core competencies, staffing, training, development, communication, rewards, and employee advocacy into a single department.[17] "Internal communication is viewed as one aspect of managing employee relations and building employee commitment," says Pfizer's director of employee communication.

In the United States, large, multidivisional companies often have internal communication representatives within each division who report jointly to the chief officer for divisional management and to a firmwide corporate communication department. Ideally, each division shares best practices for delivering high-level messages to the employees in their respective areas. However, the channels of operation may differ across divisions; for instance, some divisions may have more of a voice-mail culture, where others may pay more attention to e-mail. However, in India, internal communication as a specific job function is randomly a portfolio of either an HR functionary or corporate communication person, or it may be a shared portfolio between people of the two departments, and no exact trends are decipherable.

In some cases, companies look outside their own organizations for help with internal communications. In January 2001, for example, General Motors announced that its employee communication professionals would report to a New York–based consultant specializing in management-employee relations.[18] The new reporting structure was implemented after surveys revealed that employees did not adequately understand management's key messages. The practice of relying on outside experts is becoming less restricted to times of crisis. In fact, by the mid-1990s, the Public Relations Society of America added an internal communication section to its organization.[19] In India, too, as the importance of internal communication gains recognition, it is not surprising that PR and consulting firms are developing capabilities in the area of internal communication, or that companies are increasingly turning to them for assistance.

IMPLEMENTATION OF AN EFFECTIVE INTERNAL COMMUNICATION PROGRAM

Once goals for an internal communication program are established and decisions are made about to whom the function should report, the program is ready for implementation. In smaller organizations, internal communications may be a part of everyone's job since the ideal method of communicating with employees is one on one or in meetings with small groups of employees.

Even in larger organizations, however, this intimacy in the internal communication effort represents a good start for building a more formal program. In this section, we explore some of the key steps to implementing an effective internal communication program, from personal, one-on-one mechanisms to programs that use technology to distribute messages broadly and instantaneously.

The Necessity for Upward and Downward Communication

Many large companies are perceived as being faceless, unfeeling organizations, an impression that is only reinforced when no communication exists from employees to management. When high-level managers isolate themselves physically and psychologically from their employees, effective communication cannot take place.

A nationwide survey of over 5,000 employees in U.S. firms conducted by a major consulting firm showed that the biggest criticism employees have of companies is that they encourage neither upward nor downward communication. A minority of employers seeks workers' opinions about key issues, and a quarter of those surveyed do not feel free to express their opinions at all.

The best approach for communicating with employees is through informal discussions between employees and supervisors. Employees need to feel secure enough to ask questions and offer advice without fear of reprisals from top management.

In the United States, Continental Airlines CEO Gordon Bethune is recognized for his effective leadership, which includes his high visibility among front-line employees and openness to communicating with them regularly. Each month, Bethune holds an "open house" in his office, where employees are invited to show up to speak with him about anything—issues, suggestions, complaints. Several times a year, he travels to the airline's major hubs to meet with employees.[20] With this kind of open communication and concern for employees as a hallmark of his leadership style, Bethune has been credited with a significant improvement in employee morale and overall corporate culture at Continental.

Southwest Airlines shares a similarly employee-friendly reputation. Its executives have implemented a number of digital communication mechanisms, including the blog "Nuts about Southwest," to allow employees to interact with each other, consumers, and the brand as a whole—and to very positive effect.

The Tata Group, the giant Indian corporation—which includes more than 90 companies in seven business sectors, and employs over 200,000 employees—places a great deal of importance on communication, which takes many forms from glossy *Tata Tea* newsletters to Webcasts with the managing director of Tata Steel to online contests and CEO chats at TCS.[21] It is not only desirable but also essential to impart a sense of unity among the workforce of the diverse companies under the umbrella of the parent company. At both Tata Steel, which has 30,000 employees, and TCS, which has 24,000 employees across more than 100 offices in 55 countries, there is an emphasis on getting information out not just quickly and consistently but in a manner that connects with people. Respecting employees as well as listening to and interacting with them form the basis for an effective internal communication program.

At Tata Steel, for example, the frenetic internal communication activity consists of six print journals, e-mail and intranet-based systems, dialogues between various levels of the organization, and the recently introduced Webcast from the managing director broadcast to all centers on the first of the month. At TCS, the monthly magazine, *@TCS*, is extremely popular, as are e-mails, posters, teleconferences, videoconferences, and online chats. There are also frequent contact programs, because, as Atul Takle, vice president of corporate communications at TCS, says, the bonding is important.

Hewitt Associates (www.hewitt.com), a global outsourcing and consulting firm, launched a "best employers in India" 2003 study in which three companies from the Tata group figured prominently in the top 25 best employers list (see the sidebar for the results of the 2007 survey), where internal communication was an important parameter for arriving at the results.

RESULTS OF THE 2007 SURVEY[22]

The following list presents the 25 best employers in India in order of rank:

1. Aditya Birla Group
2. Satyam Computer Services Ltd.
3. Marriott Hotels India
4. Eureka Forbes Ltd.
5. Cisco Systems (India) Pvt. Ltd.
6. Godrej Consumer Products Ltd.
7. Agilent Technologies Ltd.
8. Standard Chartered Scope International—India
9. Tata Consultancy Services Ltd.
10. Kotak Mahindra Bank Ltd.
11. Wipro BPO
12. Covansys (India) Pvt. Ltd.
13. Ajuba Solutions India Pvt. Ltd.
14. Pantaloon Retail India Ltd.
15. Text 100 India Pvt. Ltd.
16. Domino's Pizza India Ltd.
17. Ford India
18. Becton Dickinson India Pvt. Ltd.
19. Hardcastle Restaurants Pvt. Ltd.
20. HCL Technologies Ltd.—BPO Services
21. Dr. Reddy's Laboratories Ltd.
22. Johnson & Johnson Medical, India
23. GlaxoSmithKline Consumer Healthcare Ltd.
24. HSBC
25. Monsanto India Ltd.

Making Time for Face-to-Face Meetings

One means of ensuring that employees have access to senior management is for managers to hold regular, in-person meetings with fairly large groups of employees. Such meetings should take place frequently (at least quarterly) and should be used as opportunities for managers to share company results and progress on key initiatives. Most importantly, such meetings should provide employees with an opportunity to ask questions of management in an open forum.

Topics for these types of gatherings should be limited. Rather than tackling everything that is going on at the company, managers should survey employees beforehand to find out what is most important to them. Then a presentation can be built around one or two critical issues from the employees' perspective, plus one or more messages that management wants to share. Too often, management sets up such meetings only when the company has an important announcement to make, thus reducing the likelihood of relevant dialogue.

At i-flex, the major Indian IT company, all of its 2,300-plus employees are part of interactive initiatives such as an open house,[23] which is basically an open forum in which employees across the different i-flex centers and the company heads converge on business-related issues and voice their opinions. Such sessions are conducted annually and quarterly. The challenge in this program is to get everybody to focus on problem-solving and team-initiative efforts. Apart from this, there is the rewards program, where a series of credits are awarded across different groups of employees. Then there is the intranet, with very customized information that is again interactive, besides off-the-cuff pep sessions.

Certainly large-scale events are an effective means of reaching out to the majority of employees at one time, but managers should not overlook the importance of meeting with employees in smaller groups. If they are seeking feedback or opinions about key initiatives, managers may find that employees are more forthcoming when they are not in a large group setting. Smaller groups are also more conducive to resolving specific problems.

In just two and a half years, Rourkela Steel Plant (RSP) has achieved one of the most dramatic turnarounds in Indian corporate history.[24] Rourkela, which was in a dismal financial condition just a few years ago, is now firmly in the net profit mode. While RSP's turnaround started on a modest note in the year 2001–2002, it gradually picked up speed, and in the first 10 months of 2002–2003, RSP surpassed the production levels of all previous years. A lot of the credit can be given to the confidence-building measures, which top management took, to boost the morale of the employees through planned communication exercises and to contribute toward reviving the sinking steel company.

Now RSP is following the path of resurgence. This transformation of Rourkela from the brink of extinction to the realm of prosperity is a result of detailed planning and immaculate implementation of effective communication for the most important constituency in this case—the employees.

Soon after taking over as the chief executive of the company, Dr. Sanak Mishra reached out to the employees in various forums. While he found a lack of synergy and synthesis in the organization, he was impressed by the potential of the company's collective workforce. To enable the employees to understand, assimilate, and internalize the organization's priorities and implement them in day-to-day work, the chief executive launched a massive communication campaign that had no precedence in Indian corporate history. Under Mishra's leadership, a series of communication exercises, workshops, and interactive sessions were held involving the employees' participation in large and small groups. Discussions were held on day-to-day technical bottlenecks in open sessions in which hundreds of employees participated in expressing their commitment and concern for the company. The massive "mass contact" exercise on "Regenerating strength with people for the survival and future of RSP" launched by Mishra in 2002–2003, made history with its impact. Keeping in mind the changed vision of RSP, in the year 2003–2004, the objective of the mass contact program was changed to, "Regenerating strength with people for the profitability and prosperity of RSP."

The Rourkela Collective (employees' association) has adopted a mission statement that reads: "The future of our steel plant lies in our own hands. It is our individual and collective responsibility to rebuild our plant into a profitable, harmonious and vibrant organization. We will do whatever things are necessary which are good for our plant. We shall never do anything that hurts our plant." In order to focus discussion among the employees of the unit in the context of current priorities, make them understand their individual roles in the turnaround of the plant, and elicit their commitment for positive contributions to achieve the growth plan of the plant, a new weekly forum called a "general manager communication meeting," popularly known as GMCM, has been launched at the managing director's initiative.

To further enhance the synergy and synthesis achieved as a result of the communication interventions launched by him, Mishra has formulated another unique strategy, which he refers to as "Samskara." This revolves around a philosophical code of leadership practice: "We have to create and sustain a peaceful work environment where every employee can contribute to the plant in an assigned area of work, with full freedom and dignity and without fear." In tune with the philosophy of Samskara, RSP initiated several enlightened reforms, many of which owe their genesis to suggestions made by employees in the various interaction sessions they had with the top management. Employees in general have welcomed these measures and have expressed confidence that these innovative steps will provide an added impetus to the company's efforts at improving the work culture.

Creating Employee-Oriented Publications

While meetings are an important way to communicate with employees, the most common form of information sharing in many companies is through print. Unfortunately, most internal company publications are bland and boring. How can companies make monthly newsletters or magazines more interesting to employees?

Companies need to realize that their publications are competing with the national and local media for their employees' attention. Creating an employee publication is an ideal job for a former journalist. The most senior communication official and the CEO should also take an interest in company publications to ensure that employees are getting the real story about what is happening to the company and the industry and that the information is presented in an interesting way.

Reliance Energy[25] has the corporate objective of establishing good employee relations and thus promises to, "Establish a free-flowing information network of communication through exclusive use of the Company's newsletters, formal/informal forum of employees' association. . . . Have satisfied and motivated employees proud to be associated with Reliance Energy Ltd. (REL) with an overall feeling of having achieved 'Common Goals' through 'shared efforts' and 'participation.'"

REL has an in-house quarterly magazine, *REL REVIEW*, that includes articles from the chairman's desk, editorials, articles on community development, and cultural/technical/sports events in which REL employees have participated. REL has also set up a suggestion system, which is used as a channel for employee-management communication.

The overall objective of this communication process is to encourage employee participation in the company's endeavor to improve the organization.

Another way to reach employees through company publications is to send the magazines to their homes rather than distribute them at the workplace. Although this is more expensive, it helps make the company a part of the family, something that will be a source of pride for the employee and his or her spouse.

Above all, these publications must be honest about anything that might affect employees. Nothing will hurt morale more than having employees find out about a major corporate event from a source other than the corporation itself. The goal is to make employees feel like a part of the team and on the cutting edge of what is happening within the firm and its industry.

In the United States, General Motors' monthly report, *Messages from the Marketplace*, communicates with employees about how the company is responding to changes in the auto industry and the economy, and what this means to them.[26] While Microsoft communicates frequently with its employees via e-mail, it also produces a weekly newspaper, *Microsoft News*, which is delivered nationwide to every employee's desk. Reader surveys receive a high level of response, and in turn, the content of the paper has evolved based on readers' thoughts and suggestions. Candid letters to the editor are encouraged, reenforcing to employees that their thoughts and ideas are highly valued.[27]

The messages that go into these periodicals will vary by industry and company, but managers must strike the right balance between what employees are interested in and what they really need to hear from top management. Employees should look forward to the next issue of the company publication in the same way they do their university's alumni magazine. In fact, alumni magazines are excellent models in terms of style and tone for company publications.

Other print materials are also produced from time to time in response to important events that directly affect employees. For example, health or retirement benefit areas need a special set of publications. If a company is gearing up for a reduction in health benefits, it may start communicating with employees months before the actual changes take place to put these changes in context for employees. In this situation, the corporate communication staff would likely work with human resources to craft a communication strategy for what could be a yearlong communication process.

Management can also use memos and letters to communicate to employees about internal changes, such as management succession, new group structures, or important deals or contracts. These written communications should come out frequently enough so that employees do not feel that they are unusual, but not so often that they stop paying attention to management's messages. Certainly in the case of major events such as a takeover or merger, employees need to be informed ahead of external constituencies.

The timing gap between internal and external communications about such events must be narrow, however, as it can be damaging to the company if employees communicate sensitive information haphazardly to external constituencies before the company can make an official statement to the media or its client base. With the advent of rapid IT tools for communication, like instant messaging (IM) and short message service (SMS), this particular issue has become even more complex and sensitive, and therefore, minute strategic planning has to be in place in anticipation of turbulent times.

Communicating Visually

People worldwide are increasingly turning to television rather than newspapers to get their news. Similarly, employees are becoming more visually oriented in their consumption of information. As a result, many companies have developed ways to communicate with employees through television.

Most large corporations have elaborate television studios with satellite capabilities staffed by professionals. Such sophisticated systems are the best mechanisms for communicating with employees in visual ways. Even if your company does not have its own studio, outside vendors can provide these services.

These studios are often used to create "video magazines" that can be made available to employees in outlying areas, helping them feel a part of the organization even when the company headquarters is 1,000 miles away. At TCS, bonding a wide base of 24,000 employees with the CEO seemed like a challenging task. So to help everyone in the company get a better idea of Chief Executive Officer S. Ramadorai,[28] who is going to propel the company into the future, a 10-minute video was made, catching him on a walk, reading John Lennon's biography, and listening to Hindustani vocal music. The effort was well appreciated and promoted a better understanding of the man at the helm of the corporation.

Managers should not see expenditures on such communications as frivolous or wasteful but rather as an investment in the firm, a way to make each employee feel connected. If these productions are well done, they can be tremendous morale boosters, and they can create a visual history of the company that can be used for years to come. Moreover, they can be used for training purposes, thus justifying any expenditure as an investment in talent. For example, PricewaterhouseCoopers executives used visual communications to address various internal issues in a fun, conversational manner. They produced *The Firm*, a reality TV-inspired series that starred real employees and addressed everything from navigating uncomfortable conversations with fellow workers to handling internal conflicts. The video segments were e-mailed to 30,000 employees via a live link, and it illustrated a level of interaction that is often unheard of in such large, multinational organizations.[29]

However, visual communications do not always have to be high tech. Writing highlights on the white board, pinning up notices on the soft board, and circulating letters are visual communications that are inexpensive, easy to implement, and virtually impossible for any employee to miss.

Communicating Online

The advent of company intranets in the late 1990s provided a new way for companies to reach their employees quickly with important news on events and key management initiatives. Many company intranets also serve as an interactive platform for employees to share their views on company programs, which contributes to building trust.

Communicating through company intranets can offer many of the same benefits as live discussion groups. For example, in the United States, JC Penney's managers ask their peers questions online that can be answered instantaneously. All these questions and answers are stored in a Q&A database for future reference. The program has been so well received that more than 500 managers use this "knowledge management system" daily, with 300 employees actively participating in discussion groups.[30] Organizations as diverse as IBM, Xerox, State Farm Insurance, and Wells Fargo have active intranets to communicate with employees who are not centrally located.

The well-known Indian IT company Wipro has an interestingly packaged intranet communication program called Channel W.[31] The channel seeks to promote bonding among employees across the board, not as a bland must-use channel but one that attracts attention by being stimulating and enriching. The portal was designed after several rounds of focus group discussions and interviews with the employees covering what they would like their own channel to be like.

Channel W aims to be topical and dynamic and to enable two-way communication with the company through an interactive medium. The inspiration behind the idea was the myriad TV channels that are friendly and contemporary in their tone and content. The Wipro Channel W operates on the dual concerns of being convenient and user-friendly; the channel is on every employee's desktop and features various subchannels and programs that cover multiple topics.

The W in Channel W denotes several things. Besides "workplace," it stands for "we" (emphasizing the togetherness of all Wipro employees) and for "world," meaning contemporary. This channel promotes employee empowerment and creates a distinct feeling of My Wipro.com. By launching this internal communication channel, the software giant set about achieving its objective of promoting employees' personal and professional growth through corporate and community interaction. The sections of Channel W are designed to cater to the diverse needs of an employee: business channels (where the company news is profiled), personal sections for entertainment purposes, corporate news and views, current affairs, and a section solely dedicated to employee concerns, where workers can host their personal pages.

Internet technology, while extremely powerful, must be used with care if it is to enhance communications rather than detract from the impact of management's messages. These days, employees are bombarded by information, especially given the near ubiquity of e-mail and voice mail.

Further enhancing constant connectivity, instant messaging has acquired a new dimension. It is a medium for enhancing employee productivity, fostering team-building efforts, and enabling cost-effective and speedy communication. Indian corporations are now consciously eyeing IM tools for improving the communication process, thereby building close-knit teams and improving employee relationships. Instant messaging, experts believe, is coming of age—from being a teen fad to a corporate must-have.

Take, for instance, the case of Newgen Software. The company uses a host of IM tools, the most prominent ones being Yahoo! and MSN Messenger, for all its formal and informal communications that range from discussions and query responses to employees and clients to fixing up the menu and venues for birthday parties and get-togethers.

However, managers should resist the impulse to move all communications online unless it is certain that all employees will use this medium. Surveys can reveal how employees would like to receive different types of information, which helps determine what types of information a company's intranet will be the best channel for. An effective internal communication strategy should focus on content and distribution channel, recognizing that using multiple channels (some traditional and some more innovative) has the best potential for success.

Hewlett-Packard (HP) in the United States, for instance, found the optimal balance of old and new media after a certain amount of trial and error. For almost four decades, HP employees received hard copies of *MEASURE*, a bimonthly employee publication that has received several Gold Quill awards from the International Association of Business Communicators.[32] But in 1999, after HP announced that it would spin off Agilent Technologies to focus on printing and imaging products, management examined ways to improve every part of the HP business, and the company magazine was no exception.

Within the company's corporate communication area, the decision was made to transform *MEASURE* into a strictly online magazine accessible via the company intranet. When this move was announced, it was met with stiff opposition from employees, many of whom reportedly like to "curl up on the couch" with the magazine. Even former HP CEO Carly Fiorina agreed that "there are things you can do in print that you can't do as well in any other medium."[33]

The idea of having an online magazine was then dropped, and instead HP revamped the print version of *MEASURE* with innovative design elements and improved content. The magazine is now used as a means to direct employees to the company's popular intranet site, hpNow. While *MEASURE* offers employees a sense of familiarity and continuity, the company intranet is serving as an effective vehicle for follow-up stories and as an archive made up of past articles from the print publication. HP recognized that its print publication was effective and that employees had a strong connection to it so it used the intranet to enhance rather than replace it.

FOCUSING ON INTERNAL BRANDING

In this chapter, we have discussed the importance of a clear, two-way communication relating to the strategy and direction the company is taking. Internal branding is also important for building morale and creating a workplace where employees are engaged with their jobs. While communicators do inform employees about new advertising campaigns, they seldom recognize the need to sell employees on the ideas they are trying to sell to the public.[34]

Internal branding is especially critical when an organization is undergoing changes such as a merger or a change in leadership. When British Petroleum merged with Amoco and then ARCO, it rebranded itself as BP and launched an internal branding campaign that was simultaneous with an external program. Proclaiming that the merged entity was going "beyond petroleum," the campaign reinforced the rebirth of an oil company into an energy company with an open, collaborative, "new economy" culture. Employees of the three companies that merged to become BP now have a solid identity to relate to.

New advertising campaigns are also appropriate times to think of internal branding. Employer branding is all about the company's value in the market, a timeless process that in today's world has gained even more significance. It is essentially a combination of the reputation of the organization, the career opportunities, and the corporate culture existing in the company. HCL Comnet, whose brand value signifies exuberance, has developed a "force of one" campaign that signifies an innovative attitude and the ability to individually make a difference.

In the United States, Mark Levine, director of employee communications at networking giant 3Com, created the "3Com More Connected World Expo" in 1998 as an internal, traveling trade show geared toward employees. The trade show went on the road at the same time that 3Com was launching its "more connected" campaign to the public. "We wanted our employees to understand why we were rolling out that brand," Levine said. "We wanted them also to understand . . . how that brand connected with the vision, strategy and mission of the company."[35] According to surveys 3Com conducted at the end of each local event, 85 percent of participants said that they understood the "more connected" message, and 78 percent understood the company's vision.[36]

Internal branding campaigns can also be launched when results of internal audits reveal that employees are not connecting with a company's vision or when morale is low.

When internal and external marketing messages are misaligned, the customer experience will suffer; this will have adverse effects on the company. For example, one health-care company marketed itself as putting the welfare of its customers as its number-one priority, while telling employees that the number-one priority was cutting costs.[37]

Even when employees understand the company's brand promise or key customer deliverable, it is not until they believe it that they can really help the company carry it out. Just as external branding campaigns aim to create emotional ties between consumers and companies, internal branding's goal is to do the same with employees.

Focusing attention on this important area will generate improved employee morale and ultimately better results for the company.

CONSIDERING THE COMPANY'S GRAPEVINE

When considering channels of internal communication, we cannot neglect the importance of its informal counterpart. The company grapevine—an informal communication network including everything from private conversations between two employees to the latest anecdotes shared in the cafeteria—should be considered as much of a communication vehicle as a company's house organ or employee meetings. An estimated 70 percent of all organizational communication occurs through the grapevine, which distributes messages faster and in more credible forms than formal channels. For this reason it is crucial that managers tap into it.[38] Yet, statistics reveal that over 90 percent of companies do not have a policy to deal with the grapevine or to manage any other informal communications network.[39]

Managers can find out about what employees think by simply asking questions. Union Carbide, for example, uses overnight polling to gauge employee reactions to its programs. In one study, 89 percent of managers conceded that the grapevine transmits negative information, indicating of a lack of trust of employers concerning other employees, supervisors, or organizational policies.[40] The stronger the sense of trust and commitment between employees and management, the rarer it will be that employees will resort to the grapevine as the chief means of expressing their voice and hearing that of fellow employees.

The following points indicate how a company can succeed in building a good rapport with its employees:

- Create an atmosphere of respect.
- Treat employees as insiders.
- Build up corporate loyalty.
- Capture more discretionary time.
- Increase two-way communications.

- Invest in decent publications.
- Listen to and use the grapevine.

MANAGEMENT'S ROLE IN INTERNAL COMMUNICATIONS

A common thread in the examples discussed in this chapter is the involvement in internal communications of CEOs and other senior leaders within organizations. This is critical because these individuals are the "culture carriers" and visionaries within a company, and all communications relating to organizational strategy start with them. They need to work closely with internal communication professionals to ensure that their messages are received and understood by all employees.

The "understanding" component is important, but sometimes overlooked. Donald Sheppard, CEO of Sheppard Associates, an independent consulting agency specializing in internal communication strategy in the United States, says, "You can have a vision of 'we want to be this'—that's nice, but the person out there in the plant in Michigan or in India needs to understand how that applies to him or her and what he or she needs to do differently. That can't be done at any macro level."[41]

To achieve this "micro" level of understanding of what strategic goals or initiatives mean to individuals, internal communication professionals should work with frontline managers to help make messages relevant to the employees who report directly to them. FedEx focuses development efforts on frontline managers, including work in the area of communication.[42] These individuals, after all, have the greatest potential to help relate management's vision to employees' individual business areas, and to their day-to-day activities as well.

CONCLUSION

Over the last several years, "management by walking around" and other management philosophies basically have come to the same conclusion: managers need to get out from behind their desks, put down their cell phones, get away from their computers, and go out and get to know the people who are working for them. No other method works as well, and no quick fix will satisfy the basic need for interaction with other employees. With all the sophisticated technology available to communicate with employees today—e-mail, intranets, satellite meetings, and so on—the most important factor in internal communications begins with the manager who has a basic responsibility to his or her employees. That responsibility is to listen to what employees have to say and to get to know who they really are as individuals. It is a long way from Upton Sinclair's *The Jungle* to the modern corporation. Today's employees want not only high-tech and sophisticated communications but also personal contact with their managers. Thus, the cornerstone of an effective internal communication program is the understanding and implementation of this so that it becomes a reality.

Chapter 6

Corporate Advertising

In Chapter 5, we discuss the importance of creating a coherent identity and image. Of the many options available to organizations to communicate their identity, paid corporate advertising is the easiest and fastest. As a result, most large corporations use some form of corporate advertising, which acts as an umbrella covering any product associated with the company. Because of this strong association, any corporate advertising campaign should be:

1. *Strategic.* Looking toward the future of the company so that it will have longevity and won't become stagnant or "old news."
2. *Consistent.* In keeping with images of products or businesses of the company. Image advertising cannot be viewed as a separate corporate message; rather, it must fit with company vision.

In this chapter, we study the role of corporate advertising and how it can shape an organization's image. This topic is addressed by first defining corporate advertising, then looking at the history of corporate advertising, and finally discussing who uses this form of advertising and why.

WHAT IS CORPORATE ADVERTISING?

Corporate advertising can be defined as paid use of media that seeks to benefit the image of the corporation as a whole rather than its products or services alone. Because all of a company's advertising contributes to its image, both product and corporate advertising should reflect a unified strategy. Corporate image advertising should brand a company the way product advertising brands a product.

A major difference between corporate and product advertising lies in the origin of each. Typically, a company's marketing department is responsible for all product-related advertising and pays for such ads out of its budget. Corporate advertising, on the other hand, falls to corporate communication and either comes out of that budget or, in some cases, is paid for by the CEO's office.

Corporate advertising should present a clear identity and image for the organization based on a careful assessment of its overall communication strategy (see Chapter 2), and it generally falls into three broad categories: image advertising, financial advertising, and issue advocacy. Let us take a closer look at each of the three categories to understand what corporate advertising is all about.

Advertising to Reinforce Identity or Enhance Image

Many companies use corporate advertising to strengthen their identities following structural changes. As companies merge and enter new businesses, they need to explain their new vision, organization, and strategy to constituencies who may have known them in an earlier incarnation but are now struggling to understand the new organization. These typically larger organizations often need to simplify their image in order to unify a group of disparate activities. The Tata Group, which has gone through a long restructuring process under Chairman Ratan Tata, has used corporate advertising to great effect.

The year 2004 was a special and momentous year for the Tata Group of India. It marked the 100th anniversary of the death of Jamsetji Nusserwanji Tata, the founder of the house of Tata, and the 100th anniversary of the birth of J. R. D. Tata and Naval Tata. These three men are recognized as pioneers of corporate India and business leaders with vision. Over the past 100 years the Tatas have invested in industries and worked in areas that have been of specific importance to nation building and industrial development. They accomplished this while also upholding the values cherished by the organization: innovation, leadership, trust, and fair play. Thus, the organization saw 2004 as the culmination of a "century of trust." On this occasion, the Tata Group released two advertisements to mark the launch of the century of trust initiative.

The first advertisement was to commemorate the 100th anniversary of the death of Jamsetji Nusserwanji Tata. The advertisement read:

> The man who introduced steel to India. The man who brought electricity to Mumbai. The man who set up the Indian Institute of Science. The man who built India's first luxury hotel.

The second advertisement was titled, "the human face of industry," and its visual portrayed the three dynamic Tata leaders. The advertisement read:

> These are the leaders who left an indelible mark on the Tata Group, on industry and on the country. Much of their enterprise was an expression of self-belief that the country could manufacture steel, generate power and use modern technologies.... The Tata Group has been driven by the vision of its leaders. This vision also emphasized the importance of returning to society the wealth that was generated. Over the years, the Tata Group has funded and established schools, hospitals, community centers and institutions of higher learning. It has also extended support towards management of natural resources, livelihood and other welfare projects across India. Built on the cornerstones of integrity and honesty, for over 100 years, Tata stands for trust in any language or dialect spoken in this vast land.[1]

Both advertisements reinforce the image of Tata as a family of diversified companies and one that sets high standards in two areas it has been associated with for decades: business vision and high standards of corporate ethics and responsibility. Diversified conglomerates in the United States have been using this kind of advertising for years.

United Technologies Corporation (UTC), for example, used the tagline "Intelligence shared is intelligence squared" in several print ads that portrayed the company's research center as an "engine of ideas" for the family of companies that makes up UTC. The copy in one of these ads explained why you will find the same ultraviolet air-purifying system used by Carrier (a UTC company) for buildings and Hamilton Sunstrand (another UTC company) for planes. Across the bottom of the ad were the names of six United Technologies companies. Not only do the ads raise awareness that these other companies whose names you might recognize (e.g., Otis and Pratt & Whitney) are part of United Technologies, but they also highlight a whole-is-greater-than-the-sum-of-its-parts concept by explaining how the company's core research competency benefits all UTC family members.

We discussed in Chapter 4 the need for organizations to manage their identity, image, and reputation with a variety of constituencies. When companies analyze their image with constituencies, they can then apply their findings to their corporate advertising strategy.

If an organization's identity is very different from how it is perceived externally, for instance, it can use corporate advertising to close that gap.

The state-owned telecom giant BSNL (Bharat Sanchar Nigam Ltd.) has been using corporate advertising to change its image. Because it was a domestic monopoly until the late 1990s, harassed consumers turned hostile and perceived BSNL as corrupt, inefficient, and unreliable. Today, BSNL faces tough competition from mobile and landline telecom companies such as Bharati, Hutch, Reliance, and Tata and is losing hundreds of thousands of customers in the bargain. To survive competition, BSNL is reinventing itself and entering high-growth areas of telecommunications such as mobile telephony, Internet services, and high-speed data

United Technologies used this advertising campaign to clarify the organization's identity and explain how its Research Center is the hub of the UTC family of companies. *Permission granted by United Technologies.*

transfer. According to P. Singh, managing director of BSNL, by 2006 mobile telephony had become a bigger business than landlines. According to him, consumers must perceive BSNL not as a stodgy and outdated telecom monopoly but as a dynamic telecom company. The tagline used by the company in all ads is "connecting India."[2]

Corporate advertising is also an integral part of organizations' reputation management and recovery strategies. Tyco used corporate advertising to rehabilitate its image in the wake of corporate fraud by former CEO Dennis Kozlowski and former CFO Mark Swartz. Under Kozlowski, Tyco had become a confusing conglomerate of business units built by aggressive acquisitions. Even the company's own employees were unsure of what businesses Tyco was in. Following operational improvements, new CEO Ed Breen hired Jim Harman from General Electric to serve as vice president of corporate advertising and branding. Harman, who had overseen GE's "We bring good things to life" campaign, was assigned the task of demonstrating the breadth of Tyco's businesses, products, and services. Tyco used the tagline "a vital part of your world" in several print ads that portray the company's products and services as integral to daily life. The ads feature a background of more than 6,500 words listing Tyco products and services. The words form a picture, such as a baby or a firefighter, demonstrating the importance and vitality of Tyco's offering. And indeed, in 2005, Tyco won an award for best corporate advertising from *IR Magazine*.[3]

Another example of corporate advertising being used for reputation rehabilitation is the case of Mattel. As discussed in Chapter 2, Mattel hit a significant road bump in late 2006 and 2007 when a string of product recalls threatened its credibility as a company whose products were safe for children—its ultimate consumer. Part of its crisis management strategy was a corporate advertising campaign with the tagline, "Because your children are our children, too." It served to reinforce to parents that Mattel executives were taking all necessary steps to ensure that proper safety measures were in place. The ad, which was released on August 14, 2007—the same day Mattel announced another recall—appeared in the *Wall Street Journal, New York Times*, and *USA Today*, and it included a letter from CEO Bob Eckert that began, "Dear Fellow Parents."[4] While the advertising initiative did not fix the problems brought on by the wave of product recalls, it remains an example of how corporate advertising can reinforce identity, enhance image, or boost reputation.

Effective image advertising also allows companies to differentiate themselves from rivals. A television spot by Maruti Udyog Ltd., manufacturer of India's largest range of cars, illustrates this point. The ad shows two young men driving high on the mountains in the Himalayan range when they come across a young shepherd. The boy replies in the negative when asked about food, toilet facilities, and a motel in this remote area. Yet, he nods yes when they ask if the locality has a Maruti service station! This ad seeks to single out Maruti as the only carmaker that has a service network across every corner of India. Many similar examples can be found around the world.

For instance, Nintendo won *Advertising Age* magazine's marketer of the year award in 2007 after it presented a blitzkrieg of corporate advertising around its new product, the Nintendo Wii. After years of languishing behind competitors like Sony's PlayStation and Microsoft's Xbox, the company depended on this product to boost sales and reinstate the brand as a leader in the video gaming industry. In November 2006, with $200 million in marketing support, Nintendo's advertising campaign incorporated traditional media with word-of-mouth marketing and digital communication platforms. It appealed to nontraditional audiences, like mothers, and empowered these groups by making them official Wii ambassadors. The complementary TV and print ads (crafted by Leo Burnett, Chicago) all featured the signature phrase, "Wii would like to play." However, most important to the success of the marketing effort was its application of strategy (by looking toward audiences that represented the future success of the company) and its consistent messaging.

According to NPD Group analyst Anita Frazier (as quoted in *Advertising Age*), "Marketing played a huge role in the success of the Wii and DS (dual screen), and I think the power of having a focused message executed throughout all the elements of the marketing campaign is evident. It's sort of like Marketing 101, but too many marketers forget that having a solid positioning and messaging is the most important thing to do before you spend the first dollar on executing the campaign."[5]

In India, the shaky state airline, Air India, leveraged its falling corporate image by aligning with its visionary corporate leader J. R. D. Tata and other Tata Group companies. The corporate advertisement had a portrait of J. R. D. Tata and his signature blazoned in the sky, with the Air India plane in full flight as the background. This reminded consumers of the connection between Air India and J. R. D. Tata, which the readers had almost forgotten because of the airline's falling fortunes and reputation. Now by paying homage to its leader, Air India effectively incorporated and reflected the values of its dynamic leader.

Advertising to Attract Investment

In Chapter 8 we look at the importance of a strong investor relations function. One of the tools that companies use to enhance their image in the financial community is financial relations corporate advertising. This kind of corporate advertising can stimulate interest in a company's stock among potential investors as well as buy-side and sell-side analysts (see Chapter 8 for more on analysts). Given the hundreds of companies that analysts cover, a good corporate advertising campaign can stimulate analysts' interest and lead them to take a closer look at a particular company. In India, there is special emphasis on launching corporate advertising campaigns when the company wants to raise money from the markets. Virtually every large company unleashes an expensive image-building campaign before an IPO (initial public offering). The obvious aim: attract more investors and get a better price for the share.

One of the most visible examples in recent years is the campaign launched by India's largest IT and IT services company, Tata Consultancy Services (TCS). The company released a series of ads, even in international publications like *The Economist*, in June and July 2004. With a tagline, "truly global," the campaign asks the question: "'IT' put India on the world map. But who put 'IT' on the Indian map?" Since the TCS stock will be listed in global stock markets, the campaign is targeted at investors worldwide.

Another example of a lavish campaign before an IPO is ONGC Ltd. (formerly the Oil & Natural Gas Commission). The company released a full-page ad in *The Times of India* on January 26, 2004, India's Republic Day. The advertisement made all the positive noises: "Today is the 26th of January, 2004. Today, we celebrate the pride of our nation. Tomorrow, our pride will soar even higher. Today, we are India's largest integrated Oil and Gas Corporate. Tomorrow, we will go further." It further adds that, "We carry the flame of knowledge, ideas and energy. A flame that shines on technologies for growth, and opportunities for tomorrow. A flame that leads the way, and enriches the quality of life. A flame that touches every Indian, every day. It's a flame for making tomorrow brighter."[6]

Globally, companies target investors even when they are not raising money for the markets. While analysts do focus heavily on company financials, in a survey of 200 research analysts—each of whom covered approximately 80 companies—"strength of management" was the number-one factor found to be influencing decisions to invest in a company.[7] Analysts place a high value on CEOs who express a coherent vision for their organizations, and as James Gregory of Corporate Branding LLC explains, "The CEO's ability to paint a picture of the company's future is the linchpin of a successful corporate advertising campaign."[8] For these reasons, companies' CEOs are often featured in corporate advertisements targeted at the financial community.

Some corporate advertisers in the United States assert that a strong, financially oriented corporate advertising campaign can actually increase the price of a company's stock. A W. R. Grace campaign that ran in the early 1980s is often cited as evidence of this. The television campaign, which ran as the company's "look into Grace" series, highlighted the company's financial and business attributes and then asked, "Shouldn't you look into Grace?" Attitude and awareness studies of the ad campaign in test markets showed that the company's awareness and approval ratings were much higher after this campaign ran. In addition, the company's stock price increased significantly during the test campaign, although it did not go any higher with later campaigns. Corporate advertising expert Thomas Garbett, writing in the *Harvard Business Review*, stated that:

> I interpret the relationship between corporate campaigns and stock pricing this way: advertising cannot drive up the price of a reasonably priced stock and, indeed, doing so might not be entirely legal; it can, however, work to ensure that a company's shares are not overlooked or undervalued.[9]

Professors at Northwestern University's Kellogg School of Business studied this trend using econometric analysis of the link between corporate advertising and stock price. They determined that, indeed, corporate advertising does have a statistically significant positive effect on stock prices. They further determined that the positive influence from such campaigns averaged 2 percent and was particularly strong during bull markets such as in the mid- to late 1990s. Similar studies are not available for the Indian market, but many analysts privately admit that a sustained corporate campaign does raise the profile and attractiveness of a company.

The implications of this study, if true, are exciting for companies. Even a one-point increase in the stock price can translate to the tens or hundreds of millions of rupees (or hundreds of thousands—or even millions—of dollars) for large companies with many shares of stock outstanding. In addition, an improvement in stock prices that improves the company's price-earnings ratio can present opportunities for stock options and dividends for employees.

Advertising to Influence Opinions

Advertising to influence opinions is often called *issue* or *advocacy advertising* and is used by companies to respond to external threats from either government or special-interest groups. Issue advertising typically deals with controversial subjects; it is a way for companies to respond to those who challenge the status quo.

Star News, part of the Star Network in India and controlled by Rupert Murdoch's NewsCorp, had an arrangement with content provider NDTV that began in 1998. The agreement was simple: NDTV would produce all the news bulletins and related programming that would be aired on *Star News*. In 2003, both parties terminated the deal and Star Network decided to launch a news channel with in-house employees rather than depending on an outside content provider.

Just days before the relaunch of *Star News*, the government of India changed the law relating to foreign investment in news media. The new rule stipulated that no foreign person or organization could hold more than 26 percent equity in a media outlet. *Star News* had to offload 74 percent of equity to Indians in a hurry. That was not the end of its troubles.

Two Indian media houses, the Times of India Group and the India Today Group (which runs the leading Hindi news channel Aaj Tak), ran stories that accused *Star News* of violating and subverting Indian laws. Virtually all media outlets in India picked up the story, and there was a lot of flak. *Star News* and Star Network were portrayed as foreign influences subverting Indian democracy. The network retaliated by releasing big ads in newspapers and magazines that challenged this contention. The ads kept hammering home the point that Star Network was very much Indian and accepted as Indian by viewers.[10]

Something similar happened to Coke and Pepsi in 2003 when they had to resort to corporate advertising to try to convince consumers that their soft drinks were safe. Tests conducted by a nonprofit body, Center for Science and Environment (CSE), on soft drinks found traces of pesticides far in excess of norms set by the European Union. There was a huge media outcry, and Pepsi and Coke had to face what KFC had faced in the mid-1990s in India. Both companies saw a fall in sales, and the alarm bells were loud and clear. To counter this bad press, both companies released a series of ads informing the public that two highly prestigious labs—TNO of the Netherlands and CSL of London—had concluded that the CSE findings were wrong.[11]

In the next few months, Pepsi and Coke invested heavily in celebrity-endorsed campaigns that sought to portray the pesticide controversy as a tempest in a teacup.

Other global organizations have also adopted this op-ed style for their advocacy ads including Amway, the U.S. company, which typifies the more positive approach used by companies dealing with environmental issues. Amway ran a series of ads that positioned the company as environmentally aware. One had a photograph of five Amway distributors and the headline: "Find the Environmental Activist." The copy goes on to explain that everyone in the ad is an environmental activist and that all Amway distributors are committed to environmental awareness. The tagline reads: "And you thought you knew us."

This advertisement also reveals the problem with much issue advertising. As David Kelley points out in an essay on the subject of issue advertising in the *Harvard Business Review*, most companies "Pay too much attention to the form and too little to the content of the message." Does the tagline in the Amway ad, for example, imply that, "You thought we were a bunch of polluters because we specialize in detergents that come in huge containers"? Or does it mean that, "You thought we were just selling detergents when what we are really doing is protecting the environment"? Either way, the advertisement seems to be playing into the hands of critics rather than setting the agenda for the company's position. Since the advertisement is so short, it never gets across the point that this company is trying to make. That is, it would like to argue directly with critics who charge Amway with environmental neglect.

Since companies typically are more conservative than their noncorporate adversaries, their arguments often fall short of the mark. It is extremely difficult for a large corporation to take on a tough issue in the marketplace without offending someone. When companies try to please everyone, they ultimately dilute the power of their own message.

If a company decides to pursue an advocacy campaign, senior management must have the courage to argue forcefully for its ideas and must not be afraid to alienate certain constituencies in the process. For example, in the United States when the major booksellers took on the conservative groups that called for a purging of all "dirty" books, the booksellers won the argument with advocates of first amendment rights but lost with family-oriented fundamentalist groups. Organizations should thus proceed into the world of issue advertising with extreme caution and with a full understanding of its inherent risks.

THE HISTORY OF CORPORATE ADVERTISING

Corporate advertising of all the types discussed in this chapter was first seen in the United States, and interestingly enough, one of the earliest documented corporate advertisements was issue-oriented. According to expert Thomas Garbett, the earliest corporate ad, paid for by the American Telephone and Telegraph Company, started its run in June 1908. The ad had as its headline "Telephone service, a public trust" and went on to defend the company's point of view as:

> The widespread ownership of the Bell Telephone System places an obligation on its management to guard the savings of its hundreds of thousands of stockholders. Its responsibility for so large a part of the country's telephone service imposes an obligation that the service shall always be adequate, dependable and satisfactory to the user.... There is then in the Bell System no incentive to earn speculative or large profits. Earnings must be sufficient to assure the best possible service and the financial integrity of the business. Anything in excess of these requirements goes toward extending the service or keeping down rates.

Obviously, even in the early part of the century, AT&T had to defend its (then) monopoly status and combat the assumption that it couldn't possibly be acting in the public's interest given the lack of competition. AT&T hoped that the public, as a result of reading the advertisement, would have more faith in the company and its honest intentions.

A decade later, many companies were running corporate advertisements. Herbert F. de Bower's 1917 textbook, *Modern Business*, defines issue advertising in a way that is still relevant today:

> Copy that is intended to make people "think something" is termed "molding public opinion" copy. It is used for pure publicity—to direct public sentiment for political or legislative purposes, and frequently to advertise an industry.
>
> An advertisement, which aims to induce a general impression favorable to some policy, act, or product, obviously employs copy designed to influence public opinion.[12]

By midcentury, "institutional advertising" (as it was called) was widely used throughout the United States. Garbett describes one of the most interesting reasons for the increased use of this form of advertising during World War II:

> [Corporate] advertising was broadly used during the [second world] war. Although few peacetime products were available for sale to the public, some advertisers realized that if they stopped advertising for several years, it would be difficult to regain their prestige after the war. A younger generation of consumers would come into the market unfamiliar with their products. The advertising of the period frequently took the form of telling what the company was manufacturing for the Armed Forces.... In many cases the advertisers expressed regret that their products were not available to the public and promised improved products after the war.[13]

One advertisement that captured the essence of what companies were doing was a hybrid product and image ad. Lucky Strike cigarettes at the time had a green package that was made from some derivative of copper. The cigarette company was forced to give its copper to the government for the war effort. In changing its packaging to white from green, the company adopted an innovative ad campaign with the headline: "Lucky Strike goes to war!"

After World War II, corporate advertising faded from view until its revival in the 1970s when oil companies found themselves battling allegations of exorbitant profits during the oil crisis. As special-interest groups gained power throughout the 1970s and 1980s and media interest in corporations also increased, companies again turned to corporate advertising to defend themselves.

Today, corporate advertising is highly visible and intensely scrutinized by constituencies. Magazines from *Advertising Age* to *BusinessWeek* feature annual "best of" lists praising corporate campaigns that are deemed to be the best overall or most memorable. Advertising has also gained recognition from investors and Wall Street analysts whether or not ads are explicitly targeted at the financial community. In fact, a study in the *Journal of Advertising* indicated that when a company announces a relationship with a new advertising agency, investors perceive this as a sign of strategic changes within the company.[14] Additionally, equity analysts often discuss companies' advertising campaigns in their research reports and share opinions on new campaigns with the press.

The Indian story is a little different. As mentioned in Chapter 1, India followed socialist economic policies that created monopolies and oligopolies—in both the public and private sectors. Hardly any organization spent any money on corporate advertising. Even product advertising was restricted to a handful of companies.

It was in the 1980s that corporate advertising took off in India. Led by companies like Reliance, the Indian stock markets experienced a boom in the mid-1980s, and hundreds of companies went public, raising thousands of crores of rupees (billions of dollars) from retail investors. Virtually all these companies resorted to corporate advertising to enhance their image with investors. Most of the ad campaigns hit newspapers and magazines before the public issue and were withdrawn soon after the issue.

With liberal economic policies launched in 1991, India witnessed an increasingly competitive marketplace. As globalization gathered momentum in the 1990s, companies started feeling the need for corporate advertising. The target was no longer the direct consumer and investor. Environmental and consumer activism made it necessary for Indian companies to project a humane image to the world at large. In fact, this happened to such an extent that corporate advertising has become the norm for all large companies.

WHO USES CORPORATE ADVERTISING AND WHY

According to recent studies, over half of the largest industrial and nonindustrial companies in the United States have corporate advertising programs of one sort or another. Usually, a direct correlation exists between size and the use of corporate advertising—the bigger the company, the more likely it is to have a corporate advertising program. Since large corporations tend to have more discretionary income, this makes sense. In addition, larger companies tend to be more diversified and thus have a greater need to establish a coherent image from a variety of activities, products, and services.

In India, although no detailed analytical studies have been conducted on the direct linkage that exists between corporate advertisements and the size of the advertising corporation, consumers can clearly see the strong correlation between the two. For example, the two home-grown Indian majors—Reliance Industries and Tata Group—enjoy high media visibility as their corporate advertisements appear frequently in all the national dailies. Readers can easily identify these companies with their image-boosting taglines— Reliance encapsulates its corporate philosophy with "growth is life," and Tata endorses its corporate image with "improving the quality of life." Similarly, the large Indian public sector units (PSUs), such as the Fortune 500 company Hindustan Petroleum Corp. (HP) promotes its holistic image with the campaign, "Where there's energy, there is HP," and Gas Authority of India Ltd. (GAIL) reinforces its growing portfolio of products by increasing the number of its advertisements with the corporate tagline "gas and beyond." The multinationals in India, with a large and diverse range of products and services, use corporate advertising to create consistent and unified images. In the United States, GE regularly advertises under the corporate umbrella tagline "ecomagination," and all Philips products enjoy a strong recall as a result of the company using the slogan "sense and simplicity."

Corporate advertising is also used heavily by companies in more controversial industries: tobacco and liquor companies, oil companies, utilities, and other large industrial companies all have image problems to deal with, from concerns about health to allegations of monopolistic behavior to pollution. A perfect example is Reliance Industries, whose corporate advertisement had a visual of a dewy fresh rosebud ensconced in green leaves and the body copy reads, "low emission, low waste, low pollution, low noise, low fuel consumption." The intrinsic values of the rose visual, which implies freshness, nature, and harmlessness, reinforces the copy used to project Reliance's heavy industry as something desirable and in consonance with nature. Overall, heavy industry spends more on corporate advertising than consumer-packaged goods firms do. In fact, they lead all other industries in product advertising. This may be related to the presence in consumer products companies of a strong marketing focus that concentrates more on the four Ps— product, price, promotion, and place (distribution)—than on developing a strong corporate image.

In India, gutkha (a variant of chewing tobacco) companies like Simla, Goa 1000, and Pan Parag skirt the ban on tobacco advertising in television channels by resorting to surrogate advertising in the name of pan masala (betel leaf chewy) bearing the same brand name. Cigarette companies resort to tobacco-sponsored cultural events like the Red & White Bravery Awards.[15]

Many other examples of surrogate advertising abound in India, since a ban on liquor advertising also came into effect in October

2000. Today, liquor companies in India spend close to Rs. 100 crore (approximately $23.5 million) in sponsoring various sporting events.[16] Royal Challenge whiskey, Foster's beer, Chivas Regal, and Kingfisher have emerged as avid sponsors of elite sports like golf, polo, and car racing over the last few years. With the ban on direct advertising, liquor brands have increased their focus on promotions through sports in order to directly connect with their target customers and promote lifestyle image. Shaw Wallace, for example, has a long-standing association with golf and has associated itself with professional golf associations to promote the game. Shaw Wallace's Royal Challenge Indian Open is a very popular event on the national and international golf circuits. Seagram, too, has been sponsoring events such as the Chivas Regal Polo Championships and the Chivas Regal Invitational Golf Challenge for corporations. Seagram's Royal Stag has been associated with India's most popular sport, cricket, on the domestic front. One can see Foster's association with the Formula One international car-racing events through all its strategic corporate communication activities. Similarly, Haywards 5000 beer has associated itself with darts and is sponsoring the National Darts Championships.

A good corporate advertising program can clarify and enhance a company's image, and the absence of one can hurt packaged goods companies and retailers as well. Kmart Corp. in the United States has struggled with its corporate image in recent years, and, critics argue, failed to differentiate itself from rivals such as Target and Wal-Mart. The company seems to have vacillated between trying to compete on price (it revived its "blue light specials" with much fanfare in 2001) and marketing brand names such as Martha Stewart (who went to jail for obstruction of justice in 2004). This lack of clarity left customers with no clear, differentiated perception of the company.

Let's now take a closer look at some of the reasons companies invest in corporate advertising campaigns.

In India, the Korean multinational LG has managed to position itself clearly amidst the clutter of consumer goods market, which already is overcrowded with well-entrenched companies like Usha

Lexus, Godrej, BPL, Videocon, Philips, and National Panasonic. LG's unique positioning as a company, which focuses on the health and fitness of its consumers, has bought huge benefits and increases in sales for the company. LG launched its range of products under the umbrella benefit of being a health-giving company, while its competitors could not create distinct platforms of communication and thus floundered in the marketplace.

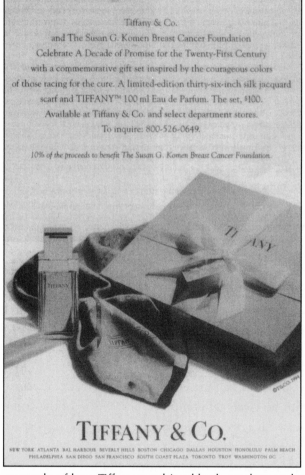

This is an example of how Tiffany combined both product and corporate advertising. It represents the best of how philanthropic efforts can be used to foster goodwill with constituencies. *Courtesy Tiffany & Co.*

INCREASE SALES

The relationship between corporate advertising and sales is less clear than that between product advertising and sales because corporate advertising is meant to do things that eventually boost sales rather than do something that will have an immediate and direct result. This creates a problem for managers who are trying to introduce corporate advertising into companies that have a heavy financial orientation. The numbers-oriented manager will often use the lack of a direct connection between corporate advertising and sales as the best reason not to use it.

In the United States, however, there are growing efforts to identify a closer relationship between corporate advertising and sales. Robin Webster, senior vice president of the Association of National Advertisers (ANA), remarked, "As has been seen in other marketing communications areas, corporate advertising managers are becoming more concerned with determining the return on investment (ROI) of their efforts."[17]

While measuring the return on investment for individual marketing disciplines began 75 years ago with the monitoring of results from direct-mail campaigns, attempts to determine the ROI from integrated marketing campaigns are more recent. Several agencies, including Grey Global Group, McCann-Erickson WorldGroup, and J. Walter Thompson are using new tools to better quantify results for clients, including measures such as cost per sale or cost per lead.[18] This sort of analysis can help companies make a stronger case for advertising budgets in difficult economic times and may also aid with their financial projections.

In 2000, AT&T Business Services took the unusual step of asking agencies competing for a $100 million business-to-business advertising assignment to project the return on investment of the company's proposed campaigns, and also to recommend which of the company's services should be most heavily advertised. In the future, "Advertising won't be treated as an expense, but as a strategic investment," said former marketing vice president Bill O'Brien.[19]

Through corporate advertising, companies can highlight aspects of themselves that they think will appeal to the public and, as a result, make consumers more likely to buy products from them. For instance, SC Johnson, the manufacturer of such brands as Glade, Pledge, Windex, and Ziploc, learned that 80 percent of consumers believe that family-owned companies made products they could trust, versus only 43 percent who said the same of publicly owned companies. In response, the company rolled out a $450 million campaign highlighting the family heritage of SC Johnson, with the tagline, SC Johnson—a Family Company.[20]

Returning to our Kmart example, after entering bankruptcy proceedings in 2002, the company looked to corporate advertising as a mechanism to bring customers back and revitalize sales, pouring $40 million into its "the stuff of life" corporate advertising campaign. With television spots directed by filmmaker Spike Lee, the campaign attempted to make what the company's marketing chief called "an emotional bond" with customers.[21] By positioning itself as a part of the lives of everyday families, Kmart hoped to attract sales by projecting a staying power that would overcome the public's perception that it was going out of business.

In India, such specific figures and data that relate corporate advertising to increased sales are perhaps even harder to get (see Table 6-1). However, an instance of corporate advertising by Airtel, mobile service, and the correlational figures of sales in that time period, does illustrate the importance of such advertising

Table 6-1   Operating Highlights for Bharti's Airtel Indicate Correlation between Corporate Advertising and Sales

| | Number of Units (000 omitted) | | |
	June 30, 2004	June 30, 2003	Year-Over-Year Growth
Mobile	7,672	3,751	105%
Fixed line	704	424	66%
Total	8,376	4,175	101%

Source: Press releases July 23, 2004, www.bhartiteleventures.com/news&events/news.htm.

rather sharply. One of the Airtel corporate advertisements read, "With Airtel, you are among friends . . . 137 countries, 337 global networks" to emphasize its international networking. The campaign seems to have achieved an important objective.

CREATE A STRONGER REPUTATION

We discussed the importance of reputation in Chapter 4. The best corporate advertising creates goodwill and enhances reputation by letting constituents in on what the organization is all about, particularly if it does beneficial things that people might not be aware of.

In the United States, Amoco Chemical Co.'s campaign, which won an award from *Business Week* in the late 1990s, is a good example. One of the print ads for this campaign showed an airplane landing at night with the headline: "Amoco helps make coming home a little safer." The ad went on to explain that the lighting masts use durable resin compounds based on material from Amoco Chemical. While the advertisement was visually appealing, another reason this campaign made it into *Business Week*'s "most memorable" list that year was the concept that chemicals are used to make our life better in ways that most people don't even think about. The tagline, also memorable, reads: "The chemistry is right at Amoco." Learning more about the good things that come out of Amoco shifted some people's perceptions away from thinking of Amoco as another "big oil" company and a producer of environmental pollutants.

Companies also look to build credibility and enhance reputation by using endorsements from a third-party organization (TPO).[22] Just as individuals rely on the Zagat survey to confirm their choice in restaurants, many find this type of "seal of approval" advertising helpful in assessing companies, particularly lesser-known ones. An endorsement by a trusted and recognized TPO can inspire confidence in the consumer. Third parties can provide ratings or rankings of a company or its services, or they can be used as the subject of a story that illustrates how the company provided a service to them.

Another example from the United States is an advertisement for a Van Kampen mutual fund that mentions the fund's five-star rating by the Morningstar investment guide. Xerox Corp. launched a series of print ads using the other approach. One of these shows the Xerox name in large print with a car key sitting on top of it. The copy reads, "Enterprise Rent-A-Car wanted to reduce operational costs. Xerox found the key to success by moving 1.7 million documents onto their intranet every month." Another ad talks about how the company helped Honeywell lower its operational costs by millions of dollars.

While Xerox already had the name recognition that many smaller companies using TPO advertising do not, it was largely known for its photocopying equipment. This series of ads, with the tagline "There's a new way to look at it" revealed a much broader set of capabilities. Being able to talk about projects it had undertaken for large, well-known companies provided Xerox with more credibility as it attempted to boost its image as a more comprehensive service provider.

In India, corporate advertising is increasingly being used to leverage conglomerates, as a whole, mostly in case of an impending initial public offering (IPO) or raise public awareness about the group's activities and enhance reputation. For example, there is heightened awareness of the Aditya Birla Group of companies because of the ongoing corporate campaign, which boldly states the company's mission as, "Taking India to the world means the world to us." The tagline occurs amidst a collage of foreign locations like the Egyptian pyramids and Thailand's pagodas. Clearly, the company is proclaiming its international reach plus voicing its patriotic sentiments. Also, sometimes by hitching corporate advertising to a national event, the corporations manage to create instant awareness and project the companies' image in a different light. Philips released a corporate advertisement on India's 50th Republic Day, in all national dailies, proudly proclaiming, "We at Philips pledge to share your vision in one voice: The new millennium belongs to India."

Corporate advertising is also widely used by companies to publicize their philanthropic activities, which, as discussed in Chapter 4, can also lead to an enhanced reputation. These advertisements can create bizarre associations between otherwise diametrically opposed sectors of society such as cigarette manufacturers and the arts (Philip Morris), opera and oil (Texaco), and supertanker manufacturers and blue whales (Samsung).

In India, tobacco companies usually fight for sponsorship rights of various sporting and cultural events. For a long time, the Indian cricket team was sponsored by Wills, the flagship brand of Indian Tobacco Company (ITC). The sponsorship lasted until March 2001, when it could not continue because of the government's ban on such sponsorships by tobacco companies. ITC's corporate campaign of 2004 highlights its philanthropic endeavor ITC e-Chaupal—a community help program for the farmers—by making available the latest information technology. The tobacco company reiterates its intent with its tagline, "Let's put India first."

On the cultural front, Manickchand, manufacturers of gutka, the tobacco chew, sponsors the Filmfare Awards (the Indian version of the Oscars). Additionally, in several parts of India, major Hindu festivals like Ganesh Chaturthi and Navratri are celebrated with great fanfare because of funding and patronage by gutka companies. The earthquake that ravaged parts of Gujarat (India) in January 2001 was fully exploited by gutka manufacturers as they distributed food packets with gutka sachets to build up their social image. Ironically, even the national Red & White Bravery Award recognizing heroes for courage capitalizes on the positive image and the goodwill the event fetches despite its injurious product—cigarettes.

Organizations using corporate advertising to enhance reputation must be prepared for their opponents to respond negatively to what they may perceive as the companies' attempt to smooth over a history of corporate wrongdoing or to apply a quick fix to a serious image problem. For example, after increasing spending on positive corporate image building by a staggering 1,712 percent between 1998 and 2000, Philip Morris still ranked 56 out of 60 corporations in the 2006 Harris interactive reputation survey published in the *Wall Street Journal*.[23]

The company's aggressive advertising campaign touting its philanthropic activities, coupled with its new identity program (see Chapter 4 for more on the Altria name change), actually worked to alienate critics further. Many viewed both as attempts to mask the company's true identity as a cigarette manufacturer responsible for thousands of cancer deaths. In fact, at Philip Morris's 2002 shareholder meeting, demonstrators waved a giant canvas banner depicting a skeletal Marlboro Man in a bandana marked Altria.[24]

It is important then, when using corporate advertising to enhance reputation, that the advertising be credible. Corporate advertising risks not being perceived as credible if, for instance, it ties closely to corporate vision when that vision has not been properly communicated to the organization's constituencies through other channels. This highlights the point made earlier that corporate advertising must be strategic and closely aligned with a company's overall communication strategy. In isolation, it will not have the power to change perceptions about the organization.

Recruit and Retain Employees

One of the most critical communication activities for any company is communicating with its employees (see Chapter 5). If a corporate advertising campaign succeeds in explaining in simple terms what a large, complex organization is all about, this can be as helpful to employees as it is to the outside world. Corporate advertising is also an indirect way of building morale among employees. Trying to quantify this is very difficult, however. Garbett says:

> Putting a dollar figure on the savings attained by reducing employee turnover is difficult. Some say you should add recruitment and training costs, next multiply by the

turnover rate, and then estimate the percentage of employees who might be persuaded to stay if they felt more positively about the company. Whatever the real figure, if corporate advertising can effect even a modest reduction in turnover, the saving to a large corporation is well worth the expense and effort of a campaign.[25]

Such advertising also helps companies attract the best and the brightest both at the entry level and for senior positions. A good corporate advertising campaign can create excitement among both potential and current employees. GE launched a corporate print advertising campaign with four employee-related themes: diversity in leadership, the GE Fund, the GE mentoring program, and volunteerism at the company. Many of the ads show photographs of current GE employees as children. In one ad, a girl is pictured holding a globe; the text reads: "Introducing Eugenia Salinas who has traveled throughout the world as GE's General Manager, Americas Marketing for GE Medical Systems. She's part of the group of minority and women leaders across GE responsible for over $30 billion in annual revenues."[26]

Other ads include more recent photos of GE employees who are involved in mentoring through the company-sponsored program or who participate in volunteer projects along with members of their local community. Many such ads, ostensibly focused on employees, enhance a company's image with nonemployee constituencies as well. Consumers, for instance, may be impressed with GE's social responsibility programs or the caliber of its employees, which they read about in these print ads.

The Indian software giant Tata Technologies attracts attention with its surprising visual in its recruitment advertisement—employees gathered around a table-tennis game in progress, and the headline reads, "Thought we'd warn you about the occupational hazards beforehand." This advertisement for recruiting software technologists apparently promotes the image of the company and its working environment as being young, friendly, and stress free. In a scenario where employee retention is becoming increasingly difficult in the BPO sector, this advertisement aims for a friendly corporate image, promoting team spirit and camaraderie.

CONCLUSION

Corporate advertising helps companies communicate their message to a wide audience quickly and efficiently, but at a rather high price. Some managers will shy away from it because of the costs involved and the difficulties inherent in measuring its near-term effect on sales. However, all the goals discussed for corporate advertising—increasing sales, enhancing reputation, and attracting and retaining employees—if met, will ultimately improve a company's financial situation.

The decision to run a campaign should be based, above all else, on a firm's overall communication strategy. Whether the company is changing its image, is suffering from erroneous perceptions in the marketplace, or simply wants to continue a successful, well-received campaign that solidifies its identity, corporate advertising can be a tremendous resource in positioning the organization for future success.

Chapter 7

Media Relations: A Key Ingredient in Global Businesses and Emerging Markets

he media relations department is one of the most critical areas in any corporate communication function. The media are both a constituency and a conduit through which investors, suppliers, retailers, and consumers receive information about and develop images of a company. Consumers, for instance, might see a business update of a particular firm on CNBC or CNN, or read an article about it in *BusinessWeek* or *Business India*. This role of the media as disseminator of information to a firm's key constituencies has gained increasing importance over the years. Virtually every company has some kind of media relations department, whether it comprises one part-time consultant or a larger staff of professionals.

In this chapter, we look at what media relations professionals do and how companies should approach increasingly sophisticated media. We examine who the media are, how firms communicate with them through relationship building, and what constitutes a successful media relations program in today's changing business environment. Before we consider media relations on a global level, we look at how the media environment in India has changed dramatically in recent decades.

THE NEWS MEDIA IN INDIA

Today, the news media are omnipresent in Indian society. With the advent of television in the late 1960s, of color television in the early

1980s, and the tremendous growth of the Internet in the late 1990s, what had once been the domain of the print medium has increasingly become part of the visual realm through television sets and computers.

The arrival of television moved "headline news" formerly found in newspapers to a new, nearly instantaneous medium. Newspapers adapted by taking over the kind of analysis that previously appeared in weekly news magazines like *Business World* and *India Today*. News magazines, in turn, took over the feature writing that used to appear in older weeklies like *Illustrated Weekly*.

The media are a powerful part of society. The Indian constitution guarantees the right of free speech, and over the years, the media have helped shape attitudes on issues as diverse as uniform civil law and reservation quota (a form of affirmative action that reserves seats in the public sector for underrepresented classes), female feticide, and pollution-control measures. A free press also makes politicians accountable for their actions in public and private life. And even politicians would argue that the media bring the distant world of politics into the home of the average citizen.

While most Indians feel strongly about the right of free press, that is, to say or print whatever the press likes as long as it is not malicious, business has always had a more antagonistic relationship with the press. This stems in part from the privacy that corporations enjoyed in earlier times. Unaccustomed to dealing with the news media, most companies simply acted as if the media did not matter. But toward the latter part of the twentieth century, companies were forced to rethink this isolationist approach because of a number of developments, including laws governing the disclosure of certain information by public companies at regular intervals, laws requiring proof of malicious intent to win libel cases against the media, more public interest in business undertakings (see Chapter 1), and more media interest in business enterprises.

These last two events in particular—increased public and media interest in what companies were doing—have had a profound effect on business and its dealings with the media. Which came first? Although it is difficult to determine whether the media generated heightened interest in business or were simply responding to changes in public attitudes, what is certain is that some time in the 1980s business coverage started to change. Since then, the private sector has become much more public.

Part of what perpetuated this shift in attitudes was the public's realization that business had a tremendous effect on their lives. Incidents like the Harshad Mehta scam,[1] the coffin controversy,[2] and the Telecom scandal[3] were precursors to India's first major sting operation, famous now as the *Tehelka* scandal.[4] People began to perceive companies as controlling important parts of their lives yet not answering to anyone in the way the government did to voters. Special-interest groups emerged to deal with this problem and to make business more accountable.

Business leaders, on the other hand, were used to the privacy they had maintained for decades and were reluctant to admit that times had changed. Even in the new millennium, some older business professionals resist accepting the importance of communicating through the media and would rather maintain little or no relationship with what they see as an institution that tries to tear down everything they built up. This kind of attitude is increasingly risky, though less common, as each industry—from oil and gas, to chemicals, to financial services—has found itself the subject of some level of scrutiny from the public and the media, and many companies have learned the hard way that having poor or nonexistent relationships with the media in these situations will only make things worse.

THE GROWTH OF BUSINESS COVERAGE IN THE MEDIA

Before the 1980s, business news was relegated to a few pages toward the back of the newspaper (consisting mostly of stock quotations) and to a handful of business magazines; it received virtually no coverage at all in national and local television news broadcasts. Financial dailies like *The Economic Times* and *Financial Express* have been around since the early 1960s, but they remained niche players until the 1980s. India's first major business magazine, *Business India*, was launched in 1978, followed by *Business World* in 1982. All these publications tried hard to critique India's socialist policies and consistently asked for more liberal economic policies. As public attitudes changed, however, the business news sections in newspapers gained recognition and began to expand.

When Rajiv Gandhi became India's prime minister in 1984, the government did make some minor economic reforms—particularly in the consumer goods sector and stock markets. The stock markets witnessed meteoric growth in the mid-1980s, with businessmen like Dhirubhai Ambani of Reliance pulling millions of retail investors into the equity markets. The stock market boom led to many magazines, including *Dalal Street Journal* and *Capital Market*, which have survived the many ups and downs in the markets.

Around the same time, the *Times of India* developed *Business Times*, a separate section published every day devoted to business issues. This is now widely read for business updates.

The 1990s saw a maturing of the business news market, with dailies like *Economic Times* emerging as the second largest circulated financial daily in the world after the *Wall Street Journal*. There was a virtual explosion in the number of newspapers and magazines that were launched to cash in on the growing middle-class love affair with stock markets, consumerism, and enterprise.

Today, so many magazines and Web sites are devoted to business news that it is nearly impossible to find a topic not thoroughly covered by one media outlet or another. In recent years, news of corporations, the stock market, and business personalities have often become the lead story on national news television and radio broadcasts. With the 24-hour networks like CNBC India devoted to business news, stock exchange buzz, and special business capsules you can find on NDTV and Zee News network, corporate news is virtually impossible to ignore. In fact, four exclusive business news channels compete with CNBC for eyeballs.

Compared to decades past, business news today is actually exciting. The magazines found in doctors' clinics in the 1980s were basically dull vehicles for companies to express their viewpoints. Today, cover stories appeal to a wider audience. *Business Today*, *Business World*, and *Business India* gain attention from a broad readership by publishing the salaries of top CEOs and features such as the widely read rankings of business schools and corporate brands.

As coverage of business increased, however, the media industry was consolidating in a way that was different from the way it was consolidated in the United States and other nations around the world. There is no doubt that the big players like *Times of India*, Living Media, Hindu, Zee, and Star networks grab the lion's share of readership, viewership, and advertising revenue. In this, the media industry in India reflects global trends. At the same time, since the 1980s, dozens of new media entrepreneurs have sprung up in regional languages. In this respect, media are not consolidating, but fragmenting, in India.

In addition, buyouts and layoffs in the media industry have led to smaller newsrooms operating on tighter budgets. As a result, many reporters have to produce stories by themselves—the TV reporter who did only on-camera work is now responsible for the development of an entire story. Print reporters need to think more today about photos and graphics if they want to capture the attention of a public inundated with information.

Most executives today recognize that the media are typically not going to get very excited about the good things that companies do. Instead, the worse the news about a company or CEO, the more likely it is to become a major news story that will capture the media's (and public's) attention, if only for a short time. In the United States, a research study revealed that the public wanted more reporting on corrupt business practices by a margin of 60–28 percent.[5] This information lends further support to corporations that want to develop a thoughtful approach to their media relations.

BUILDING BETTER RELATIONS WITH THE MEDIA

To build better relationships with members of the media, organizations must take the time to cultivate relationships with the right people in the media. This might be handled by employees within the company's media relations department (if one exists) or given to a public relations firm to handle. Either way, companies should be sure to avoid falling into some of the common pitfalls of what has historically been media relations standard practice.

For example, most of the old-style public relations experts rely on a system of communication with the media that no longer works. That system is to send out press releases (or video news releases) to a mass audience and hope that someone will pick up the story and write about it. Why is this system no longer valid? The vast majority of press releases go unread by reporters in India and the United States—because of the quantities of releases reporters receive daily and their time constraints. The same is true for mail, e-mail, and voice mail from public relations agencies. Journalists who write about business for national publications such as *Business Today* or *Economic Times* can receive hundreds of such releases in one day. The persistent buzz of all the mail, faxes, and phone calls clutters the writer's mind, and barely 10 percent of it actually succeeds in making it to print.

When DHL and fax machines first came into daily use in the 1980s, many public relations professionals started overnighting and faxing releases to reporters, thinking that they would look more serious than others and thus get read. While this may have worked for a while, reporters caught on to what was happening and began screening overnight letters for the "round file" just as they had with regular mail for years. The analogy to what many people face each night when they come home to a mailbox stuffed with catalogs is appropriate here—people are now almost programmed to jettison everything in their mailbox and look at only the mail that is delivered directly to the door via courier service.

A public relations professional made a stir by facing allegations that PR executives are flacks, even as he attacked the sacred institution of press releases. "We don't like it when we're called flacks, but as a profession we play right into the image when we spray press releases like machine-gun fire at anything that moves."[6]

While they can be very effective, press releases are overused by public relations professionals because they are relatively easy to write—even formulaic in terms of composition—and they can be widely distributed to certain segments of the media thanks to sophisticated computer programs that now allow companies to target specific audiences. There are even firms that will provide such services.

Many such service providers can be found on the Internet. The U.S. media outlet eReleases, for instance, pulls from its database of over 10,000 journalists to target and submit a company's press release; it will also write the release for an additional fee. Public relations agencies in India charge thousands of rupees (anywhere between $20 and $250) for the same kind of service. In-house public relations professionals also create and send out hundreds of press releases to the same people over and over again for such mundane stories as the promotion of a midlevel executive.

With such wide distribution to an audience that is already saturated with information, how can anyone expect that this strategy would work? Yet public relations firms claim that the system is still quite valid and embraces its similarity to the direct-mail system mentioned earlier. Response rates of 2 percent are considered a success in the direct-mail business, so public relations professionals are thrilled if their release gets picked up by a handful of publications.

Part of the problem is that the measure of success in the media relations business has for years been the amount of "ink" (coverage) that a company gets, whether aided by in-house professionals or an outside consultant. Yet no one has ever stopped to figure out what value a "hit" (as they are called in the business) in a relatively unimportant publication has in terms of a firm's overall communication strategy. Getting lots of ink, which means lots of articles written about a company, may not have any value if it does not help the company achieve the communication objective (see Chapter 2) it started out with in the first place.

The message to companies about press releases is: use mass-mailed releases sparingly. Organizations should reserve this method for stories that they are sure will have a wide audience. In such cases, the same result can be achieved by sending the story out on a public newswire, such as PR Newswire in the United States, or trying to sell the story to a national newswire like the Associated Press. Most of the time, what works better is to probably find out who the right journalists are for a given story. Companies seldom use this tactic, however, because it takes more time to conduct such research, and senior executives outside the corporate communication function may be reluctant to pitch a major story to just one journalist at a time.

In a field cluttered with information coming from a variety of sources, however, this is actually the best approach. Ron Alridge, publisher and editorial director of *Electronic Media*, makes his point in his article, "A Few Tips on Having Good Media Relations." He emphasizes, "Understand the news organization you are dealing with. I wouldn't bother to list this seemingly obvious rule if so many media relations types didn't break it so often. Ignorance is always a turnoff."[7]

CONDUCTING RESEARCH TO TARGET MEDIA FOR PITCHING

The way a typical media research operation might unfold for a company is as follows. First, senior managers working with the members of the corporate communication department determine what objectives they have for a certain story. Let us assume, for example, that the story is about a major company that is moving into the business process outsourcing (BPO) market. The managers' objective might be to create awareness about the move into the new market and also to discuss how the firm has changed its global strategy. Thus this story is part of an overall trend at the company rather than a one-shot, tactical move. Given these considerations, the company would begin to search for the right place to pitch the story.

To do this, the corporate communication professionals look in their files to find out who covers their industry and their company specifically. This is relatively easy for most companies to do since the same reporters typically cover the same beat for a period of time and have established relationships with the companies on their beat either directly or indirectly. Some of these reporters—typically those from print journalism—would definitely be interested in the story. If the company is maintaining its records properly, it can determine at a glance which reporters will most likely cover the story and more importantly who will be likely to write a "balanced story" (code words for a positive piece) about this strategic move.

How do companies determine who is going to write a positive piece before rather than after pitching the piece? This is where ongoing research pays off. Each time a journalist covers a firm in the industry, the corporate communication professionals need to determine what angle the reporter has taken. To continue with our example, suppose a look at the records shows that the *Economic Times* reporter who covers the company's beat has recently written a piece about a competitor firm moving into a different market as part of its new global strategy. The chances are that this reporter will not be interested in writing the same story again about another company. Therefore, the company should not pitch its story to this reporter.

By conducting this kind of research, companies can avoid giving reporters information that they are not interested in, and communications need occur only when a company's media audience is most likely to be receptive. While this system is not foolproof, it generally yields better results than sending out a story to dozens of reporters hoping that four or five may pick it up, with no idea who they are or what angle they are likely to take.

Today, most companies can easily access information about the journalists who cover them. In the United States, consultants generate computer analyses of reporters' articles, ask industry sources to provide critiques of writers they know, and even find out personal information about writers. In India also, with the increasing ease of Internet access, a detailed electronic database of media professionals is being compiled by major corporations to facilitate targeting the media. While earlier generations of PR professionals worked hard to get such information at long lunches with reporters, new technology allows corporate communication professionals to access such information through electronic databases with ease.

In addition to figuring out who is covering a company's beat, members of the firm's corporate communication team need to determine what kind of a reporter they are dealing with. For a television network like CNBC, this means knowing who the producer for the piece will be. Then a communication professional from the company can retrieve the last two or three stories from the head office and review them. For a business magazine such as *Business Today*, electronic databases contain stories that reporters have written over a period of time. Those written in the last two years are most likely to be useful to a company.

What can corporate communication professionals learn by looking at previous stories the producer at CNBC has filed and earlier stories that the *Business Today* reporter has written? An individual tends to write about things or put together reports in a particular way. Very few reporters change their style from one story to the next. They have found an approach that works for them—a formula, so to speak—and they tend to stick with formulas that work.

What an analysis usually reveals is that the journalist tends to write or present stories with a particular point of view. One such analysis performed for a company on a certain reporter's work showed that he liked to write "turnaround" stories. That is, he liked to present the opposite point of view from what everyone else had written about. So, if a company is trying to make a case for being an example in such a turnaround story, this reporter would be likely to write the kind of article that would be helpful to the company despite the potentially negative tone.

Watching the CNBC producer's work could help determine how interviews are conducted, how stories are edited, whether charts and graphs are used as part of the story, and so on. Let us say that the producer, for example, seems to present balanced interviews, as opposed to antagonistic ones, and likes to use charts and graphs. It seems that this producer could turn out a positive story for the company and should be pursued.

Corporate communication departments should perform the type of analysis discussed earlier for each media call that comes in. Many executives complain about the amount of time such analysis takes, but the benefits of handling an interview with this kind of preparation make the effort involved worthwhile.

RESPONDING TO MEDIA CALLS

In addition to doing their homework on reporters, companies can strengthen their relationships with the media by the way they handle requests for information. Many companies willingly spend money on advertising but are unwilling to staff a media relations department with enough personnel to handle incoming calls from the media.

This can be a costly mistake, as responding to such requests carefully can make a powerful difference in how a company comes off in a story.

Let us say that a company has gotten negative press over the last couple of years because it has not kept up with the times, but it is now working on a campaign to change its image. A call regarding this campaign comes in from a reporter at CNBC and another call comes in from a reporter at *Business Today*. What should the communication staff do to ensure that both of these calls are responded to in a timely manner and will reflect well on the company?

To begin with, calls should come into a central office that deals with all requests for information from important national media. While this sounds like common sense, calls from the media are often answered by people who cannot distinguish between important and unimportant calls. Many an opportunity has been lost because the wrong person failed to get the right message to someone in the corporate communication department.

Next, the person who takes the call should try to find out what angle the reporter is taking on the story. In our example, the CNBC reporter may or may not have a particular point of view, but the *Business Today* reporter probably does, since that publication prides itself on taking a particular approach to its stories. The company needs to find out what that approach is before it responds to the request. Let us assume that the CNBC reporter wants to look at the company's activities as part of an industry trend toward more upscale positioning. The *Business Today* reporter, on the other hand, seems to imply from the conversation that she sees the company's new approach in a less than positive light.

The person responsible for that telephone call should try to get as much information as possible while being careful not to give in return any information that is not already public knowledge. The tone of the conversation should be as friendly as possible, and the media relations professional should communicate honestly about the possibilities of arranging an interview or meeting other requests. At the same time, he or she should find out what kind of deadline the reporter is working under.

This is often a point of contention between business and the media. Particularly with senior executives who are accustomed to arranging schedules at their own convenience, a call from the media at an inconvenient time can be an annoyance. But all reporters must meet deadlines. This means that they have to file their stories—whether on television or radio, in print, or on the Web—on a certain date, by a certain time. These deadlines usually have little flexibility, so knowing in advance what the deadline is allows you to respond within the allotted time. The conversation should end with the media relations professional agreeing to get back to the reporter within the allotted time. Being aware of deadlines is similarly critical when a company is proactively pitching a story. This will avoid irritating reporters who are working under deadline crunches.

PREPARING FOR MEDIA INTERVIEWS

Once the research and analysis is complete, the executive who will be interviewed needs to be prepared for the actual meeting with the reporter. If the interview is to be conducted by phone, as is often the case for print articles, a media relations professional should plan to sit in on the interview. The following approach works best.

First, the executive should be given a short briefing on the reporter or producer's prior work, with examples gathered in the research phase discussed earlier, so that he or she develops a clear understanding of the reporter's point of view. For example, if the reporter tends to write turnaround pieces, the appropriate passages from relevant stories should be shown to the executive.

One Fortune 500 CEO prepared for an interview with a major TV network in the United States by watching the last two or three major stories the producer had filed. Having done so, he was able to begin the conversation with the producer by saying how much he liked one of the stories. This positive beginning set the tone for the rest of the interview. Additionally, after learning that the producer always used a bulleted list as part of each story, the CEO developed a list of points he wanted to communicate about the company in bullet form and handed it to him before he left. When the story was broadcast, it was positive about the company, and the bulleted list was right up there on the television screen, which delighted the CEO, who had worried for days about the interview.

Once the executive has been briefed on the reporter's background and likely angle, he or she should be given a set of questions that the reporter is likely to ask. These questions can be developed from what the communication staff member working on this interview has gleaned in previous conversations with the reporter, from an analysis of the reporter's work, and from what seem to be the critical issues on the subject. If possible, the communication specialist should arrange a trial run with the executive to go over answers to possible questions. The executive should understand that the agenda for a news story is hard to change—once the reporter has decided to write or produce a particular kind of story, it is difficult to introduce a new topic into the discussion.

In preparing for a television interview, a full dress rehearsal is absolutely essential. The interview should look as if it is totally natural and unrehearsed when it actually occurs, but the executive should be prepared well in advance. This means thinking about what to communicate to the reporter no matter what he or she asks during the interview. While the executive cannot change the agenda for the interview, he or she can get certain points across as the dialogue moves from one idea to the next.

In addition to thinking about what to say, the executive needs to think about the most interesting approach to expressing the message. Using statistics and anecdotes can help bring ideas alive in an interview. What is interesting, however, depends on the audience. Many people mistakenly assume that the reporter is their audience. But it is the people who will watch the interview that they are really communicating with. Communication professionals and executives must keep this in mind when determining the best approach for a television interview. (See Chapter 2 for more on communication strategy, especially analyzing constituencies.)

Finally, the executive needs to be prepared to state key ideas as clearly as possible at the beginning of the interview. Answers to questions need to be as succinct as possible. Especially in television, where sound bites of three or four seconds are the rule rather than the exception, executives need training to get complicated ideas into a compact form that the general public can easily understand. As a well-known PR professional advises: "A chief executive must distill the company into a story he or she can tell over lunch and a journalist should be able to walk away and write it down on the back of a cigarette packet."[8]

Interview Tips

U.S. communication expert Mary Munter suggests the following tips when preparing for a media interview:[9]

- Keep answers short; think in 10-second sound bites.
- Avoid saying "no comment," explain why you cannot answer, and promise to get back to the reporter when you can.

- Listen carefully to each question; think about your response; answer only the question you are asked.
- Use "bridging" to move the interviewer from his or her question to your communication objective.
- Use anecdotes, analogies, and simple statistics to make your point.
- Keep your body language in mind throughout the interview.

GAUGING SUCCESS

As mentioned earlier, the amount of "ink" a company gets does not indicate whether it is achieving its communication objectives. Effective Web sites keep records of all hits, looking at not only where the ink has landed but also how well the company's key messages are communicated. A former director of media relations explains, "My entire department's compensation is tied to our ability to elevate our media scores."[10] Part of elevating your media score is finding out where the media hits have landed (with what constituencies), not just determining that the media carried a story on the company.

Most major corporations actively track their media score. The media-savvy companies launch new measurement initiatives aimed at revealing how effective their communication is with the media. The research focuses not only on the number of media hits but also the effectiveness of the hits to enhance the corporate image. In addition, companies contract with research and consulting firms to conduct an annual survey of business journalists to gauge perceptions of the client company and its media relations staff.[11] In contemporary terms, this exercise is called an "image audit."

Lubna Markar, the corporate communications manager of OM Kotak Mahindra Life Insurance Company, explains the concept: "Image audits are important; they help you gauge if the communication is working. How often they should be conducted is a matter of choice; again, the rule of thumb is to conduct them before, during, and after any major activity. A periodic audit helps you to decide on the course of action as well as points out issues that need attention."[12]

If an opinion poll were held to decide on the most media-friendly group in India, the Pune-based Kinetic group would probably win hands down.[13] If you scour through the Indian newspapers, magazines, and Web sites, you would not be surprised to find that a major chunk of information is devoted to the Kinetic group and the people who run the company. The group is not known to waste money on advertising, but its proactive attitude toward the media does the trick effectively. Surprisingly, such an attitude flows directly from the promoter's family. As Vismaya Firodia, the vice president of corporate communications for Kinetic group, says, "To me, corporate communications is everything from owners' manuals that are handed out to the corporate Web site."

Not only is this information useful for improving a company's media relations, but the information provided by all the measurement research also allows the company to benchmark its results against those of its competitors. A media relations manager rightfully concludes, "The media tracking ignited changes and improvements in the client company's media relations department."[14]

MAINTAINING ONGOING RELATIONSHIPS

By far, the most critical component in media relations is developing and maintaining a network of contacts with the media. Building and maintaining close relationships is a prerequisite for generating coverage. A company cannot simply turn the relationship on and off when a crisis strikes or when it has something it would like to communicate to the public. Instead, firms must work to develop long-term relationships with the right journalists for their specific industry. This usually means meeting with reporters just to build goodwill and credibility. The media relations director should meet regularly with journalists who cover the industry and should also arrange yearly meetings between key reporters and the CEO. The more private and privileged these sessions are, the better the long-term relationship is likely to be.

One example of a company's successful efforts to build strong media relations is ICICI Bank. Top managers of the bank are usually available for friendly chats with media professionals and respect the tight deadlines of journalists. The result is that in virtually every story about banking or financial services, an ICICI Bank spokesperson is prominently quoted and featured, giving the impression that ICICI Bank is a leader. In contrast, the public-sector banks of India operate with a bureaucratic mindset and are not as readily accessible to media professionals. As a result, they are featured more in negative stories than positive ones on banking.

Many companies take a less "integrated" approach than ICICI and use the more typical venue of a meeting between a member of the media and a company executive. Since these meetings often have no specific agenda, they can be awkward for all but the most skilled communicators. Within organizations, people assigned to handle media relations should enjoy "meeting and greeting," be tapped into the company's top-line strategic agenda, and be able to think creatively.

Often, these kinds of meetings occur at lunch or breakfast and should viewed as a time to share information about what is going on at the company, but with no expectation that a story will necessarily appear anytime soon. In the course of the conversation, the skillful media relations professional will determine what is most likely to interest the reporter later as a possible story. Without being blatant about it, he or she can then follow up at the appropriate time with the information or interviews that the reporter wants.

Media relations professionals should expect to be rebuffed from time to time. They may get turned down for lunch several times by reporters who are particularly busy, only to find them very receptive to a long telephone conversation. As is true with personal relationships, media relations professionals will find that they simply do not get along with every journalist with whom they come into contact. Unless the reporter is the only one covering a company's beat at an important national media outlet, this should not be an insurmountable problem. Where personality conflicts do occur, professionals can and should work around them to ensure that the overall relationship of the company with that media outlet is not jeopardized and that media opportunities are not missed.

One hotel executive at a major chain did not think that he needed to have any sort of relationship with the reporter covering his beat. After almost two years of being left out of nearly every major story on the industry, a consultant persuaded him to try again to establish a relationship with this reporter. The reporter was only too happy to make amends as well, since she needed the company's cooperation as much as it needed hers. Nonetheless, that attitude cost the company nearly two years of possible coverage that it could not get back.

BUILDING A SUCCESSFUL MEDIA RELATIONS PROGRAM

What does it take, then, to create a successful media relations program? First, organizations must be willing to devote resources to the effort. This does not necessarily have to mean huge outlays of money; an executive's time can be just as valuable.

Timex, the global brand of watches, pulled a PR coup of sorts, bringing a new collection into the national limelight through skillful use of media relations with the help of an outside consultant (eLexicon) at a fraction of the cost of a national advertising program. In May 2004, Timex's brand ambassador speedster Brett Lee's visit to India snowballed into prominent coverage by planning creative and strategic events—Brett's Victoria ride in Kolkata, attending the Confederation of Indian Industry (CII) meet as a special invitee, stepping out of a spaceship in Delhi—all worked to increase media hype. As eLexicon vice president Achal Paul—who was handling the account—summarized the PR function succinctly: "One should always keep the pot boiling."[15]

More recently, on a much smaller scale, a couple who started a food store that specialized in fresh, healthy cereals and processed foods to be sold to an upscale, urban, informed audience was interested in building a relationship with the media. Through the couple's efforts—writing letters and reading the newspapers to find out who the best reporters would be for their message—they were able to get hits in major business papers. In both cases, the media relations effort paid off in sales, which was the ultimate goal.

But for many larger companies, the media relations effort will involve more personnel and often the use of outside counsel. What follows is what is needed, at a minimum, for the effort.

Involve Media Relations Personnel in the Company's Strategy

As one public relations executive at a large U.S. company put it: "They like to keep us in the dark, like mushrooms, and then they expect us to get positive publicity, usually at the last minute." Companies need to involve someone, preferably the most senior corporate communication executive, in the decision-making process. Once a decision has been made, it is much more difficult to talk management out of it because of potential problems with communications.

While the communication point of view will not always win in the discussions that take place at top-management meetings, having these individuals involved will at least allow everyone to be familiar with the pros and cons of each situation and decision. Communication professionals who are involved in the decision-making process also feel more ownership of the ideas that they need to present to the media.

Develop In-House Capabilities

While using consultants and public relations firms may be beneficial in some cases, by far the best approach over the long term is to develop an in-house media relations staff. As we have seen throughout this chapter, there is no magic to what communication professionals do, and the company can save thousands of dollars a month by using staff within the company and investing in the right databases to conduct research for analyzing the media.

One problem for many companies, however, is that they do not consider media relations to be important enough to hire professional staff. Lawyers, executive assistants, and even accountants often handle communications because of the unfortunate assumption that, since "anyone can communicate," it does not matter who you put on this assignment. Companies must recognize that building relations with the media is a skill and that individuals with certain personalities and backgrounds are better suited to the task than others.

Companies should also not make the mistake of thinking that a former reporter will be the best person for the job. After all, if the reporter had been good at reporting, he or she probably would not be looking to change professions. And journalism graduates are also more likely to have been trained by people with doctorates, but who have little or no experience as reporters or editors.[16]

Use Outside Counsel Sparingly

Companies should hire outside counsel for advice or information (i.e., as consultants) to help out with a major story or when a crisis arises. Otherwise, what you are typically hiring when you hire a major public relations firm is the time of a recent college graduate who is getting training to one day take the in-house job that you have waiting in your own company.

Another important use for outside firms is to help with the distribution of press releases and to create video news releases. This type of communication can be valuable for a company trying to get its message across to a wide audience. What these firms do is put together what looks like a real news story. It is then sent out via satellite for anyone to take for nightly news broadcasts. The better firms usually do a finished version of the story with a reporter and then send a "B-roll," which is backup tape, so that the local station or network can put together its own story.

DEVELOPING A MEDIA STRATEGY
FOR THE INTERNET AGE

Until recently, media coverage—newspaper headlines or more in-depth profiles on television shows—was the primary means for exposing corporate flaws. Accordingly, companies with well-managed media relations programs had some leverage to get their own side of the story communicated to the public. Over the last decade, however, wireless communication and the Internet have transferred an enormous amount of power into the hands of individuals. As a public-interest activist explains, "The Internet is a very effective new weapon for the consumer. Before the Internet, unless you had a lot of time or money, there wasn't any way to get the public's attention to a problem. Now, you can broadcast it to the entire world in an instant."[17]

In the United States, one disgruntled Dunkin' Donuts customer created a crisis situation for the company by launching his own anticompany Web site. This same thing has happened on a massive level for retail behemoth Wal-Mart, which is the target of countless sites and blogs created solely to trash its reputation. Digital communication platforms, including blogs, social media networks, virtual worlds, "mash-ups" (Web application hybrids), and wikis (collections of Web pages whose content can be modified by anyone, rather than just those who have access to the content management system), have enabled consumers to seize control of corporate messages and reputations and, in effect, have their way with them. This has a significant consequence for organizations: with real-time communications around the world happening on a 24/7 basis and with consumer-generated media pushing its way to the forefront of communications, "journalists" are now anyone with an Internet connection and something to say.

Accordingly, companies' media strategies need to be augmented with tactics for dealing with this new dimension of "coverage," including establishing a forum for constituencies to share opinions, concerns, and complaints about the company, and a proactive effort at monitoring information circulating about the company in various media channels. There are many examples of companies that are successfully harnessing the power of the digital medium to reach consumers and media alike. For example, Microsoft has built an online newsroom called "PressPass" within its main Web site, which brings corporate information, news, fast facts, PR contact information, image galleries, and broadcasts into one central location for journalists to access. Likewise, General Motors' European arm built a social media newsroom to archive news, aggregate recommended blogs, offer multimedia downloads, and consolidate RSS (real simple syndication) feeds.

Because of the widespread reach of the Internet across borders and demographics, a growing number of companies are paying more attention to the Web as a prospective medium of communication, realizing that bad publicity online can legitimately threaten their bottom line. Large corporations allot a budget to spend on monitoring the Web.[18] Some firms assign employees or obtain external specialists to gather this kind of information. Search engines such as Yahoo! and Google are good places to start investigating, as the consumer opinion section on Yahoo!'s site alone lists over 300 consumer opinion sites—criticizing multinational companies from American Express to Ford to Nike to Wal-Mart and even to Yahoo! itself.[19]

Failing to embrace the Internet as a viable and potentially potent communication tool has serious implications. In addition to the aforementioned critical sites created by consumers, huge multinational companies across the global have been forced to go up against single individuals to protect their brands and to get the true story out to media. Dell's reputation was thrown for a loop when, in June 2005, an irate blogger by the name of Jeff Jarvis lambasted the company for poor customer service. Within hours, hordes of consumers who were in agreement with his claims posted comments, thus creating a maelstrom of negativity throughout the blogosphere. The company remained in the doghouse for months after failing to properly address the discontent in cyberspace; however, beginning with the launch of its own blog (Direct2Dell) in July 2006, executives finally joined the online conversation and began to slowly rebuild Dell's tarnished image.

The blog was put to good use when another potential crisis—a widespread battery recall—hit. Dell's chief blogger Lionel

Menchaca addressed the issue in a human voice and enabled customers to comment freely. The blog also offered information on how customers could get a replacement battery. Michael Dell even launched IdeaStorm.com in February 2007 and implored customers to give the company advice. New metrics show that Dell's customer service rating has risen significantly.

Just as the Internet can present problems for companies, it can also offer opportunities. Tapping into the information circulating on the Internet can give companies extraordinary access to information about customer needs and complaints. Monitoring Internet "chats" on social networks and blogs can enable companies to learn about current constituency needs and help tailor actions to meet those that are most vital to the company's reputation and bottom line. By using the Internet proactively, companies can glean valuable insights about constituency attitudes, feelings, and reactions to what they might otherwise not have access to. In many ways, a company should view the Internet as an unprecedented and ideal survey group. The head of an Internet monitoring firm comments, "Watching the Web is like competitive intelligence. You need to keep track of who is saying what to stay ahead."[20]

Without a doubt, online monitoring can help companies gauge the feelings of constituencies and allow them to respond to constituencies effectively, and stay on top of the information surge before us today. However, companies should not become so consumed with the power of the Internet that they neglect other important media channels, such as newspapers and television.

HANDLE NEGATIVE PRESS COVERAGE EFFECTIVELY

When a company does stumble upon bad news circulating about it—be it a condemning Web site, blog, or hostile op-ed article in the daily newspaper—the communication department should quickly assess the potential damage that the news might cause. Who is the person who has issued the complaint, and are his or her comments valid? Is the person speaking for himself or herself only or does the person represent a broader constituency such as investors or employees? How widespread are the complaints? If a rogue Web site has been constructed, how many hits per day has it received, and how have people generally responded to the negative message? If an unflattering newspaper article has been printed, how wide is the paper's circulation?

Once these questions are answered, a company's task force or permanent crisis communication team—including members of senior management—must brainstorm about actions to take. Company lawyers should be consulted to discuss what legal stance the company might need to take. Lawyers will be able to offer advice about whether statements or Web sites are defamatory, thus warranting a lawsuit against the perpetrator.

CONCLUSION

As technology develops new mechanisms for disseminating information and communication professionals are able to develop databases through the use of sophisticated software, the media relations function will continue to evolve away from the old PR "flack" model into a professional group that can help organizations get their message out quickly, honestly, and to the right media.

Companies today are under constant scrutiny from many of their constituencies. A demand for instantaneous information accompanies this public watchfulness, and the pressure is increasing with each new technological innovation. Managers must be prepared to answer this demand by considering all constituencies—on- or off-line—when dealing with the journalists who inform them. By crafting messages with care and using proper media channels, companies can tap into this powerful "conduit constituency"—the media—to ensure that their voices are heard.

Chapter 8

Investor Relations: Reaping Rewards in the Corporate Setting

ompanies must continually communicate their progress to the investing public as they strive to maximize shareholder value. Accordingly, investor relations is an essential subfunction of a company's corporate communication program. While explaining financial results and giving guidance on future earnings are critical investor-relations activities, companies need to go "beyond the numbers," as Collins and Porras explain in their book *Built to Last*:

> Visionary companies pursue a cluster of objectives, of which making money is only one—and not necessarily the primary one. Yes, they seek profits, but they're equally guided by a core ideology—core values and sense of purpose beyond just making money. Yet, paradoxically, the visionary companies make more money than the more purely profit-driven comparison companies.[1]

Investor relations (IR) professionals therefore need to link communications to company vision as frequently as possible. Increasingly, IR is getting involved in activities traditionally handled by PR and media relations professionals and communicating with many of the same constituencies. In addition to a solid understanding of finance, then, IR professionals need strong communication skills.

In this chapter, we begin our examination of this important subfunction with an overview of IR and a brief look at its evolution over the years. We then turn to the goals of IR and provide a framework for them. After discussing important investor constituency groups and how IR reaches them, we look at how the function fits into an organization and conclude with a discussion of IR in the changing business environment.

INVESTOR RELATIONS OVERVIEW

The National Investor Relations Institute (NIRI) of the United States defines investor relations as, "A strategic management responsibility using the disciplines of finance, communication and marketing to manage the content and flow of company information to financial and other constituencies to maximize relative valuation."[2] The chief financial officer of a U.S. corporation explained the task of the IR professional as follows: "You're competing for the investment dollar. Your company's story must appeal to the investment world more than the next guy's, or you can't expect to win the coveted shelf space for which everyone is fighting."[3]

As these descriptions illustrate, IR is both a financial discipline and a corporate communication function. Changes in the business and regulatory environment over the past decade have affected the way corporations decide how, to whom, and to what extent they convey financial and operating results.

Investors want understandable explanations of financial performance as well as nonfinancial information about companies. According to a report from Ernst & Young's U.S. Center for Business Innovation, investors give nonfinancial measures, on average, one-third of the weight they give financial measures when deciding to buy or sell a stock.[4] Examples of nonfinancials include the credibility of management, the company's ability to attract top talent, and quality and execution of corporate strategy. A survey by McKinsey & Co. found that three-quarters of institutional investors from the United States, Europe, Latin America, and Asia said that board practices are as important as financial results when considering investing in a company.[5]

Worldwide, IR is a young industry—just a decade old—and only a handful of firms engage in it. In terms of emerging markets, Indian corporations are increasingly realizing its importance in ensuring healthy value creation for one of the company's most important but often ignored constituencies—the investors. Citigate Dewe Rogerson (CDR), a public relations company that is part of the London-based Incepta Group, specializes in IR and offers its professional services to some of the Indian majors.

But how do you measure the success of an IR program? "If a company uses investors relations, then the stock is the last one to bottom out when the markets fall and the first one to move up when the market revives," says Nitin Tandon, managing director of CDR's Indian operations.[6]

To ensure that a company presents itself clearly and favorably on all these fronts, then, IR professionals must have both financial acumen and solid communication skills. Access to senior management is also necessary so that the IR function is connected to the company's vision and strategy. An IR department organized in this way is positioned to instill confidence in investors in good times and bad.

THE EVOLUTION OF INVESTOR RELATIONS: FROM A U.S. TO A GLOBAL PERSPECTIVE

In the early part of the twentieth century, corporate secrecy was a great concern for companies in the United States. Disclosure of any kind was seen as potentially harmful to the interests of the corporation. This all changed in the 1930s with the passage of two federal securities acts that required public companies to file periodic disclosures with the U.S. Securities and Exchange Commission (SEC). Despite the new reporting responsibilities brought about by the enactment of the Securities Act of 1933 and the Securities Exchange Act of 1934, corporations were interested in only mandatory disclosure which required little in the way of an IR function.

Investor relations did not begin to resemble the discipline we know today until the 1990s. In the 1960s in the United States, the National Investor Relations Institute officially recognized the IR function. NIRI was established as a professional association of corporate officers and IR consultants who were responsible for communicating with corporate management, the investing public, and the financial community. Around the same time, the Chicago-based Financial Relations Board (FRB, now FRB/Weber Shandwick) became the first public relations firm dedicated to helping its clients develop relationships with investors.

By the 1970s, FRB had pioneered the distribution of investment profiles that laid out a company's long-term financial goals and strategies. Prior to this innovation, information reached potential investors through presentations by company representatives to local stockbroker clubs or analysts' societies.

Further regulatory changes altered the landscape for IR in the 1970s. With the enactment of the Employee Retirement and Income Security Act (ERISA) in 1974, pension fund managers were held legally responsible for acting in the best interests of their beneficiaries. This new responsibility made pension fund managers more demanding of their portfolio companies. For instance, they sought more detailed explanations of company results, particularly when companies underperformed.

In the 1980s, state and local laws in the United States enabled pension funds to increase the equity allocation in their portfolios. That share rose to 36 percent in 1989 from 22 percent in 1982, making institutional investors an even more important constituency for the IR departments of corporations. At the same time, inflation caused many individual investors to flee the stock market, and by the end of the 1980s, institutional investors represented 85 percent of all public trading volume.

Conference calls were held for hundreds of institutional investors at a time in the 1980s. Soon thereafter, quarterly conference calls were standard practice at many companies. A decade later, the Internet provided yet another channel for communicating company financials to large numbers of investors. Organizations began to create IR areas within their corporate Web sites to post information such as news releases, annual reports, 10-Ks (annual reports that must be submitted annually to the Securities and Exchange Commission) and 10-Qs (quarterly reports), and stock charts.

Even with mass communications such as conference calls and Webcasts, however, IR professionals still arranged for periodic private meetings between large institutional investors or sell-side analysts and the CFO or CEO. This allowed the analysts to ask specific questions and get management's feedback on their own earnings models and projections.

These practices changed with the enactment of legislation designed to put individual investors on a level playing field with large institutions. The 1990s saw a resurgence of individual investor participation in the stock market and, at the same time, deepening concerns that these individual players were not afforded the same access to company information as their institutional counterparts. This theory was supported when two studies showed that volatility and trading increased immediately after quarterly conference calls (which were only open to institutional investors).[7]

In response to this, in late 2000, the SEC passed Regulation Fair Disclosure, commonly referred to as "Reg FD," which prohibits companies from disclosing "material nonpublic information" to the investment community (e.g., institutional investors and analysts) that has not already been disclosed to the general public. One of the immediate effects of this legislation was the opening of conference calls to all investors, inviting individuals into a previously closed forum that allowed them to hear about company results and strategy directly from senior management. Generally, it set a more formal and coordinated tone for guidance—companies could no longer give "selective guidance," that is, provide some investors with information on earnings projections before others. Some of the other implications of Reg FD for IR are discussed later in this chapter.

Over the years, IR has gained the respect and attention of senior management, who increasingly acknowledge it as a vital corporate communication function. The majority of the largest publicly held corporations in the United States and a growing number of small and midsized companies are now members of NIRI; by 2008, NIRI had more than 4,300 members in 33 chapters around the United States.

Beginning in mid-2007, investor relations became an even more prominent force in business, both for the United States and, as globalization continued to break down borders, the global economy. A global recession, kick-started in part by the subprime mortgage crisis, prompted markets in North America, Europe, and Asia to sink at alarming rates. The turbulence that began in the United States quickly spread around the world, throwing investors and financial analysts into a frenzy. Equity markets both in the United States and abroad tumbled; in January 2008, world equity markets saw a $5.2 trillion loss according to Standard & Poor's; emerging markets fell by 12.44 percent, and India alone experienced a 12 percent decline.[8]

This brief review has a number of implications for business executives in the current environment: investor relations is all the more important as local markets shift and merge into a global economy and as increased globalization enables one country's recession to initiate a domino effect around the world. For communicators, this reality mandates an understanding of the global economy, as well as the economies of emerging markets.

THE INDIAN IR EVOLUTION

In India, since family businesses have long dominated the corporate scene, the issue of corporate secrecy was even more magnified and information was disclosed to only a select few, mostly the faithful family retainers in top management positions. Therefore, professional and reformist corporate governance concepts have been slow to catch on in India. However, with the advent of new-age industries in India (the IT and ITES in the 1990s, as discussed in Chapter 5), good communication practices as well as catering to every constituency are being adopted rapidly. Now, even the home-reared companies, noticing the robust impact IR has on the share value of the company, are active practitioners of IR, the most prominent example among them being the Reliance Group.

The evolution of the IR function in India began with the introduction of the Companies Act in 1956 which provided for standard disclosure in public issues of capital, particularly in the fields of company management and companies listed under the same management and additional information about the risk factors as perceived by the management.

However, the companies complying with the investors security act followed the act just in the letter of the law, not in its spirit. Mandatory activities like conducting an annual general meeting and posting the annual audits in national publications were complied with as required by law. The reforms and liberalization era wherein company information would be available in a free and transparent way was yet to come.

The 1990s was a decade of high-profile financial scams that rocked the trust of the investment community, and the government ushered in new vigilant regulators for the capital market. The scams that have stuck in public memory include the ones involving the stockbrokers Harshad Mehta, C. R. Bhansali, and Ketan Parekh.

Harshad Mehta, nicknamed the Big Bull, manipulated the market in 1992 and fraudulently rigged stock prices with the help of the management of various companies and the Bombay Stock Exchange. Mehta succeeded in wiping out substantial share value of the retail investor. Next, in 1997, Bhansali's CRB mutual fund managed to hoodwink the new regulator, the Securities Exchange Board of India (SEBI), and again retail investors bore the brunt of the losses. In this case, CRB's mutual fund licensed and regulated by SEBI absconded with investors' money. New vigilant acts and regulations by the Institute of Chartered Accountants of India—ICAI, SEBI, and other market regulators—were put in place, but the Ketan Parekh scam ripped up the facade of a re-formed and secure equity market in 2001 by unethical speculative practices.

Another event resulting in a substantial wealth loss for investors was the announcement of the suspension of the redemption of the largest mutual fund scheme US-64 by the financial intermediary—UTI—in 2001. When the dust had settled, the market had dropped by 15 percent in a week. Newspaper headlines spoke about malpractices at exchanges and thought that the SEBI had been caught napping. This led to the imposition of another round of stringent regulations by the SEBI.

The SEBI Act of 1992 worked for the protection of investor interests and for promoting the development and regulation of the securities market. The SEBI took on the role of advising the stock exchange to amend the listing agreement in order to ensure that the listed companies furnish an annual statement to the stock exchanges showing the variations of funds in the offer documents and the actual utilization of said funds. This would enable shareholders to make comparisons between promises and performance.[9] To begin with, despite the new reporting responsibilities brought about by the enactment of the SEBI act, companies were only interested in mandatory disclosure, which required little in the way of an investor relations function. With numerous fraudulent practices being exposed, as discussed earlier, the government and SEBI further sought to rein in the market intermediaries by issuing stringent guidelines and circulars. This helped regulate the market and proved to be a deterrent to those indulging in unfair trade practices such as insider trading.

The regulators ensure that the markets continue to be a major source of finance for corporate and government sectors, and simultaneously work toward protecting the interest of investors. The responsibility for regulating the securities market is shared by the department of economic affairs (DEA), the department of company affairs (DCA), the Reserve Bank of India (RBI), the Securities and Exchange Board of India (SEBI), and the Securities appellate tribunal (SAT).

In October 2001, the central government established a fund called the investor education and protection fund (IEPF) for the promotion of awareness and the protection of the interest of investors.

DEA, DCA, SEBI, and the exchanges have set up investor grievance cells for redress of investor grievances. The exchanges maintain investor protection funds to take care of investor claims, which may arise out of nonsettlement of obligations by a trading member for trades executed on the exchange. The DCA has also set up an investor education and protection fund for the promotion of investors' awareness and protection of the interest of investors. All these agencies and investor associations are organizing investor education and awareness programs.[10]

The focus on investor education and awareness got a tremendous boost with the launching of the securities market awareness campaign (SMAC) by the SEBI. Under the aegis of SMAC, short workshops on various aspects of safe investing in the stock market that provide investors with skills and expertise are to be conducted in various centers across the nation.[11]

The Indian mutual fund industry is also governed by SEBI (mutual fund) regulations, 1996, which established detailed procedures for the launching of disclosures in the offer document, advertising material, restrictions on business activities, obligations of the asset management company and its directors, and other related terms. The performance of the scheme is reflected in its net asset value (NAV), which is disclosed daily for open-ended schemes and weekly for close-ended schemes. The NAVs of the mutual fund must be published in newspapers and on the mutual funds' Web sites.[12]

The golden mantra sweeping across reformist corporate India and its regulators is good corporate governance (GCG). GCG is considered helpful in summarizing the various factors that direct the government, SEBI, and corporate sector toward a liberalized era. These factors are:

1. Significant participation of foreign institutional investors (FIIs) in Indian bourses (stock exchanges), demanding greater professionalism of Indian companies.

2. Awareness on the part of lending institutions, particularly with regard to income recognition (conditions under which income becomes realized as revenue) and nonperforming assets (NPAs).
3. Integration of India with the world economy, forcing Indian industry to adopt a standard set of international rules rather than continue with anachronistic policies.
4. Assertion of rights by shareholders.
5. The need for Indian companies seeking listing in foreign bourses, particularly in the Nasdaq, to prove that they have a system of GCG in operation and that they are following generally accepted accounting principles. Indian companies must ensure that their associates follow internationally accepted accounting standards and management principles.

In India, Pressman Public Relations was the first PR firm to execute communication programs that influenced investors' decisions, both institutional and retail. But the IR function has come a long way from "investor-friendly," meaning publicizing the statutory information and perhaps holding a press conference or two in order to get positive press and oblige stockbrokers with giveaways.

Given that investors today demand more communication, more transparency, and more access to companies than they have in the past, corporations competing for their investment dollars need to create IR programs that deliver on these demands. In the next section, we explore how organizations can accomplish this.

A FRAMEWORK FOR MANAGING INVESTOR RELATIONS

How do companies attract and retain investors? When you consider that in 2000, 76 percent of the average U.S. company shares listed on the New York Stock Exchange had turned over in the previous year, you begin to appreciate the challenges facing investor relations officers (IROs). In India, in the year 2000–2001 the number of listed companies in the secondary market was 9,954, which decreased to 9,644 in the year 2001–2002.[13] The following section addresses the key objectives of investor relations and also provides a framework for the implementation of a successful IR program.

While the structure of an IR program will vary from one organization to the next based on the size of the company, the complexity of its businesses, and the composition of its shareholder base, the main goal of any IR program is the same: to position the company to effectively compete for investors' capital. To achieve this goal, companies need to focus on the following objectives:

1. Explain the company's vision, strategy, and potential to investors and "conduit constituencies" such as analysts and the media. One of the most critical duties of an IR professional is to get messages about company results and potential future results across as understandably as possible to the investing public. We further examine the various investor constituencies later.

2. Ensure that expectations of the company's stock price are appropriate for its earnings prospects, the industry outlook, and the economy. IROs need to understand investor concerns and expectations for their organizations and relay this information to management so that there is a high-level understanding of what the market anticipates from the company. If management does not see the company being able to meet market expectations, it needs to work with IR to craft a communication plan to explain why and to manage expectations appropriately. Conversely, if management feels that the company's potential is not reflected in its stock price (that the stock is undervalued), an IR strategy should be developed to help investors see that potential and, accordingly, drive the stock to appropriate levels.

3. Reduce stock price volatility. Particularly in a "sell-now-ask-questions-later" environment, having strong IR capabilities is critical to maintaining a stable stock price and shareholder base. This can be accomplished through the related goal of optimizing the company's shareholder structure to include primarily

long-term owners of the stock. Companies with stable share prices typically enjoy a lower cost of capital and thus can issue new equity more economically. In addition to the more strategic goal of stabilizing share price over the long term, IROs often have to respond to market news or events that have the potential to affect stock price negatively in the short term. We provide some examples of this later in this chapter.

Now that we understand what investor relations is designed to accomplish, let's look at how it achieves these objectives. Figure 8-1 depicts how the IR function communicates both directly and indirectly with investors. The indirect communication occurs through "intermediaries" such as analysts, the media, and rating agencies. Communication with these constituencies influences stock price, volatility, and, in turn, the firm's cost of capital and its reputation.

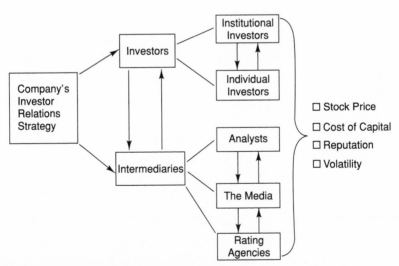

Figure 8-1 Investor Relations Framework
Source: Adapted from Markus Will and Anna-Lisa Wolters, "Interdependencies of Financial Communications and Corporate Reputation," Proceedings of the 5th International Conference on Corporate Reputation, Identity, and Competitiveness, Paris, France, May 17–19, 2001, p. 14.

TYPES OF INVESTORS

A company's IR strategy should address both retail investors (individual shareholders) and institutional investors (foreign institutional investors, mutual funds, insurance companies, endowment funds, and banks). These constituencies, however, place different demands on the IR department and require the use of different communication channels. For example, individuals often require substantially less detailed information than do institutions because of their relative lack of sophistication, but they require more "hand-holding" with respect to routine matters such as stock splits. In addition, compared with individuals, institutions provide companies with access to larger, fairly concentrated pools of capital, thereby affording them greater efficiencies in message delivery and market impact (defined as the combination of trading volume and price movement).

Institutional Investors

In the fourth quarter of 2001, U.S. institutions owned $7.5 trillion of the approximately $13.3 trillion U.S. equity market.[14] The 2007 Institutional Investment Report released by the Conference Board reported that U.S. institutional investors as a whole have increased their share of U.S. equity markets substantially—rising from holding 37.2 percent of total U.S. equities in 1980 to 51.4 percent of total U.S. equities in the year 2000, and then to 61.2 percent of total U.S. equities in 2005—at a total of $24.1 trillion in assets.[15] While the effect of the recession discussed earlier in this chapter is still unclear, we do know that institutional investors have larger holdings than do individuals and that they trade more actively. Thus they can have a greater effect on stock price volatility. Their block trading activities can have a tremendous short-term effect on a company's stock price performance, particularly for small to medium-sized companies.

IR departments can identify and target multiple categories of institutional investors. For instance, institutions can be broken down into groups based on portfolio turnover (high, moderate, and low) as well as investment styles (e.g., growth, value, income, and index). By grouping investors into smaller constituencies with similar characteristics, IROs can efficiently communicate their message to appropriate target audiences. For example, explaining a company's vision and outlook to index investors will yield little benefit because index fund managers do not have the discretion to change portfolio holdings away from index weightings.

IR professionals (or their agencies) can use databases to gather information on institutional stock holdings, turnover rates, and basic portfolio characteristics to identify institutions whose portfolio characteristics closely coincide with their company's price/earnings (P/E) ratio, yield, market capitalization, and industry classification. A company with a low price-to-book ratio, for instance, might focus on marketing itself to mutual fund managers who specialize in "value" investments. A small company will similarly target small-cap managers and possibly start raising awareness among mid-cap managers if it is approaching a larger capitalization. This kind of research will prevent the company from spending too much time communicating with uninterested investors.

Having identified those institutions whose investing criteria match their characteristics, the company should develop a plan to interest these institutions in investing for the long term. IROs can then reach those institutions in a variety of ways, including day-to-day phone contact and one-on-one meetings with analysts. For meetings with representatives of large, influential institutions the company would like to have a relationship with, the CEO and/or CFO are often involved.

More formal gatherings are another way to access large groups of institutional investors. For example, CEOs often address analyst or brokerage societies, industry conferences, and conferences geared toward particular kinds of organizations (such as small-cap, high-tech firms). Companies also host their own meetings in major financial centers such as Mumbai and New Delhi and invite institutional investors who either own or might want to buy the company's stock.

Individual Investors

Individual investors in the United States owned approximately $5.8 trillion in equities in 2001.[16] Like institutions, individual investors are not a monolithic constituency group. They may own stock directly or through mutual funds, company stock plans, or employee stock option plans (ESOPs). They may actively trade securities to generate trading profits on an intraday basis, apply "buy-and-hold" strategies to save for retirement, or anything in between.

Compared to institutions, individual investors have smaller account sizes and generate lower trading volume. In addition, as mentioned earlier, they tend to require information that is different from the kind institutional investors require.

Chapter 2 discusses the blurring lines between a company's constituency groups. As an example, individual investors can also be employees of the company whose stock they are investing in, either through ESOPs, bonus compensation that comes in the form of company stock, or options. Employees read about the financial performance of their own companies in the media and expect to see that information is consistent with what they are hearing internally. Companies should thus be prepared to respond to employees' concerns about inconsistencies between what appears in the press and messages management sends them.

Reaching individuals is more difficult than connecting with institutions because they are more numerous and harder to identify. The channels companies use to communicate with individual investors include direct mail to affinity groups (e.g., current shareholders, employees, customers, suppliers), the use of the brokerage community to promote their stocks with individuals, and the generation of visibility through the media and advertising (see Chapter 6 for more on financial advertising).

In recent years, the Internet has also proven to be a powerful channel for providing investors with real-time information about companies. The Internet is certainly used by institutional investors as well as individuals; portfolio managers and analysts can now use it to quickly and easily obtain baseline information about a company's financials and see up-to-date press releases. But for individuals who do not also have relationships with company IROs or CFOs, it has provided previously unparalleled access to company information.

Intermediaries

Investors often learn about corporations through sources other than the company itself. In particular, the media and the analyst community are key conduits. Companies provide information to investors through conference calls to highlight quarterly achievements, press conferences to announce annual financial results, and face-to-face meetings to discuss company developments and strategy. Reporters and analysts often present management with probing and difficult questions and report the company's responses to the investing public. Accordingly, management should present honest answers and messages that are consistent with what the organization is communicating to investors directly.

THE MEDIA

We learned in Chapter 7 that the business world is increasingly attracting print, television, and online media coverage. Business network news hosts regularly discuss earnings announcements on their programs and often invite equity research analysts to appear and comment on developments in companies they follow.

Media coverage of business can have a dramatic effect on a company's stock price. As an example of this, consider South African beer producer SABMiller PLC. The company had long maintained a stellar reputation among investors for its ability to manage acquired brewers in emerging markets. However, a year after taking over Miller Brewing Company in 2002 for $5.6 billion, its stock began to plummet. In an effort to understand the reasons behind this sudden decline, executives enlisted the help of Echo Research to analyze financial media coverage of the company in order to pinpoint a potential catalyst. Based on Echo's findings, which compared coverage and analyst commentary with SAB's stock movement, the executives gained insight into which journalists and analysts had the most influence over the strength of the stock. Furthermore, the research identified the biggest factor contributing to the stock's decline: Miller's ongoing and consistently poor performance. With this information in its arsenal, SAB executives retooled their communications strategy to restore investor confidence. Since then, the stock has been on the rise. This illustrates that media coverage and investor relations are key drivers of financial performance.[17]

Likewise, ITC, the tobacco giant in India, gained a noteworthy 2.4 percent on its scrip, as listed on the National Stock Exchange (NSE) on September 10, 2004, as the newspapers splashed the news of it getting a huge relief on excise duty. As further evidence of the power of the media in the realm of IR, about one in two retail brokers surveyed in the United States by FRB/Weber Shandwick stated that what they read in the media influenced them and their clients when making investment decisions.[18] Certainly, having a strong media relations function that is coordinated with the IR department will be beneficial to a firm's investor relations effort by maximizing access to media outlets and ensuring consistency in the messages each group is sending to the media.

Additionally, for low-visibility companies looking to attract investors, obtaining the right kind of media coverage can be a critical component of an IR strategy. In response to the rising influence of the financial media, some IR and PR consulting firms offer financial media relations programs to help companies target media strategically.

As is discussed in the next section, the media also play an important role in bringing the views of prominent analysts to the investing public, thus giving a voice to this other very influential intermediary.

SELL-SIDE ANALYSTS

IR functions target the financial community through buy-side and sell-side analysts. Buy-side analysts typically work for money management firms (mutual funds, for example) and research companies for their own institutions' investment portfolios. They sometimes use sell-side research in their analysis, but many perform proprietary analysis, including company visits and their own review of company financials. As such, for the purposes of our investor relations framework, buy-side analysts belong in the institutional investor constituency group and are not intermediaries.

Sell-side analysts, however, cover stocks within certain industries and generate detailed research reports that offer buy, sell, or hold recommendations. This research is then provided to clients of investment banks such as DSP Merrill Lynch or retail brokerages such as Motilal Oswal Securities Ltd., in India. Thus, sell-side analysts are intermediaries between a company and existing and potential investors.

Corporations communicate with analysts through many of the same channels they use for institutions. One-on-one meetings or lunches with the CEO or CFO are common, and conference calls are frequently used to target larger groups. On a day-to-day basis, IR professionals spend a great deal of time on the phone with analysts going over specific issues or providing feedback on their models.

Because of vigilant market regulators however, corporations are no longer free to give specific feedback on analysts' earnings models beyond corrections to factual data, much to the dismay of the analyst community.[19] Providing this kind of feedback had long been standard practice and a key mechanism for analysts to formulate their own estimates for companies. Many companies responded to the new rule by providing their own models to analysts instead of providing specific feedback on models the analysts provide them.

Sell-side analysts have come under fire in recent years for continuing to issue buy recommendations on severely underperforming stocks. The media have raised awareness of the inherent conflicts of interest in the job of a sell-side analyst working for an investment bank. Often, companies covered by a firm's research team are also important banking clients who could take their business elsewhere or cut off the analysts' access to information if offended by an unfavorable rating. Critics also point out that analysts are compelled to focus on stocks characterized by large trading volume, as this is what generates commissions for the brokers in their firm. As a result, sell ratings historically have made up only 1 percent of analysts' ratings according to Thomson Financial/ First Call, U.S.[20]

In the United States, the dot-com boom of the 1990s and the subsequent bursting of the bubble gave another fillip to IR. During the dot-com high, as the Internet economy was thriving and stock prices seemed to be on an unstoppable upward trajectory, many sell-side analysts enjoyed near-celebrity status. Merrill Lynch, U.S., entertainment analyst Jessica Reif Cohen could, in her own words, "instantly add—or subtract—billions in market value."[21] Salomon Smith Barney telecommunications analyst Jack Grubman was viewed with similar awe. As business coverage received increasing attention in the media, these analysts became household names. At the height of the dot-com boom, Morgan Stanley's Mary Meeker was even profiled in *The New Yorker* magazine.

This kind of visibility meant that analyst recommendations carried a great deal of weight. According to Zacks Investment Research, between 1985 and 2000, stocks that attracted coverage by three or more analysts fared 37 percent better over the ensuing six months than stocks that did not receive the same coverage.[22]

Even when the Internet bubble burst in early 2000, many analysts maintained sky-high valuations on companies whose stocks were plummeting. Investors, who had come to view these analysts as trusted advisors, felt betrayed and misled. Media coverage of these "star analysts" was just as prevalent as it had been in the dot-com heyday, but its angle on the analysts was decidedly changed. A *Vanity Fair* article characterized the group as "superstar analysts who were no longer objective observers of the market: they were insiders with inherent conflicts of interest."[23] Mary Meeker, once dubbed "Queen of the Net," appeared on the cover of *Fortune* magazine in a feature article titled "Can We Ever Trust Wall St. Again?"[24]

Analyst reports contain much more than a simple buy or hold recommendation, however. Despite the recent crisis of confidence in the objectivity of these ratings, other information about companies contained in these reports is often used by institutional investors to help them with their investment decisions. Analysts remain an important conduit constituency for a company's IR strategy. IROs should also be prepared to handle downgrades or other warnings that analysts may publish about their company's stock.

RATINGS AGENCIES

Ratings, usually expressed in alphabetical or alphanumeric symbols, are a simple and easily understood tool that enables the investor to differentiate between debt instruments on the basis of their underlying credit quality. The credit rating is thus a symbolic indicator of the current opinion of the relative capability of the issuer to service its debt obligation in a timely fashion, with specific reference to the instrument being rated. The primary objective of a rating is to provide guidance to investors and creditors for determining a credit risk associated with a debt instrument or credit obligation. It does not amount to a recommendation to buy, hold, or sell an instrument, just as it does not take into consideration factors such as market prices, personal risk preferences, and other considerations that may influence an investment decision.[25]

In India, examples of ratings agencies include Credit Rating Information Services of India Ltd. (CRISIL), Credit Analysis & Research Ltd. (CARE), Fitch Ratings India Pvt. Ltd., and ICRA Ltd. These agencies analyze companies in much the same way that buy-side and sell-side analysts do, but with a specific focus on their creditworthiness. The ratings that these agencies assign to a company reflect agencies' assessment of the company's ability to meet its debt obligations. This, in turn, determines the company's cost of debt capital (the interest rates at which it borrows).

These agencies make their ratings available to the public through their ratings information desks and published reports. The highest ratings are AAA (S&P, Fitch, Duff & Phelps) and Aaa (Moody's), and the lowest ratings are D (S&P, Fitch, Duff & Phelps) and C (Moody's), representing companies that are in default of existing loan agreements. Companies rated BBB/Baa or above are considered "investment grade," and those below not investment grade or "high yield." The term "junk bonds" also refers to below–investment grade bonds. The lower the rating, the higher the agency's assessment of the company's potential to default on its loans, thus making it more expensive for the company to raise capital through issuing debt.

Debt ratings affect more than a firm's cost of capital. Senator Joseph Lieberman, chairman of the Senate Committee on Governmental Affairs, said:

> The credit raters hold the key to capital and liquidity, the lifeblood of corporate America and of our capitalist economy. The rating affects a company's ability to borrow money; it affects whether a pension fund or money market fund can invest in a company's bonds; and it affects stock price. The difference between a good rating and a poor rating can mean the difference between success and failure, prosperity and bad fortune.[26]

Some examples of credit ratings of companies in India follow.

Crisil assigned AAA rating to Tata Sons' Rs. 75 crore (approximately $17.6 million) nonconvertible debenture (NCD) issue. The ratings continue to reflect Tata Sons' leading business position in the Indian software industry as well as its significant financial flexibility arising from its status as the principal holding company of the large and diversified Tata Group. Crisil has also reaffirmed the existing ratings of its Rs. 1,750 crore ($409.5 million) worth NCD issues, fixed deposit program and Rs. 150 crore ($35.1 million) commercial paper program.[27]

Conversely, the rating agency Care has downgraded Industrial Finance Corporation of India's (IFCI) long- and medium-term debt ratings to junk status. While the agency has retained the Care

BB rating on the fixed deposit program of the financial institution, it has reduced its preference share issue to default status (Care D), a press release from the agency said. According to Care, the downgrade follows persistent delays in debt servicing on IFCI's bonds. It has also skipped dividends on preference shares. The institution's financial position has been very weak for the past few years, with a high level of nonperforming assets, large asset-liability maturity mismatches, low-capital adequacy, and declining spreads. The ratings agency goes on to add that in view of its weak financial position, it is unlikely that IFCI would be able to meet its debt obligations in a timely manner.[28]

In the United States, examples of the ripple effects that debt ratings can have on a company and, in turn, the global economy, are the cases of many bond insurance companies that fell victim to the credit crisis started in large part by 2007's subprime mortgage collapse. Take FGIC Corp.: on January 30, 2008, Fitch Ratings slashed the bond insurer's rating from AAA to AA after its capital shortfall ballooned to $1.3 billion. Ambac Financial Group Inc. was also downgraded after its aborted attempt to raise the $1 billion necessary to satisfy Fitch's requirements. Ambac's stock value alone dropped from a 2007 high of $96.10 (on May 18, 2007) to a 52-week low of $4.50 on January 17, 2008.[29] In February 2008, Berkshire Hathaway chairman Warren Buffett stepped up to offer backup insurance on up to $800 billion in municipal bonds to help the troubled industry, but only time will tell if his support will be a long-term solution or a superficial panacea.

Credit rating analysts are similar to equity research analysts when it comes to their relationship with a company, with the obvious exception that they will focus a great deal more on the company's debt structure. Additionally, many buy-side and sell-side analysts rely on the research and ratings of credit analysts as a component of their assessment of the company overall, especially for firms in capital-intensive industries characterized by heavy debt loads.

For these reasons, ratings agencies are an important intermediary constituency for a company's IR efforts.

DEVELOPING AN INVESTOR RELATIONS PROGRAM

Now that we understand who the key investor constituencies are, let's look at how IR functions are structured to communicate with them either in-house, delegated to an agency, or some combination of the two. This section also takes a closer look at some of the activities that make IR such an important function within a company.

A company's IR function can be structured in a number of ways; it can range from fully in-house to fully outsourced. In-house IR teams are typically small; according to NIRI, the average size of a corporate IR department is between one and two people. At smaller organizations, the CFO himself or herself might handle IR responsibilities and use an agency to perform some of the more routine report-writing tasks.[30]

When companies do turn to agencies for assistance, they can choose from ones that specialize in IR work such as Pressman, Clea, and Weber Shandwick or full-service PR firms that have strong IR specialty groups such as Citigate Dewe Rogerson (CDR). Agencies can help with projects and activities across the spectrum of IR, from report writing and arranging analyst conferences to higher-end services such as bankruptcy and litigation communications, mergers and acquisitions, and initial public offerings. More recently, agencies have also focused on fully understanding regulations so that they can help companies with disclosure policy in the event there's a new regulation.[31]

The division of responsibilities between what is done in-house and what is handled by an agency depends on several factors, including the size of the firm and its IR objectives. However it is arranged, the individuals responsible for a company's IR efforts should have access to senior management, including the CEO and CFO. This appears to be the case for in-house IR professionals— two-thirds of corporate NIRI members report to the CFO.[32]

Given the increasing overlap in IR and areas such as media relations, in some organizations IR and public relations are linked or part of the same group. The advent of fair disclosure practices has also made many companies consider the merits of combining these

functions—or at least ensuring that they are closely coordinated—
to avoid inadvertent selective disclosure (disclosing material information to a limited group of people, as opposed to releasing it to
all investors at the same time).[33] However, if companies applaud
the idea of a closer partnership between IR and PR, it is not yet
broadly reflected in corporate structure. According to a recent
survey, PR and marketing departments still report independently of
IR at over 70 percent of companies.[34]

ANNUAL REPORTS (UNITED STATES): MORE THAN JUST THE NUMBERS

SEC reporting requirements have created the need for a number of
documents to be produced periodically, such as the annual report, the
form 10-K, and form 10-Q. Companies can file these reports electronically with the SEC, and investors can download them from the
SEC's online database, EDGAR, or the company's own Web site in
addition to, or instead of, receiving hard copies.

Among all of these, the annual report is the most time-consuming,
expensive, and high profile. An annual report is a company's equivalent to a "coffee-table book," and is now being used by companies as
much as an image vehicle as it is a reporting tool. Sid Cato has been
ranking annual reports since 1983 and providing "best and worst"
lists that appear in magazines like *Fortune*. While investors can obtain
the same financial information contained in a printed annual report
faster online, there is still great demand for the printed piece.

According to National Investor Relations Institute (NIRI) surveys,
95 percent of its 5,000 member companies posted annual reports
online in 2005; 88 percent still produced a paper version.[35]

Executives surveyed by Roper Starch ranked the printed annual
report as the single most important document their company produces.
One executive said that the annual report "should be the face of the
firm."[36] An annual report gives a company the opportunity not only to
share results for the prior year and explain them but also to communicate the company's vision.

(continued)

Annual reports typically have themes that are carried throughout the piece in graphics and text. Ford Motor Company's 2000 annual report, ranked number one by Sid Cato, had the theme of "connecting with customers." The theme was picked up in then chairman Jacques Nasser's shareholder letter, as well as through a series of photos of satisfied customers. Ford produced eight different covers for the report, each showing a real customer family.

In 2001, Ford ranked number one again on Mr. Cato's list, with the theme "building our future." Chairman and CEO Bill Ford's letter to shareholders began, "Our results in 2001 were unacceptable," and goes on to acknowledge that the company lost sight of what was important in 2001—its products and people—in the midst of the Ford Explorer tire recalls and a bleak economic environment.

Ford pledges a "back to basics" approach for the future that is echoed in the imagery throughout the report. Photos of shiny new Ford cars and trucks are superimposed on sepia-toned prints of cars, assembly lines, and employees of years past. The last section of the report, titled "What We've Learned in the Last 100 Years," includes lessons such as "be courageous" and "show passion," each supported by quotes from founder Henry Ford, his son Henry Ford II, Edsel Ford, and current chairman Bill Ford. The report clearly delivers more than financial results—it is an articulation of the company's vision.

Today, annual reports are used as reporting vehicles, brand builders, recruiting pieces, marketing brochures, corporate image books, and strategic positioning tools.[37] Even as more companies post their annual reports online, it doesn't appear that the hard copy version will go away. Sid Cato estimated that the average annual report budget was around $955,181, with an average of 234,113 reports produced per company per year.[38]

In the relatively new world of good corporate governance in Asia, however, the art of transparency and disclosure has yet to be perfected. Given such circumstances, the results of CFO Asia's second best annual reports survey, done in partnership with

Table 8-1 Best Annual Reports for Indian Companies[39]

Ranking in India	Ranking in Asia	Name of the Company
1	23	Reliance Industries
2	25	Rolta India
3	35	Hindalco Industries
4	36	Infosys
5	37	Indian Rayon
6	38	Indo Gulf
7	53	Indian Aluminium
8	54	Grasim Industries
9	65	Dr. Reddy's Laboratories
10	68	BPCL
11	78	Wipro
12	86	Hero Honda
13	90	SSI
14	97	Ranbaxy Laboratories
15	100	Larsen & Toubro

Belgium-based reports evaluator Enterprise.com, part of U.S.-based Corporate Essentials, is hardly surprising (see Table 8-1). Of the 144 companies that participated in the survey, only 40 achieved half the maximum score, reflecting the results last year.

In the category of share/investor information, Aditya Birla Group tops the survey. It features monthly stock prices for over 12 months compared with the index, distribution of companies' shareholdings, and categories of shareholders.

Reliance Industries Ltd. (RIL) is the only Indian company to find a place among Asia's 10 most creditworthy companies in the asset annual benchmark survey of the Asia's best credits in 2002. This extensive survey of investor opinion, featured in *The Asset* magazine, ranked RIL as the tenth best creditworthy company in Asia. Among the Indian companies, RIL leads the pack and ranks first. In fact, no other Indian company features among the top-30 list of Asia's best credits. In the 2004 survey, 153 international investors nominated 165 companies as their preferred credits in 10 markets, casting a total of 935 votes.[40]

USING IR TO ADD VALUE

As mentioned earlier, the investor relations function assumes a marketing role with respect to a company's stock, which involves much more than producing and distributing annual and quarterly reports, responding to shareholder inquiries, and sending information to securities analysts. IR plays both proactive and reactive roles within an organization.

Proactively, IR targets investors to whom to market the company's shares and provides regular information updates and explanations of performance to the marketplace. Proactive communications can go beyond traditional analyst calls and include activities such as "field trips" for analysts and portfolio managers. Plant tours and meetings or lunches with key company executives can provide investors and potential investors with a true feel for the company and its management.

IROs also craft communication strategies in response to certain internal or external events. Internal events such as mergers, acquisitions, or the sale of a part of the business require time for conferring with the CEO and CFO, developing a communication strategy around the event, and scripting answers to anticipated questions and concerns. External events such as an unanticipated crisis (see Chapter 10) require much more rapid damage control.

Charles C. Conaway, former president of the drugstore chain CVS Corp., explained, "Unless you have a very targeted investor relations program that communicates your message, you're going to get in trouble."[41] CVS underwent a restructuring in 1995 that resulted in a complete turnover of its shareholders in the course of one year. To resolve this instability, CVS bolstered its investor relations program and began actively recruiting longer-term institutional investors to suit its new growth profile.[42]

Companies with extensive IR resources can conduct research to identify their most influential shareholders and seek to understand what motivates them, allowing management to better predict the effect on share price of various events or announcements. Research on the changing stock prices of large U.S. and European public companies over a two-year period showed that a company's share price is significantly influenced by a maximum of 100 current and potential shareholders.[43] By identifying these investors and creating profiles on each of them that detail how they make decisions and what motivates them, companies can better perform scenario analysis on the potential effect on stock price of certain announcements. If necessary, management can modify plans to bring investors in line with the desires of key shareholders and minimize negative effects on stock price.[44]

Management must also be careful, however, not to become beholden to investor demands in the short term. The bull markets of the 1980s and 1990s were a major cause for the short-term orientation of the investment community. As Darrell K. Rigby, Bain & Company director, commented: "I've seen so many senior executives saying and doing things to deliver short-term news lately that it's a little frightening. . . . Their time horizons are shortening. They're thinking more about retiring rich at 45 or 50 and less about the institution they will leave behind."[45] Perhaps a certain corporate strategy will not deliver the earnings that investors and analysts are expecting in the short term, but if the strategy is one that the company believes is right for the long term, management must clearly explain the reasons for this to the investment community.

NIRI's Lou Thompson maintains that the 19 percent drop in Hewlett-Packard (HP) shares and the nearly 10 percent decline of Compaq shares that occurred the day the HP-Compaq merger was announced could have been mitigated by stronger IR efforts. If Compaq and HP had identified market skepticism over the merger, Thompson argued, the companies could have addressed these concerns before investors "voted with their feet" and took a toll on both companies' stock prices.[46]

When a crisis hits or a company undergoes some structural change that the market reacts to negatively, investors have already lost money, as the stock price usually adjusts downward nearly instantaneously. Shareholders can either join in the selling, or they can continue to hold the company's stock and hope that it will recover. To ensure that shareholders do not sell, companies must be prepared with swift, honest communications to investors when the stock price starts spiraling downward.

Management must identify the problem (or perceived problem) and what caused it. It must then determine what it is doing to address the problem. In these types of damage control situations, channel choice matters: a Webcast or conference call with the CEO or CFO will carry much more weight than a press release posted to the company Web site.

Similarly, when a company is not performing as well as it should, IR professionals should communicate to analysts and investors what management is doing about the situation. Such candor is definitely in the company's best interests. As Thomas Garbett says:

> Information reduces risk. The stock market, as a process, arrives at a stock price based upon all known elements relating to the company. Some of the unknown factors add to the price, others subtract. Areas about the company that are unknown usually contribute to the minus side of the price equation.[47]

CHARACTERISTICS OF EXCELLENT IR PROGRAMS

1. *Make IR professionals and senior management available.* Porter Sutro, vice president and director of research for Axe-Houghton Management, says, "Availability is important. To be able to get hold of someone when you need them, it is useful to have two people involved in the job. When one isn't there, the other is." This is especially true when the company has negative information to convey. "When bad news is announced and there's nobody there to talk to, it's extremely frustrating to analysts. In such instances, they'll often sell the stock," said Sutro.[48] Companies should therefore avoid making only periodic announcements and then disappearing.

2. *Avoid surprises.* Analysts and portfolio managers are most uneasy about the turbulence that comes from bad news for which they are ill prepared. Companies that go out of their way to call, fax, or e-mail about changes in expectations or impending negatives receive praise from the investment community. As institutional investor Ed Macheski of Macheski/Pappas Asset management says, "Telegraphing ahead is a good thing because there are no surprises. It's when you tell the street one thing and something else happens that you lose credibility."

3. *Maintain goodwill.* Credibility or goodwill is a hard won and fragile commodity that most institutional investors say goes hand in hand with avoiding surprises. As Kevin Murphy, an airline analyst for Morgan Stanley, says: "It's not a specific instance of good investor relations, it's a long-term rapport with someone you can trust. When the bad news hits the ticker tape, having a voice on the line that you know and can trust makes all the difference."[49]

INVESTOR RELATIONS AND THE CHANGING ENVIRONMENT

In this chapter, we discuss the evolution of the IR function over the years and some of the external developments that have shaped it. Over the past decade, technological advances and the changing business environment have been significant influences on the field of investor relations.

As mentioned earlier, many companies are creating investor relations areas on their corporate Web sites that make stock quotes and charts, news releases, and company financial statements available to anyone with Internet access. Investors find this kind of instantaneous access to information reassuring, particularly during periods of market volatility and uncertainty. Earnings Webcasts are also becoming popular. These events enable participants to witness firsthand how companies' top executives handle themselves and can bring an otherwise two-dimensional upper management to life for current and potential investors.

Web-based IR is becoming increasingly prevalent and is supported by external vendors and agencies that can help a company create effective sites. Jeffrey Parker (who founded First Call) and Robert Adler established Corporate Communications Broadcast Network (CCBN) in 1997, recognizing that "the concept of 'Internet time' has created pressure on corporations to do everything better, cheaper, sooner and faster."[50] CCBN now builds and manages the IR portions of the Web sites of over 2,500 publicly traded companies. Shareholder.com also emerged in the early 1990s to provide an array of online IR services, including Web site hosting, Webcasts, and integrated e-mail broadcasts and now works with over 750 companies, including Coca-Cola Enterprises, Delta Air Lines, and Tiffany & Co.[51]

The Internet enables greater transparency by providing nearly real-time information about companies to a wide audience, and this transparency is especially valued in the current business environment. Considering that seven of the fifteen largest business bankruptcies in the United States since 1980 occurred in 2001, investors have witnessed previously unimaginable corporate events over a short period of time. Energy giant Enron went from number seven in the Fortune 500 to the single largest bankruptcy in history.[52] In fact, BankruptcyData.com revealed that public company bankruptcies reached a record 257 in 2001—increasing from the 176 occurring in 2000.[53] Consequently, investors are keeping a watchful eye on Wall Street using both traditional and online media tools. As William Allen, director of New York University's Center of Law and Business, remarks: "There has not been such widespread scrutiny into the techniques employed in the financial markets since the 1920s."[54]

Many assessed the fall of Enron as a greater detriment to investor confidence than the bursting of the dot-com bubble. Additionally, as sell-side analysts came under fire for biased recommendations and conflicts of interest, investors became more uncertain of where they could turn for objective information about the companies whose stock they owned. Consequently, many retreated from the market altogether.

India's Sensex plunged by 25 percent after mid-February 2001 as software shares tumbled and an insider trading scandal rocked the stock market. Unit Trust of India (UTI)'s US-64, which had nearly 70 percent exposure in the equity market, was the biggest victim of the market crash (as discussed earlier in the chapter). According to finance market expert D. H. Pai Panandiker, "It was not a prudent move on the part of UTI authorities to substantially increase US-64 scheme's stock market exposure over the last few years." In response to this, UTI decided to suspend sales and repurchases of US-64 units for six months. However, suspending a popular scheme like US-64, in which millions of middle-class households have faith, for six months without any tangible exit route badly hit senior citizens, widows, and others who depend on mutual funds for ensured return on investments.

"It's like locking up the aspirations of middle-class India who had put in their savings into the family name that UTI schemes stood for. It served as a major blow to the reputation of UTI and other financial institutions as well," Panandiker said.[55]

The legendary Reliance Group founder, Dhirubhai Ambani, once said, "When an elephant walks, the dogs bark." He was responding to charges of improper business dealings against Reliance Industries, the textiles and chemicals giant he founded in 1968. In November 1995, the Bombay Stock Exchange (BSE) suspended trading in Reliance for three days because of alleged negligence by the company's in-house registrar in issuing duplicate shares. Then reports surfaced that the registrar also switched certificates in making stock transfers. After announcing a probe into the two cases, the government named a commissioner to look into the Reliance Group's alleged nonpayment of income tax. Also, the Central Bureau of Investigation charged Reliance with fraud in the import of raw materials in 1985.[56] Member of parliament Gurudas Dasgupta, a member of the then ruling Congress party, resurrected charges of insider trading over the 1994 merger of two Reliance subsidiaries with the flagship company. Although Ambani declined all interview requests, the Reliance publicity machine worked overtime. The company described Dasgupta's accusations as "baseless." Ambani also took on the BSE. He threatened to delist Reliance and three subsidiaries from the bourse, the largest of India's 23 stock markets. With market capitalization of nearly $3 billion, Reliance accounted for 10 percent of the BSE's 30-stock index (during November 1995). In the end, Ambani withdrew his delisting request but not until he had listed the four firms on the rival National Stock Exchange.

The fracas took its toll. Six months from November 1995, Reliance lost a third of its value on the BSE and was down by more than 50 percent from its highs in 1994. However, the bottom line remained solid. Analysts predicted that net profit for fiscal year 1996 would top $375 million, up by 23 percent from 1995. Trading at a multiple of just 7.4 times prospective earnings, Reliance was one of Asia's cheapest blue chips. That's not good news for the company's more than 3 million stockholders or nearly enough of an inducement for many international fund managers. "Nobody has come to grips with the full extent of the duplicate-shares problem," complained Anand Trivedi, a fund manager with Credit Lyonnais International Asset Management in Hong Kong. "There is a loss of confidence in the top management of Reliance."[57]

In another case, the BSE IT index suffered a sharp decline of over 13 percent in January–February 2004. The fall in technology shares came despite a strong earnings forecast announced by frontline software companies like Infosys, Satyam, and Wipro. The reasons for the decline were the probability of the BPO business of these firms being hit by a growing backlash in Western countries over rising protests of movement of white-collar jobs to countries like India and China. The U.S. senate had also proposed a bill banning outsourcing of federal government contracts to overseas companies. Additionally, the Bush administration froze the H1 B visa quota (a limitation on the number of H1-B visas that can be granted each year) for 2004, and Indian companies like TCS, Infosys, and Wipro were facing a lot of flak for allegedly flouting guidelines on L1 visas, which, like H1-B visas, are nonimmigrant visas that allow U.S. employers to hire noncitizens; however, L1 visas are generally valid for a much shorter period of time.

As a result, Infosys lost 14 percent from the Rs. 5,900 (approximately $140) mark. Midcap tech stocks also fell sharply. Polaris Software nose-dived by 33 percent, and NIIT shed 29 percent. Others like Wipro, Satyam (down 17 percent), VisualSoft (down 31 percent), and GTL also lost significantly.[58]

Even the United States' most admired corporations have felt the ripple effects of investor insecurity. General Electric (GE), for example, saw its shares plummet to $35 in February 2002, even though the company had not—unlike an increasing number of companies in today's media spotlight—been accused of any sort of misdeed. However, GE's financing subsector, GE Capital, came under fire for not offering substantial earnings information to the public, thus forcing the company to make reporting changes to increase transparency.[59]

And when Tyco International, U.S., faced a steadily declining stock price after a *Wall Street Journal* article in early 2002 pointed to accounting irregularities at the company, CFO Mark Swartz began weekly conference calls with investors to respond to questions and provide share information. The strategy did help stabilize the stock price, and Tyco subsequently suspended the calls, satisfied that its communication efforts were a success. "We were happy that one of our investors was recently on CNBC saying that they were now bored to tears by the calls," said Tyco's chief strategy officer and in-house IR chief Brad McGhee.[60]

IR is even more important to companies against this backdrop of uncertainty and mistrust. Clear, full disclosure of business results will put companies in a strong position in the competition for investor capital.

SOME WELL-KNOWN, INVESTOR-FRIENDLY COMPANIES IN INDIA[61]
TVS Motor

From a two-wheeler manufacturer that most people had written off (share price in September 2001: Rs. 65 [$1.50]) to India's most investor-friendly company (its share price touched Rs. 1,100 [$26] levels in late 2003, and the company opted for a 10-for-1 stock split to enhance liquidity), TVS Motor has come a long way in a short time.

"We believe the CEO is only the managing trustee of the shareholders," says Venu Srinivasan, chairman and managing director, TVS Motor—the essence of a true blue-chip IR practitioner.

Bajaj Auto

Not too long ago, Bajaj Auto was ranked number four in India's booming motorcycle market and number one in its flagging scooters market.

Today, following a product-led strategy orchestrated by joint managing director Rajivranjan Bajaj, the company is number two in the motorcycle market with a 25 percent share. And apart from taking on its opponent, the leader in the category, Hero Honda, it wants to go global. The constituency of happy investors—the company's average dividend between 2003 and 2006 is 120 percent—gives full marks to the company for its effective IR.

"Bajaj gives us information on the industry and briefs us regularly," says Kalpesh Parekh, an analyst at a Mumbai brokerage. The investor community claims that Bajaj Auto is among the few companies that give out product-wise revenue breakups. It has surely helped the company notch up impressive figures.

HDFC

"The management focus is on ensuring value creation for all its stakeholders," says Keki Mistry, managing director of HDFC. Coming from anybody else, it would have been a mere platitude. But this is true for HDFC. For generations, investors have come to trust the housing finance major. "HDFC is excellent in terms of balance sheet disclosures," notes Jigar Shah, head of research, K. R. Choksey Securities. Unlike some other companies, HDFC has had an investor grievance cell for the past 11 years and currently boasts a dozen staff members, four of whom are qualified company secretaries.

Jindal Steel & Power Steel

The Delhi-based O.P. Jindal Group company assures the investor that it is not just the rewards of the steel boom that is being doled out as rewards, but that the company itself is growing from strength to strength. The stock is up three times since 2001 to Rs 600 ($14) despite a 2:1 split because of the company's professional strength.

Says Sushil Maroo, vice president of corporate finance, "Our dividends have kept rising over the past few years, and the rationale behind the split was to get the retail investor back into our fold and not make the scrip too unaffordable." Adds Naveen Jindal, executive vice chairman and managing director of the company, "It's about doing the small things right." Apparently, the small investor is being counted in the big picture here.

Larsen & Toubro

As a company founded by technocrats and run thereafter by a board, L&T has traditionally evoked a great deal of trust among its retail investors. And that despite the battles for its control, more recently fought by the A.V. Birla Group for the cement business.

"It is our managing director [A. M. Naik]'s diktat [decree] not to have even a single aggrieved investor," says D. Shankar, the company's compliance officer. The current fiscal year had been exceedingly good for L&T. At Rs 253 crore ($5.4 million), its nine-month net profit is up by 52 percent.

Bharat Forge

The company has happily surprised many an investor with its energetic IR practices. The auto components company gives a region-wide breakdown of its financial performance. The new Bharat Forge is surely a changed company. Just a few years back, the Pune-based manufacturer of forging materials was like any other family-managed company in the industry. But over the last few years, it has taken on a totally different mindset.

Says a Mumbai-based analyst, "Bharat Forge has become very open and transparent in the last couple of years." Explains Amit Kalyani, the company's vice president and chief technology officer (CTO), "There's nothing complicated about being investor-friendly."

Tata Motors

In December 2002, when Tata Motors conducted a shareholder satisfaction survey, it scored 6.6 out of 10. The company has since conducted another survey, which suggests not only that the business does look good but also that IR plays a significant part in such an optimistic era.

"We communicate our strategy to our shareholders," says Praveen Kadle, executive director of finance and corporate affairs, Tata Motors.

BSES

The Reliance Group–owned power distribution company, which actually Webcasts its annual general meeting, has an impressive reliability rating of 99.99 percent. Now as part of a group that spawned the equity culture in India, BSES may become even more investor-savvy.

Says Anil Ambani, chairman, "Investor friendliness is a core corporate value that we pursue in order to achieve our vision of [being] one of the most admired utility companies in the world."

CONCLUSION

Many activities fall under the IR function, from planning and running annual meetings and putting together reports for SEC filings to targeting and marketing the company's shares to investors. The way all of these should be approached is no different from any other communication activity: companies need to follow a communication strategy that includes a clear understanding of the company's objectives and a thorough analysis of all of its constituencies so that appropriate messages can be crafted and delivered.

Unfortunately, efforts to quantify IR's direct effect on stock price and/or a company's cost of capital have yielded little in the way of results. Today's equity markets are influenced by many factors beyond companies' control, and thus, while it is still used as a broad indicator, stock price does not single-handedly signal an IR success or failure. Anecdotal evidence does, however, provide a basis for the simple conclusion that IR is a required communication function in today's marketplace.

No company can afford to deal with the current investment community without developing an effective investor relations function, whether it is fully in-house, fully contracted to an outside agency, or a combination of the two. The price paid for overlooking this advice is far greater than the investment made in the personnel who staff this important function.

Chapter 9

Managing Government Relations: India and the United States

In the preindependence era, the British ruled India and administered it primarily as a commercial colony, suitable for sourcing raw materials that fed the ever-hungry machines back home in England. The European industrial revolution of the 1800s needed both a source of raw materials and a market for finished goods. India, with its rich base in agrarian culture and wealth of mineral ores, proved to be the right bet in this case. The British, as a colonial power, looked after its home country's interests by actively discouraging industrial development in India. No incentives were offered to Indian industries, and many hurdles appeared in its growth phase. However, despite the negative attitude of the British government, foundations of some important industries were established in these years. Credit must be given to pioneers like Jamshetji Tata, Walchand Hirachand, Lala Sriram, G. D. Birla, and others, who laid down the foundations of modern industry in India.

Postindependence, the Industrial Policy Resolution of April 1948 contemplated a mixed economy, reserving a sphere for the private sector. This was largely a socialist-inspired policy with a large public sector and extensive controls on the private sector. Industries were broadly categorized into four areas. The first was the "commanding heights" (major industries, as discussed in Chapter 1) like the fields of defense, railways, and atomic energy—reserved for the public sector. The second category included coal, iron and steel, aircraft manufacture, shipbuilding, telephone manufacture, and so on.

New undertakings in these industries could henceforth be taken up only by the state. The third category included industries of such basic importance that the central government felt it necessary to plan and regulate them, such as salt, cotton and woolen textiles, paper and newsprint, and so forth. A fourth category, including the remainder of the industrial field, was left open to private enterprises, individuals, and cooperatives.

A second industrial policy was adopted in April 1956. The resolution emphasized the importance of the planned economy in securing a continuous increase in production and its equitable distribution and pointed out that the state must play a progressively active role in the development of industries. The new policy established three categories of industrial development based on the socialistic pattern of economic development. The objective of this policy was to expand the public sector and to build up a large and growing cooperative sector. Emphasis was placed on formulating policies to reduce disparities in income and wealth, to prevent private monopolies and the concentration of economic power, in different fields, from falling into the hands of a small number of individuals. Therefore, the planned growth model envisioned that the state would progressively assume predominant and direct responsibility for setting up new industrial undertakings.

In the ongoing context, in the late 1960s and 1970s, many banks and industries were nationalized because they were perceived as not fulfilling the aspirations of the government and the people.

The industrial policy statement of 1977 was formulated to encourage small-scale industries and cottage industries rather than the large-scale industries dominated by big industrial houses and multinational corporations (MNCs). It was thought that such encouragement of the small-scale industries would, on the one hand, lead to an extension of employment and, on the other hand, lead to a reduction in the concentration of economic power.

At this juncture, Indian industry was caught in the throes of controls, licenses, and resultant corruption. Attempting to liberalize industry from the licensing raj, the Industrial Policy Resolution of

1980 aimed to regularize the excess capacity installed over and above the licensed capacity.[1]

Although the government policies and procedures were aimed at industrial development of the country, the enactment of the Industrial Development Regulation (IDR) Act, procedures laid down for obtaining industrial licensing and various rules made under the act, served as a great deterrent to the growth of industries in the country. The bureaucracy acquired unprecedented powers and authority over all kinds of business activities, and entrepreneurs felt that they were placed at the mercy of the bureaucrats. Apart from the IDR Act, a number of other acts were also passed and served as obstacles to the industrial development of the country. Despite industrial licensing, an entrepreneur had to obtain clearance from many agencies, like the secretariat for industrial approvals (SIA), the department of industrial development, chief inspector of factories, the department of company affairs, and many others.

The fresh winds of liberalization truly began in July 1991 when the parliament announced a new industrial policy whose main aim was to:

1. Unshackle the industrial economy from the cobwebs of excessive bureaucratic control.
2. Introduce liberalization with a view to integrate the Indian economy with the world economy.
3. Remove restrictions on FDI and also free the domestic entrepreneur from the restrictions of the Monopolistic and Restrictive Trade Practice (MRTP) Act.
4. Eliminate public enterprises that show a very low rate of return or incur losses over the years.

In the sphere of industrial licensing, the role of the government changed from that of being only a regulatory body to one of providing help and guidance. In this context, industrial licensing was henceforth abolished for all industries, except those specified, regardless of levels of investment. A short list of specified industries continued to be the subject of compulsory licensing for reasons related to security and strategic concerns, social reasons, problems related to safety and overriding environmental issues, and manufacture of products of a hazardous nature. The exemption from licensing was particularly helpful to the many dynamic small and medium-sized entrepreneurs who were unnecessarily hampered by the licensing system. The primary objective was to benefit the Indian economy as a whole by letting it become more competitive, more efficient, and more modern so that it could take its rightful place in the world of industrial progress. The government assumed a new role—to ensure that essential procedures are fully transparent, to expedite industrial development, and to eliminate delays.

As discussed in Chapter 1, the government of India adopted five-year plans for the rapid and planned development of the country. The policies changed with each new government at the center. Therefore, priorities in the five-year plans also changed from time to time. One of the long-term objectives of the planning commission was based on equality and justice, addressing issues of gender and socioeconomic disparities and to protect the workforce from exploitation. As a result, the government framed various policies to control both industry and corporations.

In India, one important aspect of the private-sector development since independence has been the spectacular rise of a few large enterprises, commonly known as the *monopoly capital*. The Monopolies Inquiry Commission (MIC) of 1965 found that 75 business houses controlled 1,536 companies. A business house or business group was defined as comprising all such concerns that were subject to the ultimate decision-making power of the controlling group. The report of the MIC culminated in the passage of the Monopolies and Restricted Trade Practices Act in 1970. Under this act, a permanent statutory commission was set up to investigate, case by case, the effects of such practices on the public interest and to recommend suitable corrective action.[2]

With globalization and the opening up of the economy, some felt that the Indian market should be geared to face competition not only from within the country but from outside as well. The Competition Bill of 2001 provides for prohibition of anticompetitive agreements, prohibition of abuse of dominance (preventing firms that dominate a market from engaging in activities that harm their competitors and reduce competition), and regulation of combinations (acquisitions, mergers, and amalgamation above a certain size). The bill also establishes a competition commission of India (CCI) in place of the existing MRTP commission. Indian parliament passed the bill in December 2002.

GOVERNMENT AND BUSINESS IN THE UNITED STATES

Traditionally the government has had an adversarial relationship with business in the United States, as business attempts to minimize government involvement in the private sector and Washington attempts to manage the needs of all citizens through exerting its power over the corporate realm.

Government influences business activities primarily through regulation. Originally, government regulation managed market competition. The first regulations applied to industries such as telecommunications, where high barriers to entry facilitated the emergence of monopolies that could hurt the consumer. In these cases, regulation replaced Adam Smith's "invisible hand" to protect citizens from high prices, bad service, and discrimination.

Governmental regulation of monopolies has not prevented large corporations from wielding impressive political and social power. The predominance of global corporate giants such as Nike, Coca-Cola, and McDonald's transcends voting districts and political borders. Some of the most politically active organizations in the United States are, in fact, domestic or multinational corporations and trade associations.[3] Political largesse on the part of big business has made many Americans cynical about the integrity of the political process in Washington and its ability to govern the corporate world properly.

Many voters rank politics below business on their list of trustworthy professions. However, 90 percent of incumbents are returned to Congress each election, indicating that if this distrust does exist, Americans are not translating their dislike of politicians in general into action against particular officeholders by voting them out.[4] At the same time, as discussed in Chapter 1, action against particular corporations that the public perceives as corrupt is increasingly prevalent. Anticorporate campaigns range from boycotts and demonstrations to support of legislation to restrict corporate influence on Capitol Hill. When Congress responded to scandals at Enron, Tyco, and WorldCom in 2002 with a wave of reforms aimed at curbing corporate misdeeds and enforcing tougher standards on transparency of reporting, the government appeared to take the protestors' side.

In this chapter, we first examine the nature of the relationship between government and business through history up to the present. Next, we discuss the growing importance of government relations departments within companies and how this function itself has developed over the past few decades. After seeing how businesses today manage internal and external government affairs, we highlight some of the political activities that companies use to advance their agendas in Washington and New Delhi.

Government Begins to Manage Business: The Rise of Regulation in the United States

Government regulation began over 100 years ago with state regulation of the railroad companies. By the mid–nineteenth century, trains had triumphed over rival forms of land transportation. Railroad systems opened travel opportunities to people all over the United States and led the growth of industry, as goods could be shipped over long distances with relative ease. However, the railroads also presented the country with enormous problems. While proponents of a laissez-faire approach to the markets maintained that competition would regulate business, it failed to regulate the railroads, and corruption ensued.

In 1887, the Act to Regulate Commerce established the Interstate Commerce Commission (ICC), which began the federal government's regulation of business. Then in 1890, another critical piece of legislation, the Sherman Antitrust Act, was passed, which established a legal framework to prevent trusts from restricting trade and reducing competition; this remains the main source of antitrust law in the United States today. From the ICC and the Sherman antitrust laws to the hundreds of regulations currently in place covering issues from the environment to pornography to food quality, the government has remained actively engaged in business affairs. Each year, the federal government passes laws, and even creates new agencies, to correct what it perceives as market externalities (the positive or negative impact of a decision or transaction on a third-party stakeholder) produced by private business.

Some examples of past bills that affected business include the Cigarette Labeling and Advertising Act (1965), which requires all cigarette packages to carry warnings about the hazards of smoking, the Clear Air Act Amendments (1970), which outline procedures for monitoring air quality, and the Employee Retirement Income Security Act 1974 (also known as ERISA—see Chapter 8 for more on this law), which set new federal standards for employee pension programs.

Historically, business has resisted new regulations, especially laws that created costly additions to existing procedures. One example of these regulations is the "best available technology" clauses of many environmental laws, which demand that polluting companies maximize investment in "clean" equipment when they update their facilities. U.S. industry has complained that regulations hurt U.S. businesses and their efforts to compete with foreign rivals. Regulatory bills, they argue, add costs to U.S. companies not incurred by foreign competitors. These costs could drive up the price of U.S. products, making them comparatively less attractive than their foreign substitutes. The amount and extent of government involvement in the market has fluctuated with changes in White House administrations, but in spite of these fluctuations and the arguments against regulation, business enterprises will always have to deal with a baseline level of government regulation.

The Reach of U.S. Regulatory Agencies

Through the years, regulatory agencies have evolved into sophisticated organizations. Franklin D. Roosevelt's New Deal gave government incredible power to regulate business. The Securities and Exchange Commission (SEC) was created to stabilize financial markets, and the National Labor Relations Board (NLRB) to remedy labor problems. The Federal Communications Commission (FCC) regulates radio, television, and telephones; and the Civil Aeronautics Board regulates the airlines (the safety rule-making powers would later be transferred to a new agency, the Federal Aviation Administration [FAA] and then undergo yet another restructuring as part of homeland security after September 11). This is only a small selection of the regulatory agencies that have emerged over the last century.

The U.S. government is therefore involved in virtually all aspects of the life of a business. Many enterprises cannot begin operations until they receive a license from a regulatory agency such as the Interstate Commerce Commission, the Federal Communications Commission, or the Food and Drug Administration (FDA).[5] Once an enterprise has its license to operate, the same government agencies must then inspect and approve its products. The Consumer Product Safety Commission helps set safety standards for consumer products, and most products must pass this "test" before they ever reach the market.[6]

Beyond approving which products become available to the public, the government can also influence the prices of goods and services, such as agricultural goods, forest products, and metals. Using congressionally approved formulas, federal agencies have set floor prices, volume-based subsidies, and quota systems that shape the prices in these markets. The government also heavily influences the prices set by transportation, communications, and utility companies—industries that provide the basic infrastructure for society.

Since the days of the Sherman Antitrust Act, the government has continued its efforts to prevent monopolies and other anticompetitive business practices. One recent example is the Federal Trade

Commission's (FTC) rejection of a merger between Staples and Office Depot. The FTC argued that, if they merged, each superstore would lose its largest competitor. Without the check that direct competition between Staples and Office Depot had placed on prices, the merged office supply store would gain considerable control over what it charged its customers. The FTC viewed the joining of Staples and Office Depot as more of a threat to consumers than a benefit and thus prevented the merger.[7]

Government involvement in preventing and punishing corporate fraud gained momentum following the demise of energy giant Enron and a series of subsequent accounting scandals at other large companies in the United States. In mid-2002, two bills on accounting reform and corporate governance that provided a blueprint for overhauling corporate governance, auditing, and the rules for sell-side research analysts came before Congress. Both bills called for an oversight committee to monitor the accounting industry, and each dealt with the conflicts of interest that may arise when auditors perform additional consulting work for their clients.[8] Other elements of the bills proposed tougher prison terms for corporate criminals and closed legal loopholes used by executives to avoid prosecution. The Senate bill took a more aggressive stance than its counterpart in the House, but neither allowed businesses to escape closer scrutiny of their corporate practices. Congress was united in agreement that it must change the lax regulatory environment that had fostered corporate misbehavior in the past.

THE IMPORTANT ROLE OF GOVERNMENT IN INDIA'S INDUSTRIAL DEVELOPMENT

In India, with the development of a large public sector and socialist-inspired system, the government enacted various laws for the welfare of the workers. These laws were very helpful in protecting the workers' interests and at the same time provided the government ample ammunition to control industries. The Factories Act was enacted to ensure adequate safety measures and to promote the health and welfare of the workers employed in factories. The Employees Provident Fund Act was enacted to make provisions for the future of the industrial worker after retirement or for dependents in the case of early death. The Payment of Wages Act was enacted to ensure regular and prompt payment of wages and to prevent the exploitation of a wage earner by prohibiting arbitrary fines and deductions from wages. The Minimum Wages Act of 1948 was enacted to establish the minimum wages in industry and trade where labor organizations were nonexistent or ineffective. The Industrial Establishment Act was enacted to regulate the conditions of recruitment, discharge, disciplinary action, holidays, and the like of workers employed in industrial establishments. The Payment of Gratuity Act of 1971 makes it mandatory for any organization employing more than 19 employees to provide this benefit. Gratuity is payable 15 days per year of service on the salary at the time of exit. The Payment of Bonus Act provided statutory obligations for payment of a bonus to persons employed in certain establishments on the basis of profits or productivity. The Air and Water Pollution Act applied to all establishments discharging effluents in water or on land.

Regulatory bodies were formed to provide an effective regulatory framework and adequate safeguards to ensure fair competition and protection of consumer interests. The Indian government is committed to being a strong and independent regulator with comprehensive powers and clear authority to effectively perform its functions.

Toward this objective some of the important regulatory bodies and their chief function are listed here. The Insurance Regulatory and Development Authority (IRDA) was established under IRDA Act, 1999, to regulate insurance companies in India. The Telecom Regulatory Authority of India (TRAI) Act, 1997, was established to regulate telecommunications and related services, and for matters connected therewith or incidental thereto. The Cable Television Networks [Regulation] Act, 1995, was enacted to regulate the operation of cable television networks in the country and for matters connected to this industry. By government order, the cable television network in India is now regulated by the TRAI.

The Central Electricity Regulatory Commission (CERC) is a statutory body that regulates the tariff of companies that generate electricity. The National Pharmaceutical Pricing Authority, established in 1997, has been entrusted with the task of fixation/revision of prices for pharmaceutical products (bulk drugs and formulations), the enforcement of provisions for drug (price control) orders, and monitoring of the prices of controlled and decontrolled drugs in the country.[9]

The Essential Commodities Act, 1955, gave power to the government to control production, supply, distribution, and so on of essential commodities for maintaining or increasing supplies and for securing their equitable distribution and availability at fair prices. Using the powers under the act, various ministries and departments of the central government have issued control orders for regulating production, distribution, quality aspects, movement and so on pertaining to commodities that are essential and administered by them.[10]

With the passage of the Companies Act (Second Amendment), 2002, the law governing corporations has been fine-tuned by amending the Companies Act to create the right ambience for corporate enterprises so that they will function effectively in the era of liberalization. With these amendments, corporations are now in a position to adopt best practices in corporate governance in vogue elsewhere in the world. A committee has also been set up by the Indian government to look into issues relating to auditor-company relationships such as the rotation of auditors or auditing partners, restrictions on nonaudit work and fees, procedures for appointments of auditors, determination of audit fees, the role of independent directors, and disciplinary procedures for accountants.[11]

In the next section, we look at how business has responded to government regulation and ways in which companies work with lawmakers to ensure that their voice is heard when business-specific legislation is drafted.

HOW BUSINESSES CAN "MANAGE" THE GOVERNMENT: THE RISE OF GOVERNMENT RELATIONS

In light of the government's heavy involvement in commercial affairs in both the United States and in India, businesses eventually realized that, instead of fighting regulation, a more effective approach would be advocating their own positions to key political decision makers. Companies began to protect their interests with well-crafted lobbying and negotiating tactics, particularly when facing substantial opposition from consumer and community groups whom politicians were eager to appease.

Philip Morris, a U.S.-based company associated with the controversial tobacco industry, is a good example of a politically active corporation. This tobacco giant was the largest political action committee contributor in the 1987–1988 election cycle—distributing a total of $623,380. In 2000, over a decade later, Philip Morris still ranked tenth in a survey of the most politically active Fortune 500 firms. During this time, the company maintained its political momentum by having the second largest number of lobbyists on Capitol Hill (behind General Electric) with 28 representatives in its Washington, D.C., office.[12]

An article published in the *American Political Science Review* in December 2000 revealed that in a survey of 565 Fortune 1000 firms, 72.6 percent engage in some form of measurable political interaction with the federal government. Of the domestic Fortune 500, 56.4 percent engage in lobbying activities, and 54.6 percent have political action committees (PACs). Virtually all of the top 200 Fortune 500 companies are politically active.[13]

In the interaction between business and Capitol Hill, powerful lobbies and trade unions are prevalent, subjecting the government to a multitude of pressures. As Alfred D. Chandler Jr., a U.S. economic historian, writes, "The visible hand of management [has] replaced what Adam Smith referred to as the invisible hand of market forces. . . . [Business has] acquired functions hitherto carried out by the market, it [has become] the most influential group of economic decision makers."[14]

In Washington, businesses use a number of tactics to further their own agendas. In this section, we look at the rise of the government relations function within companies.

The Government Relations Function Takes Shape

In the United States, in the late 1960s and early 1970s, government regulations placed on certain industries significantly raised the cost of doing business. "It became apparent to American business leaders that in order to win in Washington, they would have to adapt the rules to their advantage, and that meant playing Washington's game."[15] "Playing the game" became the job of a company's government relations, or government affairs, department. This function concentrated specifically on the positive and negative effects of government policy and policy changes, as well as on monitoring shifts in ideology and agendas on Capitol Hill and accurately identifying emerging trends. By being knowledgeable about government and getting involved in the development of regulatory policy, businesses could better protect themselves from damaging regulations while taking advantage of any positive opportunities that government regulation created.

Similar sentiments, logic, and reason seem to have dictated the growing importance of government relations in Indian companies. Of course, in India one also has to remember the suffocating shadow of the license raj and the various restrictive controls that were hurdles to industrial growth and that could be surmounted only with the help of a so-called liaison officer. These liaison officers specialized in networking with government officials, and the most frequent route of taking sanctions or imposing a ban on trade was through bribes and kickbacks. At the time, the Indian bureaucracy was stuck in a quagmire, and the true entrepreneur was frustrated with all the red tape.

Since the 1990s—the most liberating decade for business in India—government relations departments have improved their effectiveness by studying the methods of other companies, hiring consultants, organizing popular support, learning to use the media properly, making alliances, creating political action committees, and establishing connections with influential capital insiders. By applying business and marketing techniques to politics and combining traditional organizational tools with advanced technology (e.g., computerized association memberships, the Internet, electronic and paper newsletters), business has increased its influence over Delhi's policymakers.

Some examples from U.S. corporate history demonstrate the costs associated with not having a Washington presence, as Bridgestone/ Firestone learned. When the National Highway Traffic Safety Administration forced Bridgestone/Firestone to recall millions of tires, the company had no Washington office in place and had lost most of its outside consultants. The company needed to seek out new representation in the midst of a highly publicized crisis. Bridgestone/Firestone learned from this mistake and now has a dedicated Washington office and several consultants.[16]

The U.S. Foundation for Public Affairs conducted a survey in 2000 to define the responsibilities of corporate affairs executives. Two-thirds of the 223 executives polled reported that they provide senior management with political and social trend forecasts, with over half reporting directly to the company CEO, president, or chairperson.[17] Sixty percent of respondents reported a direct correlation between this trend monitoring and the company's overarching strategy. The duties of government affairs executive revealed in the Foundation for Public Affairs statistics point to a greater interaction between this department and public affairs, two functions that were once separate within companies.[18]

Along with a strong internal team for government relations, a number of businesses today outsource certain functions to external groups in a "divide and conquer" strategy. The external lobbying consultants in Washington to whom companies often turn for advice and guidance on political activities can command rates of $5,000 to $20,000 per month.[19] These steep costs make relying entirely on outside counsel to oversee all government affairs activities unrealistic for most companies.

Microsoft has successfully built a strong in-house government relations function. After the justice department filed an antitrust suit against the company in 1998, Microsoft initiated a government relations overhaul of an unprecedented magnitude. The end result was a team of 15 savvy government affairs staffers in Washington, a presence three times larger than the average corporation's lobbying presence there, as well as lobbying representatives in every major state in the nation.[20] Microsoft also implemented a number of less conventional strategies, including construction of a Web site tailored to generate nationwide support for the company from individuals.

As with all other corporate communication functions, companies must measure the impact of their government affairs program to gauge whether it is properly tailored to the existing political environment. Today, businesses use a range of methods to track and evaluate their efforts. A U.S. survey revealed that 94 percent of companies use objectives set and achieved, 69 percent use legislative wins and losses, and 64 percent use costs reduced or avoided as measuring sticks for their performance in government affairs.[21] A results-focused approach will help ensure that a government affairs program stays strategically on track.

THE WAYS AND MEANS OF MANAGING THE GOVERNING POWER

An in-house staff of government relations professionals and senior leaders who are engaged in the issues that affect their companies are two important components of any business's strategy to stay tapped into the government. In this section, we look at some of the specific activities that companies use to advance their positions with lawmakers.

Coalition Building

In India, the 1990s saw a great political resurgence of business. Many methods used by government relations departments today became established or perfected during this period. In particular, coalition building emerged as a popular form of political influence. Many businesses previously acted to defend only their individual interests when faced with legislative problems without considering the ways in which their own concerns might be linked to those of other groups or organizations. When a particular company was in trouble, it often battled Delhi alone, even when the same issues applied to many other corporations within its industry.

The days of each business standing alone against Delhi ended when legislation that affected most, if not all, businesses became more common than the earlier regulations that had affected one or a small collection of industries. Laws concerning consumer safety and labor/wage reform led the wave of these broader regulations. Companies soon learned the benefits of working together. When one company was affected by new regulations, it would now find other firms in a similar position to form ad hoc committees. In these committees, the companies forged alliances of support on the business level, which then translated into channels for expressing their views in a greater number of congressional districts and states.

In the United States, the so-called big five accounting firms formed powerful coalitions to battle the SEC and lobby Congress to block legislation that would, among other things, restrict the amount of consulting work the firms could do for audit clients. These large and powerful accounting firms also joined forces with their clients to put pressure on the Financial Accounting Standards Board (FASB) not to force the recognition of stock options as expenses on companies' income statements.[22] Accounting firms lost much of their influence on these fronts when the Enron/Arthur Andersen scandal broke and the inherent conflicts of interest related to Andersen's consulting work became a focal point of the SEC investigation.

While loosely formed ad hoc coalitions are still common, companies also often join established industry associations that pool financial and organizational resources in order to represent their positions to the government. The Consumer Electronics

Association (CEA) in the United States, for example, advocates that the collective viewpoint of industries on issues that include government regulation of broadband, consumer home recording rights, and copyright protection. The National Cattlemen's Beef Association (NCBA) is another similar organization presenting the unified views of thousands of ranchers and beef producers with respect to public policy affecting the cattle industry.

By joining forces through either ad hoc coalitions or more formalized industry associations, companies can assert greater power and have a better chance of affecting legislative outcomes than they would have acting alone.

India's premier business association is the Confederation of Indian Industry (CII), with a direct membership of over 4,800 companies from the private as well as public sectors, including small and medium-sized enterprises (SMEs) and MNCs and indirect membership of over 50,000 companies from 253 national and regional associations. It works to create and sustain an environment conducive to the growth of industry in India, partnering industry and government alike through advisory and consulting processes.

As a facilitator, CII effects change by working closely with the government on policy issues, enhancing efficiency, competitiveness, and expanding business opportunities for industry through a range of specialized services and global links. It also provides a platform for sectoral (section or group) consensus building and networking. Major emphasis is placed on projecting a positive image of business and assisting industry in identifying and executing corporate citizenship programs.[23]

The Federation of Indian Chambers of Commerce and Industry (FICCI), established in 1927 on the advice of Mahatma Gandhi, was set up to garner support for India's independence and to further the interests of the Indian business community. At present, this powerful body has a membership of over 500 chambers of commerce, trade associations, and industry organizations.

The FICCI promotes business and government interface to resolve issues, ferret out new ideas, and speed up the reform process. The FICCI's annual sessions are major economic landmarks where policy issues are spelled out and two-way communication between the government and industry is fostered. The prime minister of India addresses this high-profile event each year. Various sessions are held that analyze past business trends and offer suggestions for the future.[24]

There are also industry associations in India which put forward their collective viewpoint to the government, for example, the Cellular Operators Association of India (COAI), which was organized in 1995. The main objective of the COAI is to protect, promote, and upgrade mobile cellular operations in India and also to look after the common and collective interests of its members. It helps to address the common problems of cellular operators relating to operational, regulatory, financial, or licensing issues through interaction with the ministry of communications and IT, the ministry of finance, the ministry of commerce, the department of telecommunications, the Telecom Regulatory Authority of India, financial institutions, and so on.

Similarly, the Indian Drug Manufacturers' Association (IDMA), founded in 1961, is the premier association of the Indian pharmaceutical industry. The IDMA plays a vital role in the growth and development of the industry by taking up with the government major issues such as price control, patents, trademark laws, quality and good manufacturing practice (GMP) regulations, research and development, and exports and by promoting a better understanding with the consumer organizations, the press, and other media on problems faced by the industry.

CEO Involvement in Government Relations

Large and small companies alike strengthen their government relations programs through actively involving senior management in political activities. As they have recognized the importance of gaining a seat at the policy discussion table for their companies, an increasing number of CEOs are stepping into the policy debate.

This trend does not surprise most executives. As John de Butts, former chairman of AT&T, remarked, "So vital ... is the relationship of government and business that to my mind the chief executive officer who is content to delegate responsibility for that relationship to his public affairs expert may be neglecting one of the most crucial aspects of his own responsibility."[25]

Frederick W. Smith, founder, chairman, and chief executive officer of FedEx, exemplifies the benefits of CEO involvement in government relations. Since FedEx's inception in 1973, Smith has advanced his company's interests by using ingenuity, networks of personal alliances, and strategic charitable contributions. Examples of his creative political outreach range from FedEx's maintenance of a small corporate jet fleet ready to fly members of Congress across the country at a moment's notice to Smith's preservation of his long-standing relationship with former Yale fraternity brother George W. Bush.[26] As Wendell Moore, chief of staff to Tennessee governor Don Sundquist, explained: "The fact that Smith knows his members of Congress on a first-name basis is a significant reason that the company has been so successful."[27]

FedEx continues to reap the rewards of its CEO's notable presence on Capitol Hill. For example, during the Clinton administration, Smith's rapport with the president undoubtedly led to his place as part of the official delegation on a trade mission to China. In 2002, the U.S. Postal Service announced a seven-year partnership with FedEx worth up to $7 billion, in which FedEx planes provide the postal service an air-delivery network in exchange for having its branded drop boxes installed at 10,000 post offices nationwide, a major accomplishment for Smith's well-positioned company.[28]

In 2002, the Indian telephone company Videsh Sanchar Nigam Ltd. (VSNL) was disinvested in favor of the Tatas. VSNL was the international long-distance (ILD) service provider of government-owned access providers Bharat Sanchar Nigam Ltd. (BSNL) and Mahanagar Telephone Nigam Ltd. (MTNL). After disinvestment, there was a disagreement on the outgoing rates of the ILD calls of

BSNL and MTNL. To overcome this crisis, Ratan Tata, chairman of Tata Sons, met the communications and information technology minister, Pramod Mahajan, and sorted out their differences. After a few months, VSNL signed new interconnection agreements with BSNL and MTNL.

After the electoral victory of the Congress party in 2004, as it prepared to form a government with the help of the left parties at the center, Indian industry drew up a list of demands. The Indian Steel Alliance—the association of the five largest steel companies in the country: Steel Authority of India, Tata Steel, Essar Steel, Jindal Iron & Steel, and Ispat Industries—said, "Changing world market dynamics may result in the Indian steel industry being faced with the threat of cheap imports. We hope that the new government would provide adequate protection to the domestic steel industry and not bring down the import duty on steel any further from the current 15 per cent level."[29]

Lobbying on an Individual Basis

When U.S. business leaders realized the importance of having a say in the activities taking place on Capitol Hill, they turned to lobbying groups to help them successfully advance their viewpoints with congressional decision makers. (Lobbying can be defined as any activity aimed at promoting or securing the passage of specific legislation through coordinated communications with key lawmakers.) In recent decades, as government intervention has grown, so has the number of organizations in Washington that present the views of business to Congress, the White House, and the regulatory agencies.

Using individuals in lobbying (which typically consists of activities such as letter writing, editorials, or op-ed pieces in print news media, and office visits to lawmakers) can have a significant impact on Congress. The U.S. Chamber of Commerce, for one, has conducted very effective and sophisticated grassroots campaigns to increase its influence. With state and local chapters that contain thousands of members, the chamber of commerce has a wide base from which to work. By 1980, it had established 2,700 congressional action committees that consisted of executives who were personally acquainted with their senators and representatives. These executives received information about events in Washington through bulletins from the chamber's Washington office and remained in touch with their representatives so that they might contact them when they need to.

This method of lobbying through far-reaching constituencies has produced good results: "Within a week [the Chamber of Commerce] ... can carry out research on the impact of a bill on each legislator's district and through its local branches mobilize a 'grassroots campaign' on the issue in time to affect the outcome of the vote."[30] Today, the Chamber of Commerce—once poorly regarded in Washington—has a network of 50,000 business activists, an expansive membership of 3 million businesses, 830 business associations, and 92 American chambers of commerce abroad.[31]

Microsoft's lobbying efforts, which included its grassroots Web site campaign, have clearly paid off. In 2001, Microsoft's lobby against copyright violators resulted in a government crackdown on software piracy. Later that year, in the wake of the September 11 terrorist attacks, Microsoft led the charge in persuading the Bush administration to allot over $70 million to improve "cyber security" in the United States.[32]

Success stories including Microsoft and the U.S. Chamber of Commerce have prompted many major corporations to establish campaigns that target individual legislators. In addition to achieving desired legislative outcomes, "A prudently managed grassroots program can be a team-building exercise. Providing information about legislation that will affect current and future company activities will be of interest to many employees at all ranks ... building a grassroots program with employees makes them part of the team."[33] Lobbying is the most popular method used by companies to get themselves and their employees involved in politics.

In India, when the Companies [Amendment] Bill, 2003, was introduced in parliament, the Confederation of Indian Industry and the Federation of Indian Chambers of Commerce and Industry were not happy with some of its provisions. Anand Mahindra, president, CII, in a note sent to the office of the prime minister, the finance minister, the minister of law and justice, and the minister of commerce and industry, had forcefully argued against some of the provisions of the Companies [Amendment] Bill, 2003.[34] Industrialists were upset that the bill would block the free movement of money from companies through a pyramid of investment subsidiaries, by restricting their number to just one. So they started pressuring the government to withdraw the bill from parliament. Finally, the government caved in to pressure from industry and ordered the withdrawal of the Companies [Amendment] Bill, 2003.[35]

A vivid example of a successful proactive industrial association can be cited in the National Association of Software and Service Companies (NASSCOM), which was established to initiate and maintain close interaction with the government in formulating national IT policies; it regularly initiates action against software pirates. NASSCOM's initiative to thwart piracy has helped reduce software piracy in India. According to International Data Corporation (IDC) estimates, the money lost in 2001 from pirated software is estimated to be close to $245 million, which is almost half of the legal packaged software market.[36] The government of India has further strengthened the copyright act with input from the Indian Federation against Software Theft (INFAST).

Political Action Committees

Another popular method of businesses getting involved in government is the formation of political action committees (PACs). In the United States, the idea for this movement came from organized labor, which created official committees responsible for raising and dispersing money to support political campaigns. By 1980, 1,204 companies had their own PACs. Approximately 55 percent of Fortune 500 companies currently have a PAC.[37]

To target their funding efficiently, PAC administrators need to have access to information about each political candidate and the races they support. The Business-Industry Political Action Committee (BIPAC) was formed to meet these information needs. While this group does contribute directly to candidates, its most important role is to research candidates and identify close races. During each election year, BIPAC holds monthly information briefings for PAC managers, along with providing daily updates on congressional races through a BIPAC telephone service. By utilizing their national organization, individual PACs remain well informed and are able to direct their funds intelligently.

An increased political awareness in corporate managers has led to the setting up of PACs. These committees provide a simple framework for getting employees involved in political issues that could influence their employers' well-being into the future. According to one executive, "PACs are one of the most effective vehicles to generate individual participation in the political process to come along in a long time." Another executive had further commented, "Our first goal is to involve our people in the political process. Only about five percent of our time is devoted to fund-raising and the distribution of funds; 95 percent is devoted to political education. Our philosophy is to encourage long-term understanding and continuing involvement in the political process."[38]

The Public Affairs Council in the United States estimates that of political donations, PAC contributions currently account for between 1 and 10 percent.[39] The bulk of the remaining funds streams into a number of channels that fall under the category of "soft" money, to which corporations, labor unions, and individuals can contribute in unlimited quantities as long as the funds do not go directly to any one candidate. These unrestricted donations are different from those of a PAC, which may not give a candidate more than $5,000 per election. To avoid the limits placed on donations from a PAC, companies are donating larger amounts of money that can be indirectly used by candidates, such as for identity-building strategies and campaign advertising.[40] Although recent legislative efforts have increased restrictions on soft money, these donations still allow corporations to gain political influence through more flexible, non-PAC routes.

Business organizations contribute a staggering amount of money to politicians in any given election cycle. The Center for Responsive Politics estimates that between 1989 and 2001, for instance, accounting firms had spent nearly $39 million on political contributions.[41] The flow of money from business interests to political campaigns has caused alarm to some sectors of the U.S. public, who fear that the ability of businesses to back their agenda with large sums of money gives them an unfair advantage in having their voice heard in Congress. A *BusinessWeek*/Harris poll revealed that three-quarters of Americans are of the opinion that large companies are too influential in Washington. The same poll concluded that 84 percent of the public believes that campaign contributions made by big business firms have too much influence on American politics.[42] This seems to demonstrate that not everyone views businesses' political spending as a positive trend.

Indian corporate conglomerates such as those held by the Tatas and the Birlas have set up electoral trusts to fund political parties and independent candidates. The Tata electoral trust, set up in 1996, distributes funds only to those political parties that are registered with the election commissioner of India as a political party under the Election Symbols (Reservation and Allotment) Order of 1968. However, the trust does not distribute funds to individual candidates. In years past, it distributed 50 percent of the funds on the basis of the current composition of the Lok Sabha (lower house of Indian parliament), whereas the balance was given after the elections were over and when the new composition of parliament became clear.

The Birla electoral trust, set up in 1998, also makes contributions to political parties registered with the Election Commission of India and also to individual candidates. According to Justice P. N. Bhagwati,[43] "We donated equally to all political parties during the last elections and not to any particular party only."[44]

On December 25, 1997, many industrial companies in India came together to produce an eight-page special color pamphlet on the then prime minister, Atal Bihari Vajpayee, on the occasion of his birthday. The supplement projected him as "the man India awaits." The special supplement was reported to have cost Rs. 2 crore (approximately $469,000) for the corporate houses.[45]

CONCLUSION

Corporate relationships with various levels of government extend far beyond licenses, safety standards, and product prices. Today, the influence of private businesses on public affairs, and vice versa, has become so established that we often assume that changes in one arena will lead to changes in another. Democratic reform in Latin America and Eastern Europe came hand in hand with market reform, and upon China's acceptance into the World Trade Organization (WTO), President George W. Bush declared: "I believe a whiff of freedom in the marketplace will cause there to be more demand for democracy."[46]

As we have seen, defining the roles of government and business with regard to each other is an ongoing process. In the summer of 2002, a crisis of confidence in business ethics and corporate governance had compelled President Bush to address Wall Street leaders, saying, "We must usher in a new era of integrity in corporate America."[47] Congress moved rapidly to enact a raft of bills and proposals that would regulate not only how businesses are run but also how they report their activities to the public.

On the technology front, the Internet is seen to have significantly shaped companies' approaches to government affairs. Companies may rely heavily on Web monitoring, issues-focused Web sites, and online networks of grassroots lobbyists to track important legislation and broaden the reach of their own coalitions.[48]

At the same time, as discussed in Chapters 1 and 4, the speed at which information flows over the Internet implies that news of corporate wrongdoings or legal violations has the potential to reach many constituencies before senior management can even have a chance to prepare for the crisis at hand.[49]

With the complexities of globalization and the ever-increasing speed of information flows, businesspeople must devote their attention and resources to actively managing their relationships with governments and lawmakers. Successful companies recognize the importance of staying abreast of what happens in the world's capital cities. In order to stay connected, the government relations function is critical, which, whether entirely internal or partially outsourced, must be an integrated function of a company's overall communication strategy.

Chapter 10

Crisis Communications— Lessons from Multinational Companies

Unlike many of the other topics covered in this book, a crisis is something everyone can relate to. The death of a close relative, the theft of one's car, or even a broken heart—all can become crises in one's personal life. Organizations face crises as well: pesticides at Pepsi, worms at Cadbury, the detention of Polaris's CEO in a foreign land, and lethal leaks at Union Carbide—all became crises for the companies and people involved.

Ten years ago, such events would have received some national attention but would more likely have been confined to the local and regional area where the events occurred. Today, because of changes in technology and the makeup of the media, any corporate crisis is covered in a matter of hours by the national and international media and is potentially Webcast on the Internet. A more sophisticated media environment and a new emphasis on technology in business have created the need for a more sophisticated response to crises.

This chapter first defines what constitutes a crisis. It turns next to a discussion of several prominent crises of the last two decades. Once we define what crises are all about, the focus shifts to how organizations can prepare for such events. And finally, this chapter offers approaches for organizations to follow when crises do occur.

WHAT IS A CRISIS?

Imagine for a moment that you are waiting for guests in an air-conditioned drawing room on a warm evening in Delhi, India. Suddenly, the power goes, the whole scene plunges into darkness, and it is pitch dark outside on the streets. If you are from Delhi, you would know that you are in the middle of an unfortunate but routine power cut; if you are from Mumbai, you might think that some abnormal situation is developing and some chaos or riots might follow. Or picture yourself on a friend's boat, out for a leisurely sail on a sunny afternoon. Two hours later, you discover that you have been having such a good time that you did not notice yourself moving farther and farther away from shore toward the open ocean. Storm clouds are gathering on the horizon, and the sun seems mysteriously to be setting a bit early.

All of us would agree that in these situations we, as individuals, would definitely be facing crises. If the power cut turned out to be the result of a terrorist attack or if your friend is a novice sailor and you are in fact drifting into a severe storm, these scenarios could be life threatening.

But how do crises affect organizations? Organizations also face crises that occur naturally: a storm rips through a town leveling the local waste management company's primary facility; the power cut we imagined earlier disrupts production in a dairy plant and all fresh products start souring without adequate freezing facilities; a ship is battered at sea by a storm and sinks with a load of cargo destined for a foreign port. None of these events can be planned for, and all create havoc for the organizations involved.

Although natural disasters cannot be avoided totally, there are many other kinds of crises—those caused by human error, negligence, or, in some cases, malicious intent—that planning could have prevented in the first place. In fact, most of the crises described later in this chapter—such as those that beset Tylenol, Perrier, Coke and Pepsi, and CD Universe—were human-induced crises rather than natural disasters. Such crises can be more devastating than natural disasters in terms of costs to companies in both money and reputation.

All human-induced crises cannot be lumped together, however. One type includes cases in which the company is clearly at fault, for instance, cases of negligence. One example of this was the June 2000 sinking of a Panamanian tanker, the *Treasure*, which spilled 400 tons of heavy bunker oil off the west coast of South Africa and threatened 40 percent of the world's African penguin population. The second type includes cases in which the company becomes a victim, such as CD Universe, a U.S. company involved in a cyber-blackmailing situation examined later in this chapter. In these situations, the company falls prey to circumstances, just as when natural disasters unexpectedly hit. A company's role as either perpetrator or victim in a crisis is the distinction upon which public perception often hinges.

In addition, the general public's attitude toward the company is more likely to be negative for crises that could have been avoided, such as the purported pesticides in Coke and Pepsi products and worms in Cadbury chocolate, as opposed to the kind of crisis that an organization really had no control over, as when ICICI Bank witnessed panic among customers when the bank was rumored to be near bankruptcy. In both cases, however, constituencies will look to the organization's response to the crisis before making a final judgment.

Thus, defining *crisis* for organizations today is a bit more complicated than simply saying that they are unpredictable, horrible events. For the purposes of this chapter, a crisis is defined as follows:

> A crisis is a major catastrophe that may occur either naturally or as a result of human error, intervention, or even malicious intent. It can include tangible devastation, such as the destruction of lives or assets, or intangible devastation, such as the loss of an organization's credibility or other reputation damage. The latter outcomes may be the result of management's response to tangible devastation or the result of human error.

Crisis Characteristics

While all crises are unique, they do share some common characteristics according to Ray O'Rourke,[1] former managing director for global corporate affairs at investment bank Morgan Stanley. These include:

1. *The element of surprise.* Examples of this are Polaris finding its CEO in detention at Jakarta or Pepsi learning of reports of pesticides found in a Pepsi bottle.
2. *Insufficient information.* The company doesn't have all the facts right away, but it very quickly finds itself in a position of having to do a lot of explaining. The Perrier example cited later in this chapter is instructive here, as it took the company over a week to figure out what was going on after reports of benzene contamination surfaced.
3. *The quick pace of events.* Things escalate very rapidly (e.g., even before command and control [CAC] operations center in Chennai was set up to resolve the Polaris crisis, the national media were reporting new developments in Jakarta at a rapid pace).
4. *Intense scrutiny.* Executives are often unprepared for the media spotlight, which is instantaneous, as answers and results normally take time.

What makes crises difficult for executives is that the element of surprise leads to a loss of control. It's hard for people to think strategically when they are overwhelmed by unexpected outside events. In addition, the media frenzy that typically surrounds a crisis can prompt a siege mentality, causing management to adopt a short-term focus. Attention shifts from the business as a whole to the crisis alone, forcing all decision making into the shortest time frame. The company's uncoordinated and off-the-cuff statements only increase the likelihood that the crisis will escalate. When panic sets in, this is typically what happens in organizations.

Part of the problem of dealing with crises is that organizations have tended not to understand or acknowledge how vulnerable they are until after a major crisis occurs. This lack of preparation can make crises even more severe and prolonged when they do happen. To bring our definition to life, let us take a closer look at some major crises that occurred in the United States and India during the past 30 years.

U.S. CRISES

For baby boomers in the United States, the defining crisis of their time was the assassination of President John F. Kennedy. Virtually everyone who was alive at that time can remember what they were doing when the news was announced that President Kennedy had been shot. Generation X in the United States today probably feels the same way about the explosion of the space shuttle *Challenger* in January 1986. Certainly people everywhere will remember the terrorist attacks of September 11, 2001, in the United States as a defining moment of the new millennium. These events have become etched in the public consciousness for a variety of reasons.

First, people tend to remember and be moved by negative news more than they are by positive news. Americans in particular seem to have a preoccupation with negative news. Network and cable news broadcasts underscore this. Viewers rarely see "good" news pieces because they just don't sell to an audience that has become accustomed to the more dramatic events that come out of the prime-time fare on television.

Second, the human tragedy associated with a crisis strikes a psychological chord with most everyone. A cable car detaching over the French Alps in 1999, a New York–bound Air France Concorde exploding near Charles de Gaulle airport in July 2000, the terrorist attacks of September 11, the tsunami of 2005—such events make us realize how vulnerable we all are and how quickly events can make innocent victims out of ordinary people.

Finally, crises associated with major corporations stick in the public's mind because many large organizations lack credibility in the first place. A public predisposed to distrust big oil companies would not be completely surprised by what happened to the *Exxon*

Valdez or by Texaco's racial discrimination suit. Indeed these events validated the public's suspicions, so people took as much pleasure in the turmoil these corporations faced as a result of their actions as they felt sorrow in what the *Exxon Valdez* accident did to the environment and how Texaco had treated minorities. As we look at other major crises, we will start to see more clearly why these events linger in the public psyche.

1982: Johnson & Johnson's Tylenol Recall

Johnson & Johnson's Tylenol recall in the early 1980s is held by many as "the gold standard" of product-recall crisis management. While more than 25 years have passed since the crisis, the lessons to be learned from it are still very relevant. Johnson & Johnson's handling of the crisis was characterized by a swift and coordinated response and a demonstration of concern for the public that only strengthened its reputation as "the caring company."

In late September and early October of 1982, seven people in the United States died after taking Tylenol capsules that had been laced with cyanide. At the time, Tylenol had close to 40 percent of the over-the-counter market for pain relievers. Within days of the first report of these poisonings, sales had dropped by close to 90 percent.

Certainly the irony of something that is supposed to relieve pain turning into a killer made this episode one of the most memorable in the history of corporate crises. But many experts on crisis communication, marketing, and psychology have conjectured that it was Johnson & Johnson's swift and caring response that was primarily responsible for turning this disaster into a triumph for the company. Despite losses exceeding $100 million, Tylenol came back from the crisis stronger than ever within a matter of months.

What did Johnson & Johnson do? First, it did not simply react to what was happening. Instead, it took the offensive and removed the potentially deadly product from shelves (ultimately, 31 million bottles of Tylenol were recalled). Second, it leveraged the goodwill it had built up over the years with constituencies, ranging from doctors to the media, and decided to try to save the brand rather than come out with a new identity for the product. And third, the company acted in a caring and human way, rather than simply look at the incident from a purely legal or financial perspective. Thousands of J&J employees made over 1 million personal visits to hospitals, physicians, and pharmacists around the nation to restore faith in the Tylenol name.[2]

Why did the company go to these lengths? Despite its decentralized structure, Johnson & Johnson's management is bound together by a document known as "the credo." The credo is a 308-word companywide code of ethics that was created in 1935 to boost morale during the Depression; it is carved in stone at company headquarters in New Brunswick, New Jersey, today. It says: "We believe our first responsibility is to the doctors, nurses, and patients, to mothers and all others who use our products and services." James Burke, the CEO at the time of the Tylenol crisis, made sure that the principles of the credo guided the company's actions during the crisis, helping J&J react to tragedy without losing focus on what was most important.

What is most amazing is not that J&J handled this crisis so formidably, but that the perception of the company was actually strengthened by what happened. As Burke, who was brought in early as the lead person handling the crisis, explained, "We had to put our money where our mouth was. We'd committed to putting the public first, and everybody in the company was looking to see if we'd live up to our pretensions."[3] J&J managers did, and the public rewarded them for it. Within three months of the crisis, the company regained 95 percent of its previous market share.[4] Nearly two decades later, *BusinessWeek* and Interbrand ranked Johnson & Johnson as the top brand portfolio, valuing its brand portfolio at over $68 billion.[5]

1990: The Perrier Benzene Scare

Perrier Sparkling Water faced a contamination crisis of its own nearly 10 years after the Tylenol episode. While Perrier's contamination crisis did not lead to any deaths, or even reported illnesses, it still demanded resolution and an explanation for the public and the media. Perrier's actions during the 1990 benzene scare provide as many lessons in how not to handle a crisis as J&J's did of how to effectively handle one.

In February 1990, Perrier issued the following press release:

> The Perrier Group of America, Inc., is voluntarily recall-ing all Perrier Sparkling Water (regular and flavored) in the United States. Testing by the Food and Drug Administration and the State of North Carolina showed the presence of the chemical benzene at levels above pro-posed federal standards in isolated samples of product produced between June 1989 and January 1990.[6]

This press release marked the beginning of the end of Perrier's reign over the sparkling water industry. In 1989, Perrier, one of the most distinguished names in bottled water, sold 1 billion bottles of sparkling water, riding high on the wave of 1980s health con-sciousness. Then, in January 1990, a technician in the Mecklenberg County environmental protection department in Charlotte, North Carolina, discovered a minute amount of benzene, 12.3–19.9 parts per billion (less than what is contained in a non-freeze-dried cup of coffee) in the water.[7] After receiving confirmation from both the state and federal officials, Mecklenberg briefed Perrier Group of America about the contamination.

Two full days after the crisis broke, after recalling over 70 million bottles from North America (but before identifying the source of the contamination), Perrier America president Ronald Davis confidently announced that the problem was limited to North America. Officials had reported that a cleaning fluid con-taining benzene had been mistakenly used on a production line machine.[8] The real cause of the contamination—defective filters at its spring[9]—was discovered less than three days later, and contrary to what Ronald Davis had previously announced, six months' worth of production would be affected, covering

Perrier's entire global market.[10] The firm was forced to change its story.

Without an official crisis plan of its own, Perrier relied on the media to communicate its story during the crisis, which proved to be a fatal decision. The press only served to expose the lack of internal communication and the lack of global coordination within the company. At a news conference in Paris, when Perrier-France announced that it was also issuing a recall due to the presence of benzene, the president of Perrier's international division, Frederik Zimmer, offered the explanation that "Perrier water naturally contains several gases, including benzene."[11] From the contradictory messages released to the press, it was clear that U.S. operations were not communicating well—if at all—with their European counterparts. Moreover, yet another story emerged to explain the presence of benzene, and it contradicted the previous explanations: according to Perrier officials, "The benzene entered the water because of a dirty pipe filter at an underground spring at Vergeze in southern France."[12] All of this hurt the company's credibility.

The cost of the recall and eventual relaunch of the product—ushered in by a pricey advertising campaign—meant that customers found the new 750-milliliter bottles selling at the same price as the 1-liter ones. Perrier's precrisis 1989 market share of 44.8 percent had plummeted to 5.1 percent by 1998.

The Perrier benzene crisis illustrates not only the consequences of having a reactive strategy to deal with crises, but also the problems of not having a coordinated and fact-based approach to crisis communication.

1993: Pepsi-Cola's Syringe Crisis

Another beverage company, Pepsi-Cola, faced a highly publicized contamination crisis of its own in the United States shortly after Perrier's benzene episode. Pepsi's handling of the syringe hoax of 1993 is a stark contrast to the Perrier example. In addition to showing concern for the public and demonstrating resoluteness in getting to the bottom of the problem, Pepsi also skillfully leveraged two other critical constituencies—the government and, most importantly, the media—to help it combat the bogus tampering claims and win back the public's trust.

In June 1993, a man in Washington State reported that, after drinking half a can of Diet Pepsi the night before, he had discovered a syringe in the can the following morning when he shook the rest of the contents into the sink.[13] This was the beginning of a major crisis for Pepsi-Cola.

The CEO of Pepsi-Cola North America, Craig E. Weatherup, did not let the surprise of the crisis overwhelm him when he was contacted at home by FDA commissioner David Kessler and informed of the situation. His first action was to engage Pepsi-Cola's four-person crisis management team—made up of "experienced crisis managers from public affairs, regulatory affairs, consumer relations, and operations"[14]—to swiftly deal with the unfolding situation, including opening lines of communication with FDA regulatory officials, the media, and consumers. Internally, Pepsi prevented organizational chaos by updating employees with daily advisories to over 400 Pepsi facilities nationwide.[15] Unlike Johnson & Johnson's immediate recall of Tylenol from the shelves by the next morning, Weatherup had decided not to recall the product—despite a flood of new reports to the FDA of dangerous objects found in Pepsi cans.

When television networks contacted the company looking for a response or any formal statements, Weatherup realized that the crisis was rooted in the disturbing imagery of syringes in cans and therefore decided to supply the media with an equally "visual" response. Weatherup had his staff prepare video footage of the canning process at Pepsi that showed how it would be virtually impossible to insert a syringe into the cans. Additionally, Pepsi later distributed a grocery-store surveillance tape of a woman stealthily dropping a syringe into her Pepsi can. After the footage appeared as the lead story on three major networks, no new reports of syringes were made.[16]

Weatherup also made several television appearances throughout the day, on *The MacNeil/Lehrer News Hour* and *Larry King Live*. In his last appearance, FDA commissioner David Kessler accompanied him. Both men stressed the implausibility of the claims and the criminality of making false statements (five years in prison and up to $250,000 in fines).

Pepsi's highly visible work with the FDA in investigating the crisis boosted its credibility in the public eye. Additionally, without an investigative reporting team of its own, Pepsi found that the government agency was invaluable to the company during the crisis. The FDA established a center in 1989 to provide a team of forensic science experts who could respond immediately to all tampering incidents and provide expert advice and scientific evidence to FDA officials. It was an FDA investigation that provided the evidence used to convict a tamperer who had falsely claimed to find a mouse inside a Pepsi can when she opened it. Several days later, the FBI arrested four individuals for making false claims, and the contamination scare appeared even more like the hoax it turned out to be. In the end, 20 arrests were made, and the crisis was resolved.

Pepsi-Cola did not stop there, however. To ensure that consumers knew that the tampering claims were false, Weatherup took out an ad to address the concerns of employees and customers. As he explained, "On Monday, Pepsi will run full-page advertisements in 200 newspapers around the country, including the *Washington Post*. The ad reads: 'Pepsi is pleased to announce... nothing. As America now knows, those stories about Diet Pepsi were a hoax. Plain and simple, not true.' It ends with an invitation: 'Drink All the Diet Pepsi You Want. Uh Huh.'"[17] To date, Pepsi-Cola remains one of America's leading soft drinks with a 31.6 percent market share,[18] demonstrating that negative publicity and crisis situations can be overcome when the crisis is well handled.

Pepsi is pleased to announce...

...nothing.

As America now knows, those stories about Diet Pepsi were a hoax. Plain and simple, not true. Hundreds of investigators have found no evidence to support a single claim.

As for the many, many thousands of people who work at Pepsi-Cola, we feel great that it's over. And we're ready to get on with making and bringing you what we believe is the best-tasting diet cola in America.

There's not much more we can say. Except that most importantly, we won't let this hoax change our exciting plans for this summer.

We've set up special offers so you can enjoy our great quality products at prices that will save you money all summer long, It all starts on July 4th weekend and we hope you'll stock up with a little extra, just to make up for what you might have missed last week.

That's it. Just one last word of thanks to the millions of you who have stood with us.

Drink All The Diet Pepsi You Want.
Uh Huh.

2000: Bridgestone/Firestone's Tire Recalls

Mishandled corporate crises can inflict lasting damage, even on well-respected brands with reputations a hundred years in the making, as evidenced by Bridgestone/Firestone's tire recall crisis of 2000. Harvey S. Firestone founded the Firestone Tire and Rubber Company in 1900. One of the oldest partnerships in American business history was born when Henry Ford had approached Firestone and had asked him to sell tires for Ford motorcars. Despite their historical ties, the year 2000 saw the Ford-Firestone relationship fall apart against the backdrop of hundreds of accidents and 271 deaths linked to Firestone tread separations on Ford Explorers. The majority of the 6.5 million tires were recalled because of tragic accidents on popular Ford models from which Ford derived 90 percent of its profits.[19] Since both companies feared they would suffer enormous losses if they assumed total blame for the incidents, each had motivation to blame the accidents on the other. Ford maintained that the problem was a Firestone tire issue, while John Lampe, CEO of Bridgestone/Firestone cited "significant safety concerns with the Ford Explorer," which he claimed experienced five times more separation claims than the Ford Ranger with the same Firestone tires.[20]

As a result of this highly publicized crisis, Firestone fell to the bottom of the list in Fortune's survey of the most admired companies, assuming the last spot among rubber and plastics companies.[21] While the finger-pointing reflected badly on both Ford and Firestone, the latter's reputation in particular took an enormous hit as a result of its handling of the crisis.

What elements of the crisis did Firestone handle so poorly? First, consumers lost faith in Firestone because of the company's tardy reaction to the tire tragedies, which they felt reflected a lack of concern for their safety. For instance, Firestone initially proposed a phased recall of tires—a decision based on its ability to manufacture needed replacements, which angered consumers in states not covered by the first phase, many of whom brought class-action lawsuits against the company. Firestone also tried to explain that the tire failures resulted from poor tire inflation and maintenance, effectively blaming drivers themselves for the accidents. Then Firestone blamed the problems on the design of the Ford Explorer. More and more, the company seemed to be dodging any responsibility for the accidents and instead tried to protect its own business interests.

When Firestone did come out with a proactive PR strategy to handle the crisis, it was targeted at dealers, and not the public—the group most immediately affected by the tragic accidents. Because dealers build customer satisfaction in the tire industry and manufacturers are largely removed from buyers, Firestone distributed ads to local dealers to be cosigned by both the company and the dealers. The ads used local dealers as a seemingly neutral third party to help reassure consumers that the confidence they had lost in Firestone should be restored based on the amount of faith the dealers themselves had in the company. In taking this approach, under the assumption that local dealers had strong relationships with their customers, Firestone attempted to leverage dealers' reputations to help build back its own. Instead, the company should have channeled its efforts and resources into targeting consumers directly to bolster their view of the company.

With the recall nearly seven months old, it was not until February 2001 that Firestone began to speak to consumers directly by putting information about their safety efforts online. The company launched the Web site TireSafety.com, containing pertinent information about daily tire maintenance while prominently displaying the Firestone name. Since the company cited improper tire inflation as one possible cause of the Ford Explorer accidents, the site offered free tire gauges to those people who registered and offered to provide e-mail alerts upon request to warn customers when to check tire pressure to ensure safety.[22] Woody McMillin, manager of motor sports and consumer products PR at Firestone, hoped that the site would convey to the public the fact that Firestone cared.[23]

But by acting so late and misdirecting its initial PR efforts, Firestone gave the appearance of paying attention to consumer safety only when backed into a corner, not because it was part of their corporate philosophy. Had the company acted swiftly and decisively, assuming responsibility for the mishaps with compassion, consumers may have felt more valued and thus more willing to forgive the company.

In a survey conducted in March 2001 by Total Research Corp.—a market researcher in Princeton, New Jersey—consumers were asked about the reliability of various brands. Firestone scored less than four on a zero to ten scale, plummeting 40 percent from its rankings a year earlier, prior to the crisis.[24] The Firestone tire recalls demonstrate how even venerable and established brands can fall from grace quickly and dramatically when they mishandle crisis communications.

Ford's reputation also suffered during this crisis, but public relations specialists and consumers alike generally felt that, of the two companies, Ford's response was stronger, swifter, and more sympathetic to consumers than was Firestone's. Clearly, though, both companies had a great deal of trust to rebuild.

CRISES IN INDIA
Tata Teleservices Crisis

Human insight and strategic planning can save a situation from spinning out of control. Management at Tata Teleservices in Andhra Pradesh made one such hard decision in a crisis situation and saved the company from the agony of battling with bad press.

K. S. Susindar, handling the company's communication and marketing, recalls the episode: "On a busy, working day the police entered the company premises and took into custody some of our employees from their work place on the basis of a complaint lodged by a business rival."[25] To make matters worse, the rival company had even arranged for some photographers to be present to photograph the officials being taken into custody by the police. There was enormous pressure within the company to contact the media and talk about the police action against the detained officials who were merely engaged in carrying out the company's routine business. However, Susindar's wiser counsel prevailed: "With four of my colleagues in custody, I advised against taking a strong antipolice stance."

Instead, the company contacted the regional and the national media directly through its public relations agency. The press was apprised of the situation and was requested to desist from publishing the photographs of the officials being taken into custody.

As a result of using the right communication strategy, it mitigated the ugly situation. And although some publications carried the story, it did not generate much adverse publicity for Tata Teleservices. In fact the company's statement on the episode was also published, since the media appreciated the company's stance. Importantly, the company did not antagonize the police, an important constituency, in this case.

Though the issue took some time to settle down and some publications did carry a story, Tata Teleservices made it a point to remain in touch with the media throughout, which helped to strengthen the company's image with a variety of constituencies.[26]

Infosys and Polaris Crises

Infosys, the premier Indian IT company, known for its excellent corporate governance measures, got embroiled in an unsavory crisis situation in 2002. Reka Maximovitch, an employee with the company's U.S. subsidiary, filed a case against Phaneesh Murthy, her boss and the company's director, for sexual harassment.

Infosys Technologies maintained a studied silence on the sexual harassment episode on the grounds that the matter rested in a U.S. court. Murthy said he wanted to go ahead with the sexual harassment case and fight it legally. But Infosys insisted on an out-of-court settlement. On May 11, 2003, Infosys finally announced the amicable settlement with Maximovitch by agreeing to pay $3 million as compensation. Infosys refused to give more details about the settlement.

However, an inquisitive press, much to the discomfort of the company, revealed past details. An *India Today*[27] report said that Maximovitch was fired from her job in December 2000. Between October 1999 and December 2000, she was pressured by Murthy to have a sexual relationship with him. Maximovitch further alleged that Murthy "stalked" her by tracking her to her new employer and offering to buy out the company on behalf of Infosys.

In the absence of a corporate communication strategy in place and working, the media were rife with rumors about Infosys, which were misleading to the general public. This case is an obvious example of mismanagement of a crisis situation.

One of the areas that corporations neglect during a crisis is their media relations. Many companies make the mistake of neglecting the ongoing relationship with members of the media during a crisis.

On this front, the normally reticent Polaris Software and its external media relations agency, Imagequity, worked overtime to feed the media's voracious appetite for updates on the company's CEO Arun Jain's detention in Jakarta by local police after a commercial dispute with a client, Bank Artha Graha. As discussed in Chapter 3, press releases and background information were promptly dispatched to all kinds of media—print, visual, and Web sites. This positive corporate communication strategy paid off well; the company weathered the crisis and also enhanced its reputation by efficiently handling the media.

Of the two software companies, Jain's arrest and the events that followed got better media coverage in the news dailies and magazines. Polaris Software did not lose sight of its employees and customers in its crisis communication strategy.[28]

1997: Tata Tea Crisis

In 1997, Tata Tea was under dire pressure as it was charged with funding the northeastern Indian state of Assam's banned terrorist outfit, the United Liberation Front of Assam (ULFA), and paying the bills for militants, but the company had planned a cohesive communication strategy.

Tata convinced the Assam chief minister, the union home secretary, and the home minister that the medical-aid scheme implemented in 1997 was meant to benefit his employees and their families. That an ULFA activist benefiting from it was an aberration, Tata management conferred. Ratan Tata's image of being soft spoken, introspective, and righteous helped the situation greatly.[29]

In the last decade, Tata Tea's management of the ULFA episode speaks volumes about the company's approach to perception management. It not only quelled any negative fallout for the TATA brand, but it also put the matter in the correct perspective by issuing notices, corrective advertising, and media management. The entire PR machinery was in overdrive to clear the brand name of any negative perception.[30]

2003: ICICI Bank Crisis

In the case of ICICI Bank, a situation was allowed to get out of hand by the bank officials, who, perhaps, thought the panic would be confined to Gujarat alone. However, their lackadaisical attitude hurt the bank's long-standing reputation and gave its image an unexpected jolt.

The series of events began in the second week of April 2003 when Infosys and a few other IT companies declared their annual results. While the results were good, the outlook for the next year was not very encouraging. This led to a crash in the stock market, and the value of Infosys and other IT stocks fell substantially with crores of rupees (in which one crore equals 10,000,000, and a rupee equals approximately $0.02) evaporating into market capitalization. A local Gujarati newspaper carried a story on April 11, 2003, a Friday, that ICICI Bank had huge exposure to these stocks and was likely to go bankrupt.[31]

Nothing was further from the truth, but the rumor and panic spread like wildfire. Panic withdrawals first began in the small town of Surat and the withdrawal frenzy spread to Rajkot, Ahmedabad, and soon to nearly all the towns in the state. On that particular

Friday, crowds were seen withdrawing from the bank's ATM centers until early in the morning.

The next day, similar scenes occurred at the bank's ATM centers in Maharashtra too. A string of bank holidays followed, which also saw people rush to the ATM centers.

The officials failed to gauge the depositors' mood, what with cooperative banks, nonbanking finance companies, provident funds, and importantly the Unit Trust of India tanking in recent times. Further, after the reverse merger of its parent (ICICI), in which ICICI Personal Financial Services Limited and ICICI Capital Services Limited were absorbed by ICICI Bank, the bank's nonperforming asset (NPA) went up.

Finally, it required a financial soundness certificate from the RBI (Reserve Bank of India) which put an end to depositors' cashing out. Only on April 14 did the bank come out with an official statement. Until then, it followed its avowed policy of not responding to speculation and rumors. Theories abound for the depositors' run on the bank, though the bank does not put the blame on anyone, unlike Global Trust Bank (GTB), which accused rival banks of instigating the crisis.

The RBI and other banks joined in to stem the tide. RBI issued a public statement assuring the public that its deposits with ICICI Bank were safe and that the bank was in a position to repay all its liabilities.

Other banks also helped in supplying cash to the centers where withdrawals were taking place. By Tuesday, April 15, the panic subsided and things had returned to normal. The total amount withdrawn during this period was about Rs. 200 crore ($46.7 million)—a small amount considering the bank's asset base, but big enough to leave the bank shaken.

The bank's expansion and growth strategy in the retail segment has been ATM-driven. Through ATMs, banks can offer their customers multiple products and bring down transaction costs at the same time. However, the problem with ATMs is that the amount of cash that can be stored at one time is limited, unlike in the case of a currency chest of a bank, which is the money stored in banks on behalf of the RBI. Thus, catering to the withdrawing public in Gujarat and Maharashtra also became a logistical problem.

This was also pinpointed by Crisil, a credit rating agency, which in a statement said, "This incident highlights the issues all banks face under these circumstances, including timely availability of system support, operational issues of cash management with large ATM networks, and the need for banks to maintain various sources of liquidity." Postwithdrawal, Crisil reaffirmed the ICICI Bank's outstanding ratings, but not before it lost public confidence temporarily.

Looking back, it's clear that India's number-two bank had really failed to adhere to the basic dos and don'ts of crisis management in terms of internal and external communication. Says K. Srinivasan, managing director, Prime Point Public Relations: "Unlike government-owned banks, private banks will always have to face the stability and credibility question. Yesterday it happened to GTB and today ICICI Bank faces the same wrath. And this may happen to any other private bank or private insurance company tomorrow." Terming the ICICI Bank episode as a lesson in crisis management for all corporations, he says that private banks should be more transparent and forthcoming than government-owned banks when it comes to information sharing.[32]

THE NEW FACE OF CRISES

With personal computers and the Internet increasingly a part of the fabric of business, organizations throughout the world face new challenges and the potential for crises that they have not dealt with before. The "I love you" virus unleashed in 2000 cost businesses across a range of industries an estimated total of $10 billion in damages. Companies of all kinds are also grappling with information security issues, including theft of company and customer information.

While all businesses need to be on guard against these new threats, Internet-based businesses in particular are on the front lines of the information security battle. A case in point is CD Universe, an online retailer of music CDs, that was blackmailed in January 2000 by an extortionist claiming to have copied the company's 300,000+ customer credit card files and demanding compensation of $100,000 in return for not posting the information on the Internet.[33] When the company did not respond to his demands, he followed through with his threat and created a Web site where he placed the customer credit card files.

CD Universe promptly sent e-mail notices to its customers alerting them to the situation. The e-mail explained how the company was responding to the security breach and working with the credit card companies to help customers in the event that their stolen numbers were used. The Web site displaying the credit card information was shut down the same day the security breach was discovered.

While the crisis was handled swiftly and was ultimately resolved, it cost the company in both financial and reputational terms, and arguably had a spillover effect to other Web-based businesses that rely on credit card transactions. Consumers who were already uneasy about typing this information into a Web site became even more reluctant to conduct transactions online after witnessing the CD Universe crisis unfold.

Another dimension of the new face of crises is how the Internet can be used to create "communities" where people can share information, opinions, and grievances about companies. Dunkin' Donuts experienced a crisis in the summer of 1999 when a dissatisfied customer used the Internet to share his own bad experience at a Dunkin' Donuts store. When Dunkin' Donuts advertised coffee "your way," this customer was displeased to learn that he was not offered his preference of skim milk. Since the company did not have a corporate Web site where he could formally lodge a complaint, he created his own, writing: "Dunkin' Donuts sucks. Here's why."[34]

While the site started out as a small section of this individual's personal Web page, it was not long before Yahoo! picked up the page in its consumer opinion section. Soon it was generating 1,000 hits a day. Since Dunkin' Donuts had no official forum for customer suggestions or complaints, this fledgling site—out of the company's control—effectively became that forum. The complainant eventually purchased new Web space and the domain name, www.dunkindonuts.org, moving the discussion to a place with a seemingly official name.[35]

It was a full two years after the site was launched that Dunkin' Donuts purchased it (after first writing a letter to the individual who created it, politely requesting that he close it and then threatening him with a lawsuit) and built its own corporate Web site around it. Customers now have a wide variety of options for contacting specific franchise managers or company headquarters via e-mail or toll-free numbers to share feedback.

In the end, Dunkin' Donuts learned the value of offering a Web-based forum for customer feedback, but the company could have mitigated this crisis by acting sooner to take control of the situation. Another example of a company that fell victim to the Internet's power of connectivity is Dell. As discussed in Chapter 7, Dell executives made the grave error of overlooking blogger Jeff Jarvis's "Dell Hell" posting about the company's poor customer service. His published opinion gathered a following; for months, Dell's reputation suffered as its executives failed to address the commentary in the blogosphere. It wasn't until 2006 that they finally joined the online conversation to begin mitigating the reputation crisis.

These examples demonstrate the power of the Internet to make the voice of one individual louder than that of a major corporation, and they also highlight how search engines can further raise the visibility of anticorporate sites, however small and "homegrown" they may be at first.

In the "new economy," these phenomena, coupled with widespread public concern over information security, now have the power to affect a company's bottom line substantially. Companies must recognize the increasing influence of the Internet on a growing number of its constituencies (see Chapters 7 and 8 for more on media and investor constituencies, respectively) and keep this dimension in mind in planning for and handling crises.

These are just some of the other major crises that global organizations have faced in the past 25 years:

- In early 2008, German customers boycott Nokia after thousands of employees are unexpectedly laid off from its Bochum plant so business could be outsourced to cheaper countries in Eastern Europe. Many of the employees learn of their layoffs not from Nokia managers but from radio reports of the company's plans to cut staff and outsource.

- During a snowstorm in mid-February 2007, hundreds of JetBlue passengers are stranded on runways in the New York metro area for up to 10 hours without being deplaned. The company ultimately has to invest millions in reparations and in drafting a constitution of passengers' rights, which would protect JetBlue customers in the event of future weather delays.

- In 2007, Whole Foods CEO John Mackey is caught denouncing his competitors—including one that he was in discussions with for the purpose of purchasing the company—on Yahoo! financial message boards. The messages, which he posted anonymously, date back seven years; his reputation (and, in turn, that of the company) suffered from his lack of discretion.

- Mattel recalls millions of toys throughout 2007 because of lead contamination and faulty pieces—errors largely the result of oversights of the Chinese manufacturers, but ones that cost the toy company dearly in terms of sales and efforts to manage the crises.

- The University of Michigan suspends the sale of all Coca-Cola products on its campus in 2006 after environmental concerns in India and labor issues in Colombia become public.

- Ford Motor Company recalls 6.5 million Firestone tires in August 2000 following a number of deaths and lawsuits concerning Firestone tires on Ford Explorers.

- Coca-Cola issues a recall of its soft drinks in Belgium, France, the Netherlands, and Luxembourg in 1999 after more than 200 people report illnesses.
- In 1997 FDA data suggest that diet drug Fen-Phen may be responsible for heart valve damage.
- TWA flight 800 explodes in July 1996, killing all 230 people onboard the Paris-bound 747–100.
- Tainted meat served at Jack in the Box restaurant kills two children in 1993.
- The FDA attacks Dow Corning's breast implants in 1992.
- The *Exxon Valdez* spills oil on the Alaskan coastline in 1989.
- Pan Am flight 103 explodes over Lockerbie, Scotland, in 1988.
- Sandoz Chemical plant accident contaminates the Rhine in 1987.
- Thousands die because of an explosion at a Union Carbide plant in Bhopal, India, in 1984.

These are just some of the other crises that organizations faced in the past 25 years in India:

- The RBI places a moratorium on the operations of the Global Trust Bank in 2004, limiting depositors who are now allowed to a maximum withdrawal of only Rs 10,000 (approximately $235) from the bank until the moratorium ends.
- A sex scandal engulfs Infosys Technologies in 2004.
- The Centre for Science and Environment (CSE) shows that there is pesticide content in bottled water and soft drinks in 2003.
- More than 20 employees of ONGC die in a helicopter crash in the year 2003.
- The CEO of Polaris is detained in Indonesia in 2003.
- Large-scale withdrawals from the ICICI Bank occur in 2003 after a rumor that the bank is on the verge of bankruptcy.
- Indian Airlines flight IC-814 is hijacked by terrorists from Kathmandu in 1999.
- Tata Tea is charged with funding terrorists of the ULFA by the government in 1997.

- In June 1985, a bomb explodes on Air India flight number 182; it crashes into the North Atlantic en route from Toronto to India; 329 people perish.
- Thousands die because of an explosion at a Union Carbide plant in Bhopal in 1984.

HOW TO PREPARE FOR CRISES

The first step in preparing for a crisis is understanding that any organization, no matter what industry or location it is in, can find itself involved in the kinds of crises discussed in the previous section. While these may be some of the most noteworthy ones from the last 25 years, those left out were likely just as devastating to the companies involved. Obviously, some industries are more crisis-prone than others, such as the chemical industry, pharmaceuticals, mining, forest products, and energy-related industries such as oil and gas and electric utilities. But today, every organization is at risk.

In the United States, terrorist attacks of September 11, 2001, proved to be an important test of many companies' crisis plans, and for others, it underlined the importance of having a plan in place. A U.S. survey of nearly 200 CEOs conducted by Burson-Marsteller and *PRWeek* magazine in late 2001 revealed that a full 21 percent of CEOs surveyed "had no crisis plan and were caught unprepared" by the events of September 11. Fifty-three percent acknowledged that their plan was good but "not totally adequate for such events." In response to the question of whether they had readdressed their crisis communication plan since September 11, 63 percent indicated that they would.[36]

Many companies located in the World Trade Center had also been tenants of the Twin Towers at the time of another terrorist attack. In 1993, an explosion blew out three of the underground floors of the World Trade Center, forcing the evacuation of more than 30,000 employees and thousands of visitors from the entire complex and a rescue operation lasting 12 hours.[37] After the 1993 bombing, many organizations developed or refined their evacuation plans from the Trade Center. When the second attack occurred in 2001, this preparation helped save many lives.

For example, the World Trade Center's largest tenant, Morgan Stanley Dean Witter, cited its own evacuation plan as critical to saving the lives of all but six of its 3,700 employees on September 11. A Morgan spokesman attributed the smooth evacuation to a companywide familiarity with the plan: "Everybody knew about the contingency plan. We met constantly to talk about it."[38]

Communication managers must follow these examples and prepare company management for the worst by using anecdotal information about what happened to unprepared organizations in earlier crises. There are so many to choose from that managers would not be hard-pressed to find crisis examples in virtually every industry from experiences over the last 25 years. Once the groundwork is laid for management to accept the notion that a crisis is a possibility, real preparation should take the following form.

Assess the Risk for Your Organization

As mentioned earlier, some industries are more prone to crises than others. But how can organizations determine whether they are more or less likely to experience a crisis? First, publicly traded companies are at risk because of the nature of their relationship with a key constituency—shareholders. If a major catastrophe hits a company that trades on one of the stock exchanges, the likelihood of a sell-off of the stock is enormous. In addition to the damage the crisis itself inflicts, such immediate financial consequences can threaten the organization's image as a stable, ongoing operation.

Although privately held companies do not have to worry about shareholders, they do have to worry about the loss of goodwill—which can affect sales—when a crisis hits. The owners of privately held companies often become involved in communication with shareholders during a crisis to lend their own credibility to the organization. So all organizations, public, private, and not-for-profit, are at some risk if a crisis actually occurs. The next section examines how a company can plan for a worst-case scenario no matter what it may be.

Plan for Crises

The first step in planning for crisis is for the person in charge of corporate communication to call for a brainstorming session that includes the most senior managers in the organization as well as representatives from the areas that are most likely to be affected by a crisis. For example, this would include the head of the manufacturing division in some cases because of the potential for industrial accidents during the manufacturing process. It might also include the chief information officer because computer systems are subjected to danger, be it security breaches or system failures, when accidents happen. In the case of the explosion that had occurred during the first World Trade Center attack in 1993, most of the organizations that were affected were service organizations. Aside from the loss of lives, the loss of critical information was one of the worst outcomes of the explosion.

During brainstorming sessions, participants should work together to develop ideas about how to tackle potential crises. They should be encouraged to be as creative as possible during this stage. The facilitator should allow participants to share their ideas, no matter how outrageous they may be, with the group and should encourage all participants to be open-minded as they think about possible crisis scenarios.

Once a list of possible crises is created, the facilitator should help the group to determine which of the ideas developed have the most potential to actually occur. It might be useful, for example, to ask the group to assign probabilities to the potential crises so that they can focus on the more likely scenarios rather than waste time working out solutions to problems that have a very low probability of occurring. But even at this stage, participants must not rule out the worst-case scenario. According to outside projections, the risk for an oil spill the size of the one resulting from the *Exxon Valdez* spill was very low. Thus, neither the oil company nor government agencies were prepared for the actual event.

Determine the Effect a Crisis Can Have on Constituencies

Once the probability of risk has been assigned to potential crises, organizations need to determine which constituencies would be the most affected by the crisis. This is important because some constituencies are more valuable than others, and so organizations need to look at risk in terms of its effect on the most important constituencies. Unfortunately, crisis communication experts spend too little time thinking about this question.

When the World Trade Center came under attack on September 11, 2001, American Express CEO Ken Chenault phoned the company's headquarters across the street from the World Trade Center and instructed the building security to evacuate employees immediately. As the day progressed, he contacted all his senior executives to check on their well-being.[39] Until Chenault was able to relocate the company's 3,000 employees to a new building across the river, AmEx's in-house communications staff worked from their homes to reach out to customers and let them know that the company was open for business.[40] Two concerns guided Chenault in his actions after this crisis—employee safety and customer service.[41] Employees and customers, in this example, were the constituencies determined to be most affected by these events, and Chenault's actions reflected this.

It is more difficult to determine how to rank constituencies when a crisis actually happens because so many other things could be going on. But thinking in advance about risks in terms of the effect on constituencies helps the organization further refine which potential crises it should spend the most time on and money preparing for. During the Tylenol crisis, for example, Johnson & Johnson could rely on its credo to help the company set clear priorities to deal with its constituencies.

Pearson and Mitroff's Crisis Management Strategic Checklist*

Strategic Actions

1. Integrate crisis management into strategic planning processes.
2. Integrate crisis management into statements of corporate excellence.
3. Include outsiders on the board and on crisis management teams.
4. Provide training and workshops in crisis management.
5. Expose organizational members to crisis simulations.
6. Create a diversity or portfolio of crisis management strategies.

Technical and Structural Actions

1. Create a crisis management team.
2. Dedicate budget expenditures for crisis management.
3. Establish accountabilities for updating emergency policies/ manuals.
4. Computerize inventories of crisis management resources (e.g., employee skills).
5. Designate an emergency command control room.
6. Assure technological redundancy in vital areas (e.g., computer systems).
7. Establish working relationship with outside experts in crisis management.

Evaluation and Diagnostic Actions

1. Conduct legal and financial audit of threats and liabilities.
2. Modify insurance coverage to match crisis management contingencies.
3. Conduct environmental impact audits.
4. Prioritize activities necessary for daily operations.
5. Establish tracking system for early warning signals.
6. Establish a tracking system to follow up past crises or near crises.

Communication Actions

1. Provide training for dealing with the media regarding crisis management.
2. Improve communication lines with local communities.
3. Improve communication with intervening stakeholders (e.g., police).

Psychological and Cultural Actions

1. Increase visibility of strong top management commitment to crisis management.
2. Improve relationships with activist groups.
3. Improve upward communication (including "whistleblowers").
4. Improve downward communication regarding crisis management programs/accountabilities.
5. Provide training regarding human and emotional impacts of crises.
6. Provide psychological support services (e.g., stress/anxiety management).
7. Reinforce symbolic recall/corporate memory of past crises/dangers.

*Pearson, Christine, and Ian Mitroff, "From crisis prone to crisis prepared: A framework for crisis management," *Academy of Management Executive*, 1993, vol. 7, no. 1, pp. 48–59.

Set Communication Objectives for Potential Crises

Setting communication objectives for potential crises is quite different from figuring out how to deal with a crisis itself. Clearly, organizations may need to do both, but typically, managers are more likely to focus on what kinds of things they will do during a crisis rather than what they will say and to whom. Communication takes on more importance than action does when the crisis involves more intangible things such as the loss of reputation rather than the loss of lives.

Analyze Channel Choice

Once the ranking of constituencies is complete, the participants in a planning session should begin to think about what their communication objective will be for each constituency. Whether this objective will be achieved often depends on the effectiveness of the communication channel the company selects for conveying the message.

Perhaps, in the time of crises, the mass distribution of a memo would be too impersonal for a message to have an effect on employees. The company might consider personal or group meetings or a "town hall" gathering instead. The choice of a communication channel can often reflect how sensitive a company is to its constituencies' needs and emotions. What would be the most efficient and the most sensitive way to communicate with consumers or their families during a crisis? Johnson & Johnson's caring and highly personalized reaction to the Tylenol crisis—involving a host of personal visits to hospitals and pharmacies nationwide—won the company a great deal of goodwill. In the time of crisis, constituencies crave

PROACTIVE CRISIS COMMUNICATION

University of Kansas journalism professor David Guth has recommended the following proactive approach to crises:

1. *Speak the same language.* Crisis plans fail when they cannot be understood. Adrienne Lallo, corporate media relations manager at Hallmark Inc., says that a common language is especially important for global companies with scattered operations. "People react to different situations with different levels of intensity."
2. *Cage the lawyers.* Gerald Meyers, former head of American Motors, offers this advice in his 1986 book *When It Hits the Fan*, "For [lawyers] information is a commodity to be bartered. Decline comment, they say, and save everything for battle in the

courtroom or the privacy of negotiations. Smart executives are not intimidated by lawyers who do not have to run the business once the legal skirmishing is over."

3. *Define the CEO's role.* The CEO's presence, as in the case of Peter Bijur during Texaco's 1996 fiasco, is an important symbol of the organization and top management's commitment. Timing, however, is critical. Exxon chairman and CEO Lawrence Rawl waited a week to comment on the Alaskan oil spill. He believed that public opinion issues should take a back seat to more important issues relating to the cleanup. Most critics feel that Rawls was wrong.

4. *Don't wait to act.* Proactive crisis communication is about taking action before crises hit.

5. *Employee training and counseling.* A crisis communication plan is only as good as the training that accompanies it. A University of Kansas survey found that only one in three organizations had practiced or conducted crisis training in the previous two-year period.

Source: David W. Guth, IABC's *Communication World*, October 1995

information and are often more sensitive than usual to how information is conveyed to them.

Assign Different Teams to Handle Each Crisis

Another important part of planning for communicating in a crisis is determining in advance who will be on what team for each crisis. Different problems require people with different kinds of expertise, and planners should consider those who are best suited to deal with one type of crisis or another. For example, if the crisis is likely to have a financial focus, the chief financial officer may be the best person to lead a team dealing with such a problem. He or she may also be the best spokesperson when the problem actually develops. On the other hand, if the problem is more catastrophic, such as an airline crash, the CEO is probably the best person to be in charge of the team and to serve, at least initially, as the head spokesperson for the crisis. In such crises that result in a loss of life, only the CEO will have the most credibility with the general public and the media.

But managers should avoid putting only senior-level executives in charge of communications for all crises. Sometimes, the person who is most closely associated with the crisis is the one people want to hear from. For example, when considering cultural issues, language differences, and local community concerns, the best spokesperson for a global company may be someone located in the country where the problem develops rather than a more senior manager from the head office.

By assigning different teams to handle different crises, the organization can put the best people in charge of handling the crisis and communications. It also allows the organization to get a cross-section of employees involved. The more involved managers are in planning for and participating on a team in a crisis, the better equipped the organization will be as a whole.

Plan for Centralization

Although organizations can employ either a centralized or decentralized approach to corporate communication (as is discussed in Chapter 3), when it comes to a crisis, for general purposes, the approach must be completely centralized.

Conflicting stories from Perrier's U.S. and European divisions created problems in the company's handling of the benzene contamination scare, which only compounded the crisis. If decentralized organizations do not give interdivisional communication full consideration in a crisis-planning phase, they may often find it more difficult to communicate efficiently among divisions. Planning for centralization can help strip away layers of bureaucracy, keep lines of communication open throughout the organization, and dissipate conflict, all of which are especially critical in a crisis.

WHAT TO INCLUDE IN A FORMAL PLAN

Every communication consultant will suggest that an organization develop a detailed plan for use in a crisis. These are formal in the sense that they are typically printed and passed around to the appropriate managers who may have to sign a statement swearing that they have read and agreed to the plan. This allows the organization to ensure that the plan has been acknowledged by the recipients, and permits questions and clarifications to be discussed in a noncrisis environment. The last thing one would want to happen is for a plant manager's first read of the plan to be when a real crisis occurs.

Research on crisis planning shows that the following information is almost always included in a crisis plan.

A List of Whom to Notify in an Emergency

A crisis plan must include a list of whom to notify in case of emergency. The list must contain the names and telephone numbers of everyone on the crisis team as well as numbers of external agencies such as the fire and police departments. As people leave the company or change responsibilities, this list should be updated.

An Approach to Media Relations

Frank Corrado, the president of a firm that deals with crisis communications, suggests that the cardinal rule for communicating with all constituencies in a crisis should be "Tell it all, tell it fast!"[42] Although this is true to a certain extent, one should be extremely careful about applying such a rule too quickly to the media. Perhaps an amendment to Corrado's rule might be, "Tell as much as you can, as soon as you can" so that you do not jeopardize the credibility of the organization. For example, Perrier's hasty communications with the media, in the absence of accurate information, was a crippling mistake.

Organizations must also build good relations with the media in good times so that reporters will be inclined to be understanding when a crisis occurs. Having a reserve of goodwill with the media is what helped Johnson & Johnson during the Tylenol crisis. Generally, during a crisis, it is a good idea to involve the person who has the best relationship with individual reporters. By agreeing ahead of time that all crisis-related inquiries will go to a central location, organizations can avoid looking disorganized.

A Strategy for Notifying Employees

Employees facing a crisis should be considered similar to families facing a personal crisis. Therefore, employees finding out from the media about something that affects the organization can be as pathetic as when a family member hears about a personal crisis from an outsider. An organization should take adequate measures to ensure that a plan for employee notification is created with the help of employee communication professionals and that it is included in the overall crisis plan.

A Location to Serve as Crisis Headquarters

Although consultants and experts suggest that companies need to invest money in a special crisis center, what companies really need to do is identify an area that can easily be converted before a crisis crops up. It is also important to gather the appropriate facilities (e.g., computers, fax machines, cell phones, hookups for media transmissions) as quickly as possible when a crisis hits. All key internal and external constituencies should be told of the location before a crisis arises, and all information should be centralized through this office. Other lines of communication should then flow through the headquarters for the duration of the crisis.

A Description of the Plan

It is a must that companies have their crisis plans in writing. In addition to having a communication strategy, a crisis plan should address logistical details as well; for example, how and where the families of victims will be accommodated in the case of an airline crash.

After an overall plan is developed, all managers should receive training for dealing with a crisis. Several public relations firms and academic consultants now offer crises simulation courses that allow managers to test their crisis management skills in experiential exercises. Companies including MasterCard, Southwest Airlines, and General Motors use similar simulations sessions to help their organizations work out the kinks before a real crisis hits.[43] Managers searching for the right training courses should be sure that the simulation or training session includes a heavy emphasis on communication in addition to managing the crisis itself.

Communicating during the Crisis

All the planning that an organization can muster will only partially prepare it for an actual crisis. The true measure of success is how it deals with a problem when it actually occurs. If the plan is comprehensive enough, managers will at least be in a strong position to start with. What follow are the most important steps to take when communicating during a crisis. Since every crisis is different, managers must adapt the following eight steps to meet their needs, but crises also have enough common elements for this prescription to be a starting point for all crisis management.

Step 1: Get Control of the Situation
The first step to be taken should be for the appropriate manager to get control of the situation as soon as possible. This involves defining the real problem using reliable information and then setting measurable communication objectives for handling it. As shown in the Perrier case, failing to take this seemingly obvious but crucial first step can prove to be devastating to crisis management efforts. Perrier lacked sufficient information to define its benzene problem in the first place—though its spokespeople had tried to convince the public otherwise—which only compromised its attempts to mitigate the crisis.

When a crisis erupts, everyone in the organization should clearly know whom to contact, but in large organizations this could be unrealistic. Therefore, the corporate communication department can initially serve as a clearinghouse. At the head office, therefore, the vice president of corporate communication should know who are members of crisis teams so that he or she can then turn the situation over to the appropriate manager.

Step 2: Gather as Much Information as Possible

Understanding the problem is the right step for communicators to take in dealing with a crisis. This often involves managing information coming from many sources.

Someone should be assigned to mine information as soon as it becomes available, and the following are questions that could arise. If it is an industrial accident like the one in Bhopal: "How serious is it?" "Were lives lost?" "Have families already been notified?" If the incident involves an unfriendly takeover: "What are the details of the offer?" "Was it absurdly low?" "Have any plans been made for the company to defend itself?"

Many corporations that were desperately trying to gather information about the Bhopal incident have been criticized for reacting too slowly during a crisis. When it takes longer than a couple of hours to get the right information, a company spokesperson should communicate to the media and other key constituencies right away to make it clear that the company is not stonewalling. Although no one will criticize an organization for trying to find out what is going on, a company can face harsh treatment if its constituencies think that management is deliberately obstructing the flow of information.

Step 3: Set Up a Centralized Crisis Management Center

Managers must simultaneously get in touch with the right people and gather information, and they should also make arrangements for creating a crisis center as described earlier in this chapter. This center serves as the platform for all communications during the crisis. Organizations should also provide a comfortable location that can be used by the media during the crisis; it should provide adequate computers or Internet hookups, phones, fax machines, and so on. All communications about the crisis should only come from this one, centralized location.

Step 4: Communicate Early and as Often as Possible

The organization's spokesperson needs to say whatever he or she can as soon as possible. Particularly if the crisis involves a threat to public lives and property, communicators should try to shield constituencies from panic by allaying some of the probable fears that people will have about the situation. Employees, the media, and other important constituencies should know that the crisis center will issue updates at regular intervals until further notice. Even if they retain public relations firms to assist them in handling a crisis, companies need to put good inside people on the front lines of crisis communication and should encourage managers to adopt a team approach with others involved.

Above all else, management must avoid silence and delayed responses. As seen, Firestone proved just how detrimental tardy communication can be. Larry Kamer, chairman of GCI Kamer-Singer, has noted that, "Nine and a half times out of 10 you have to communicate before the facts are in."[44] Management must therefore communicate values, such as concern for public safety, and show a commitment to coming to the aid of people affected by the crisis even if managers do not have all the details yet.

Step 5: Understand the Media's Mission in a Crisis

It is known that members of the media work in an extremely competitive environment—they all want to get the story first. They are also accustomed to a crisis environment in their work and look for a good story that involves victims, villains, and visuals.

The Pepsi syringe hoax had all these sensational elements. As we have seen, CEO Craig Weatherup recognized the impact that visuals would have in reassuring the public that the tampering claims it was facing were simply not so. The video footage of Pepsi's canning procedures and the grocery-store surveillance tape, shown on television, and the full-page newspaper ad are all examples of Pepsi using the media to help it beat a crisis.

Step 6: Communicate Directly with Affected Constituents

It is a good idea to use the media to get information, but it is more important to communicate with your employees, sales staff, organized leadership, site security, operators, and receptionists, as these will be the media's best sources of information in the crisis. External constituencies may need to be contacted as well. These include the other three key constituencies besides employees—customers, shareholders, and communities—as well as suppliers, emergency services, experts, and officials. All available technologies should be employed to communicate with them, including e-mail, voice mail, faxes, direct satellite broadcasts, and online services.

But before communicating, companies should also consider which constituencies are of "top priority." During the 2000 tire recall scandal, one of Firestone's major blunders was the targeting of its first round of PR efforts at dealers instead of appealing directly to the consumers themselves—the constituency most directly affected by the crisis in the first place.

Step 7: Remember That Business Must Continue

The crisis will most certainly remain uppermost in the minds of those managers involved in it, but others may feel that the business must go on despite the crisis. Before the next crisis occurs, managers must not only find suitable replacements ahead of time for those who are on the crisis team, but they must also try to anticipate the effects of the crisis on other parts of the business. For example, if an advertising campaign is underway, should it be stopped during the crisis? Have financial officers stopped trading on the company's stock? Will it be necessary for the organization to move to a temporary location during the crisis? These and other questions related to the ongoing business need to be thought through by managers on and off the crisis team as soon as possible.

Step 8: Make Plans to Avoid Another Crisis Immediately
After a crisis, corporate communication executives should work with other managers to ensure that their organizations will be even better prepared to face another crisis should another one arise. Companies that have experienced crises are more likely to believe that such occurrences may happen again and will recognize that preparation is key to handling crises successfully.

Johnson & Johnson's experience of dealing with Tylenol contamination in 1982 helped the company deal with another episode of Tylenol contamination four years later when a New Yorker died after taking cyanide-laced Tylenol capsules. The period immediately following a crisis is the best time to prepare for the next one because people are still highly motivated to learn from the mistakes made the first time.

CONCLUSION

We all know that crises are a normal part of our private lives. Managers must realize that the same is true for their organizations. In Chapter 4, we see that a company's reputation can be dependent on how it handles a crisis. Unfortunately, a short-term orientation may prevent many managers from acknowledging the potentially long-term damage that crises can inflict.

In this chapter, we explore some real-life examples of how companies across a number of industries dealt with crises of their own. We see that planning and preparation are key to effective crisis management and communication. As British author Aldous Huxley had put it, "The amelioration of the world cannot be achieved by sacrifices in moments of crisis; it depends on the efforts made and constantly repeated during the humdrum, uninspiring periods, which separate one crisis from another, and of which normal lives mainly consist."[45]

Endnotes

CHAPTER 1

1. TPI Index, January 23, 2008.

2. "Nokia's Big Plans for India," *BusinessWeek* online, August 31, 2007, www.businessweek.com/globalbiz/content/aug2007/ gb20070831_914354.htm?chan=search. Downloaded January 26, 2008.

3. Government of Madhya Pradesh, Bhopal Gas Tragedy Relief & Rehabilitation Department, Bhopal. Web site: www.mp.nic.in/bgtr-rdmp/profile.htm. Retrieved April 15, 2004.

4. Rajivan, Anuradha Khati, "Policy implications for gender," The India Time Use Survey, 1998–1999, International Seminar on Time Use Surveys, December 7–10, 1999, Ahmedabad. For more details see www.hdrc.undp.org.in. Retrieved July 12, 2004.

5. Singh, Roopinder, "Failure is a budge of success for 'Hotmail man,'" May 13, 2002, *The Tribune* Web site, www.tribuneindia.com/ 2002/20020513/login/main1.htm. Retrieved July 10, 2004.

6. 2008 Edelman Trust Barometer.

7. McLuhan, Marshal, and Bruce R. Powers, *The Global Village: Transformations in World Life and Media in the 21st Century*, Oxford University Press, New York, 1989.

8. Argenti, Paul A., and Janis Forman, *The Power of Corporate Communication: Crafting the Voice & Image of Your Business*, McGraw-Hill, New York, 2002, p. 83.

9. Garten, Jeffrey, *The Mind of the CEO*, Basic Books, New York, 2001, p. 24.

10. For more information see http://divest.nic.in/performance.htm. Retrieved on July 23, 2004.

11. For more information see www.financeasia.com/article.aspx? CIaNID=69258. Downloaded February 3, 2008.

12. Shell, Adam, "Mergers hit fastest pace since 2000," *USA Today*, May 9, 2006. For more details see www.usatoday.com/money/companies/2006-05-09-merger-usat_x.htm. Retrieved May 14, 2008.

13. http://money.cnn.com/magazines/fortune/fortune500/2007/flash/index.html. Downloaded January 26, 2008.

14. 10th Annual Global CEO Survey, PricewaterhouseCoopers, www.pwc.com/gx/eng/pubs/ceosurvey/2007/10th_ceo_survey.pdf.

15. Klein, Naomi, *No Logo: Taking Aim at the Brand Bullies*, Picador USA, New York, 1999, p. 327.

16. Ibid.

17. Ibid., p. 280.

18. Tanner, Adam, "Activists embrace Web in anti-globalization drive," Reuters, July 13, 2001.

19. Ibid.

20. Evaluation—World Social Forum 2004, India. World Social Forum presents real alternative to globalization. World Social Forum Web site: www.wsfindia.org. Retrieved April 14, 2004.

21. Tata Telecom Web site: www.tatatelecom.com. Retrieved July 12, 2004.

22. Vision 2020 Document, Planning Commission Web site: www.planningcommission.nic.in. Retrieved July 8, 2004.

23. Argenti and Forman, *The Power of Corporate Communication*, pp. 10–11.

24. Holusha, John, "Packaging & public image: McDonald's fills a big order," *New York Times*, November 2, 1990, p. A1.

25. www.umich.edu/news/?BG/procmemo. Downloaded October 2, 2007.

26. www.umich.edu/news/?BG/procmemo. Downloaded October 2, 2007.

27. For more details log on to www.kuttyjapan.com/no-child-labour-in-sivakasi.asp. Retrieved July 5, 2004.

28. Garten, *The Mind of the CEO*, p. 32.

29. Low, Jonathan, and Pam Cohen Kalafut, *Invisible Advantage: How Intangibles Are Driving Business Performance*, Perseus Books, Cambridge, 2002, p. 114.

30. For more details log on to www.kisanwatch.org/eng/special_reports. Retrieved July 5, 2004.

31. Low and Kalafut, *Invisible Advantage*, p. 115.

32. de Geus, Arie, "The living company," *Harvard Business Review*, March 1, 1997.

33. Ibid.

34. For more details log on to www.indiainfoline.com/comp/bata/bata.html. Retrieved July 5, 2004.

CHAPTER 2

1. Aristotle, *The Art of Rhetoric*, Harvard University Press, Cambridge, MA, 1975.

2. Munter, Mary, *Guide to Managerial Communication*, 5th ed., Prentice Hall, Upper Saddle River, NJ, 2000. Please see Chapter 1 for a full discussion of how these same ideas apply to an individual rather than to an organization.

3. Shelby, Annette N., "The theoretical bases of persuasion: a critical introduction," *Journal of Business Communication*, 23(1) (1986) 5–29.

4. For details see http://dilbert.iiml.ac.in/~prism/resources/Kellogs.PDF/. Retrieved July 21, 2004.

5. Munter, *Managerial Communication*.

6. "Council of Public Relations Firms Tests Impact of Corporate Reputation," *Business Wire*, February 7, 1999.

7. "Success stories in India," for more details see www.indiainbusiness.nic.in/business-climate/success-story.htm. Retrieved July 22, 2004.

8. Interview with Ganesh Mahalingam, New Delhi, December 16, 2002. For details see www.agencyfaqs.com/news/interviews/ganesh_mahalingam_1612_2002.html. Retrieved July 22, 2004.

9. Lahiri, Sampa Chakrabarty, "Ethics of persuasion," *Strategic Marketing*, October 1, 2006; see Web site: www.etstrategicmarketing. com/smNov-Dec2/art7.html/. Retrieved July 22, 2004.

10. "Nickel in chocolates," *The Saturday Statesman*, December 5, 1992. For details see http://members.rediff.com/saeserl/campaigns.html/. Retrieved July 22, 2004.

11. "Leader speak," India Infoline-Columns, January 05, 2000. For details see www.indiainfoline.com/view/0512.html. Retrieved July 23, 2004.

12. "Reflections on the growth of a retail chain," March 23, 2000. For details see www.domain-b.com/companies/companies_s/shoppers_stop/20000323bsnreflections.htm. Retrieved July 23, 2004.

13. Rao, S. L., "CSR goes with good governance," February 16, 2004. For details see www1.economictimes.indiatimes.com/articleshow/497922.cms. Retrieved July 23, 2004.

14. Singh, Sangeeta, "No hiccups about this job," *The Financial Express*, Sunday, July 01, 2001. For details see www.financialexpress. com/fe20010701/person2.html. Retrieved July 23, 2004.

15. For details see www.businessstandard.com/search/storypage_new.php?leftnm=lmnu1&leftindx=1&lselect=0&autono=139864. Retrieved July 23, 2004.

16. "American Eagle apologizes for Lord Ganesha flip-flops," April 27, 2003. For details see www.indiacause.com/cause/C18_AE_Ganesha.htm. Retrieved on July 24, 2004.

17. Roth, Daniel, "How to cut pay, lay off 8,000 people, and still have workers who love you," *Fortune*, February 4, 2002, pp. 62–68.

18. For details see www.alleyinsider.com/2007/09/aol-to-fire-tho.html. Downloaded November 9, 2007.

19. For details see www.spiegel.ed/wirtschaft/0,1518,528713,00.html. Downloaded January 29, 2008.

20. Megastar of Bollywood, the Indian film industry.

21. Ace batsman of the Mumbai Indians Cricket team.

22. Rising star of Bollywood.

23. "The rise and fall of Hometrade.com," *The Hindu Business Line*, May 3, 2002. For details see www.responservice.com/archives/ may2002_issue1/media/cybertlk.htm. Retrieved July 26, 2004.

24. Porter, Michael, "How competitive forces shape strategy," *Harvard Business Review*, 57(2), March 1979, pp. 137–145.

25. Hamel, Gary, and C. K. Prahalad, "Competing for the future," *Harvard Business Review*, 72(4) 1994, pp. 122–128.

26. Collins, James C., and Jerry E. Porras, *Built to Last: Successful Habits of Visionary Companies*, Harper Business, New York, 1994.

27. Slywotzky, Adrian, *Value Migration: How to Think Several Moves Ahead of the Competition*, Harvard Business School Press, Boston, 1996.

28. D'Aveni, Richard A., *Hypercompetition: Managing the Dynamics of Strategic Maneuvering*, The Free Press, New York, 1994.

29. Prahalad, C. K., and Gary Hamel, "Strategic intent," *Harvard Business Review*, 67 (3) 1989, pp. 63–76.

CHAPTER 3

1. Bhushan, Ratna, "The smiles are coming back," *The Hindu Business Line*, January 1, 2004. See www.thehindubusinessline.com/ catalyst/2004/01/01/stories/2004010100040100.htm. Retrieved July 26, 2004.

2. Personal interview with William Nielson, May 18, 2005.

3. LeMenager, Jack, "When corporate communication budgets are cut," *Communication World*, vol. 3, February 3, 1999, p. 32.

4. Ibid.

5. Ibid.

6. Ibid.

7. "The Rising CCO," a survey conducted by Weber Shandwick, Spencer Stuart, and KRC Research. Released on January 23, 2008.

8. Letter from Union Carbide's CEO, Robert B. Kennedy, to his executives, dated March 5, 1992.

9. Nemec, Richard, "PR or advertising—who's on top?" *Communication World*, February 3, 1999, p. 25.

10. LeMenager, "When corporate communication budgets are cut."

11. Bloom, Jonah, "Corporate survey 2002," *PRWeek*, February 18, 2002, p. 14.

12. Ibid.

13. Argenti, Paul, "Measuring the value of communications," *Journal of Business Strategy*, vol. 27, no. 6, 2006.

14. Branch, Shelly, "How Target got hot," *Fortune*, May 24, 1999, p. 169.

15. Polaris software lab, news archives, www.polaris.co.in/media/releases/2004_Crisis_19022004.htm. Retrieved July 28, 2004.

16. "Community relations critical to corporate reputation," Phillips Publishing International, March 4, 2002.

17. Fitzpatrick, Kathy R., and Mareen Shubaw Rubin, "Public relations vs. legal studies in organizational crises decisions," *Public Relations Review*, 1995, p. 21.

18. Clutterbuck, David, "Linking communication to business success: a challenge for communicators," *Communication World*, April 1, 2001, p. 30.

19. Leaper, Norm, "How communicators lead at the best global companies," *Communication World*, 33(4), April 5, 1999.

CHAPTER 4

1. For more details, see www.delhieducation.net. Retrieved July 19, 2004.

2. van Riel, Cees B. M., *The Expressive Organization*, Majken Shultz, Mary Jo Hatch, and Mogens Holten Larsen, eds., Oxford University Press, England, 2000, p. 163.

3. Ibid.

4. Interbrand Best Global Brand 2007 survey, www.interbrand.com/surveys.asp. Released July 26, 2007.

5. For more details see www.itcportal.com/newsroom/press_april21_04.htm. Retrieved May 14, 2008.

6. BSES was renamed Reliance Energy on June 10, 2003. See www.domain-b.com/companies/companies_b/bses_ltd/20030610_renamed.htm. Retrieved April 24, 2004.

7. For more details see www.businessweek.com/globalbiz/content/jan2008/gb20080110_468471.htm?chan=search. Downloaded January 28, 2008.

8. Branch, Shelly, "How Target got hot," *Fortune*, May 24, 1999, pp. 169–174.

9. Roberts, John, and Bill Whitaker, "Olympics too commercial?" *CBS Evening News with John Roberts*, February 10, 2002.

10. Shankar, T. S., "A maharajah, not so royal," *The Hindu*, April 12, 2004.

11. Guy, Sandry, "Consultant to launch big effort to advertise its new identity," *Chicago Sun-Times*, November 16, 2000, p. 66.

12. Wetherbe, James, *The World on Time*, Knowledge Exchange, 1996, chap. 11.

13. Ibid.

14. For details see www.prnewsonline.com/news/10910.html. Downloaded January 14, 2008.

15. For details see www.foolonahill.com/adasianpaints.html. Retrieved July 18, 2004.

16. "What's the idea," media report, *Business Standard*, August 6, 2002, For details see www.tata.com/idea_cellular/media/20020806.htm. Retrieved July 15, 2004.

17. For details, log on to the Web site of Café Coffee Day, www.cafecoffeeday.com. Retrieved, July 12, 2004.

18. Yesodaran, Devi, "Infy in new mode, with new rules," *Times of India*, July 17, 2004.

19. Lucknow, Verma, "Rin set to capture low cost segment, offers challenge," *The Asian Age*, April 10, 2004.

20. "Parle-G makes dreams come true," *Business Standard*, March 18, 2002, For details, log on to www.responservice.com/archives/mar2002_issue2/media/markting.htm. Retrieved May 10, 2004.

21. Titan's design your watch contest on Cartoon Network. For more details see www.responservice.com/archives/mar2002_issue2/media/markting.htm. Retrieved, May 10, 2004.

22. Guy, Sandry, "Consultant to launch big effort to advertise its new identity," *Chicago Sun-Times*, November 16, 2000, p. 66.

23. "No ordinary Joe," *Reputation Management*, May/June 1998, vol. 4, no. 3, p. 54.

24. Ibid.

25. Keller, Kevin L., "Building and managing corporate brand equity," *The Expressive Organization*, ed. Majken Shultz, Mary Jo Hatch, and Mogens Holten Larsen, Oxford University Press, England, 2000, p. 118.

26. Fombrun, Charles J, *Reputation: Realizing Value from the Corporate Image*, Harvard Business School Press, Boston, 1996, pp. 5–6.

27. Klein, Pamela, "Measure what matters," *Communication World*, October/November 1999, vol. 16, issue 9, pp. 32–33.

28. Boyle, Matthew, "The right stuff," *Fortune*, March 4, 2002, pp. 85–86.

29. *PR Week*–Burson-Marsteller 2007 CEO survey, *PR Week*, November 12, 2007.

30. 2006 Hill & Knowlton Corporate Reputation Watch, annual survey, www.hillandknowlton.com.

31. Aaker, David A., *Building Strong Brands*, The Free Press, New York, 1996, p. 51.

32. Klein, "Measure what matters."

33. ORG-MARG news update, press release (2002). For details see www.org-marg.com. Retrieved April 26, 2004.

34. Centre for Science and Environment (CSE), press releases. See www.cseindia.org. Retrieved April 14, 2004.

35. Hatch, Mary Jo, and Majken Schultz, "Are the strategic stars aligned for your corporate brand?" *Harvard Business Review*, February 2001, pp. 129–134.

36. "Gone to (Google) hell: Resurrecting a reputation when the devil's in the digital," *PR News*, June 11, 2007.

37. Goldstein, Lauren, "Dressing up an old brand," *Fortune*, November 9, 1998, pp. 154–156.

38. Cope, Nigel, "Stars and stripes," *Independent*, June 6, 2001.

39. *2007 Cone Cause Evolution Environmental Survey.* Downloaded December 21, 2007.

40. Harris Interactive–Reputation Institute 2006 RQ gold survey.

41. Bhan, Indu, "An act of bravery," www.financialexpress.com/ fe_full_story.php?content_id=56225. Retrieved April 24, 2004.

42. Ibid.

43. For details see CII Web site, www.ciionline.org/social-initiatives/ 177/default.asp. Retrieved July 5, 2004.

44. "Tata Steel—a benchmark in corporate social responsibility," media release, March 16, 2004. For details see www.tata.com/ tata_steel/releases/20040316.htm. Retrieved July 12, 2004.

45. See Reliance Web site, www.ril.com. Retrieved July 12, 2004.

CHAPTER 5

1. For details visit www.tcs.com/0_features/articles/ kicking_retention_strategies.htm. Retrieved August 6, 2004.

2. Roper Center at University of Connecticut public opinion online Web site. Retrieved April 5, 2002.

3. Levering, Robert and Milton Moskowitz, "The 100 best companies to work for: The best in the worst of times," *Fortune*, February 4, 2002, pp. 60–61.

4. Roth, Daniel, "How to cut pay, lay off 8,000 people, and still have workers who love you," *Fortune*, February 4, 2002, pp. 62–68.

5. For more information visit www.blonnet.com/life/2003/ 06/02/stories/2003060200080100.htm. Retrieved August 26, 2004.

6. Shellenbarger, Sue, "Workplace upheavals seem to be eroding employees' trust," *The Wall Street Journal*, June 21, 2000, p. B1.

7. Adapted from a speech given at the Tuck School of Business at Dartmouth by Rod Odham of Bell South's small business services division, October 1994.

8. "Gemini consulting study shows similar worker attitudes across cultures around the world," *Business Wire*, September 28, 1998.

9. For details see www.blonnet.com/life/2003/06/02/stories/
   2003060200080100.htm. Retrieved August 6, 2004.

10. Senge, Peter, "The leader's new work: Building learning
    organizations," *Sloan Management Review*, Fall 1990, vol. 32,
    pp. 7–23.

11. Vander Houwen, Boyd A., "Less talking, more listening," *HR
    Magazine*, August 1997, pp. 53–59.

12. For information see the Web site, www.expressitpeople.com/
    20031208/cover.shtml. Retrieved August 23, 2004.

13. For information see the Web site, www.expressitpeople.com/
    20011008/management4.htm. Retrieved August 23, 2004.

14. Troy, Kathryn, "Employee communication: Top management
    priority," Report 919 (New York: Conference Board, 1988).

15. Morley, Michael, "Corporate communications: A benchmark study
    of the current state of the art and practice," *Corporate Reputation
    Review*, Winter 1998, pp. 78–86.

16. Grensing-Pophal, Lin, "Follow me," *HR Magazine*, February
    2000, pp. 36–41.

17. Bill, Leonard, "Balancing business partnership with employee
    advocacy," *HR Magazine*, vol. 41, no. 4, January 1, 1996, p. 89.

18. Weidlich, Thom, "Getting the corporate point across to employees,"
    The New York Times, July 25, 2001, p. C8.

19. Ibid.

20. O'Reilly, Brian, "The mechanic who fixed Continental," *Fortune*,
    December 20, 1999, pp. 176–186.

21. For information see the Web site, www.blonnet.com/life/2003/
    06/02/stories/2003060200080100.htm. Retrieved August 6,
    2004.

22. For information see the Web site, http://was4.hewitt.com/
    bestemployers/india/results_2003.htm. Retrieved August 24, 2004.

23. For further information see the Web site, www.blonnet.com/
    life/2003/06/23/stories/2003062300170100.htm. Retrieved
    August 26, 2004.

24. For further information see www.steelworld.com/rour.htm.
    Retrieved August 12, 2004.

25. For details see the Web site, www.rel.co.in/career/hrpolicy.asp. Retrieved August 26, 2004.

26. Weidlich, Thom, "Getting the corporate point across to employees," *The New York Times*, July 25, 2001, p. C8.

27. Vander Houwen, Boyd A., "Resources to assist line managers: Less talking, more listening," *HR Magazine*, August 1, 1997.

28. For more information see Web site, www.blonnet.com/life/ 2003/ 06/02/stories/2003060200080100.htm. Retrieved August 6, 2004.

29. For more information see Web site, www.prnewsonline.com/news/ 10902.html. Downloaded January 14, 2008.

30. Ibid.

31. For more information see Web site, www.wipro.co.in/resources/ whitepapers/resource42.pdf. Retrieved on August 7, 2004.

32. Coleman, Boyd A., "HP forges a tight relationship between print and online communication," Lawrence Ragan Communications, Inc., Chicago, 2002.

33. Ibid.

34. Mitchell, Colin, "Selling the brand inside," *Harvard Business Review*, January 2002, pp. 5–11.

35. "Taking the show on the road—internally," *The Ragan Report*, February 22, 1999.

36. Ibid.

37. Mitchell, "Selling the brand inside."

38. Crampton, Suzanne M., John W. Hodge, and Jitendra Mishra, "The informal communication network: Factors influencing grapevine activity," *Public Personnel Management*, no. 1, December 22, 1998, p. 569.

39. Ibid.

40. Ibid.

41. Grensing-Pophal, Lin, "Follow me," *HR Magazine*, February 2000, pp. 36–41.

42. Ibid.

CHAPTER 6

1. For more details see www.tata.com/0_beyond_business/ articles/century_of_trust/20040723_cot_media_bg.htm. Retrieved July 26, 2004.

2. Mukerjea, D. N., and Anup Jayaram, "Bharat Sanchar Nigam, The New No. 2," *Businessworld*, November 2, 2003. www.businessworldindia.com/Nov0203/coverstory05.asp.

3. For details see www.thecrossbordergroup.com/pages/1109/ Award+winners.stm.

4. For more details see http://blogs.reuters.com/blog/2007/08/14/ mattel-launches-national-ad-campaign/. Downloaded January 18, 2008.

5. For more details see www.iabcfortworth.com/emma_news/ October_2007/nintendo_marketer2.html. Downloaded January 18, 2008.

6. *The Times of India*, New Delhi, January 26, 2004. pp. 1–2.

7. Gregory, James R., "The impact of advertising to the financial community," *BusinessWeek* special publication, 1999, p. 4.

8. Ibid.

9. Garbett, Thomas F., "When to advertise your company," *Harvard Business Review*, March–April 1982, p. 104.

10. Chakradaeo, Anil, "Rivals stare at the Star move," www. deccanherald.com, August 3, 2003. Retrieved April 26, 2004.

11. Khan, Ehtasham, "CSE ridicules foreign labs; flays Coke, Pepsi," February 5, 2004, www.inhome.rediff.com/money/ 2004/feb/05cola1.htm?zcc=rl. Retrieved July 23, 2004.

12. de Bower, Herbert F., *Modern Business*, vol. 7, Alexander Hamilton Institute, New York, 1917.

13. Garbett, Thomas F., *Corporate Advertising*, McGraw-Hill, New York, 1981, p. 9.

14. Coulter, Robin A., Gerald Zaltman, and Keith S. Coulter, "Interpreting consumer perceptions of advertising: An application of the Zaltman metaphor elicitation technique," *Journal of Advertising*, January 1, 2001, p. 1.

15. For details see www.consumer-voice.org/tobacco/tobacco6.htm. Retrieved July 27, 2004.

16. Sehgal, Arshdeep, "Surrogate advertising: Liquor firms are game," *Economic Times*, April 9, 2003.

17. Association of National Advertisers Web site, www.ana.net/news/ 1998/04_01_98.cfm. Retrieved April 29, 2002.

18. Hughes, Laura Q., "Measuring up," *Advertising Age*, February 5, 2001.

19. Sampey, Kathleen, "AT&T: Ads are investment; shops must project ROI," *Adweek*, July 31, 2000, p. 6.

20. Neff, Jack, and S. C. Johnson, "Ads to stress 'family owned,'" *Advertising Age*, November 13, 2001, p. 1.

21. Horovitz, Bruce, "Kmart hopes Spike Lee ads do the right thing," *USA Today*, February 22, 2002, p. 3B.

22. Dean, Dwane Hal, and Abhijit Biswas, "Third-party organization endorsement of products: An advertising cue affecting consumer prepurchase evaluation of goods . . .," *Journal of Advertising*, January 1, 2002.

23. Harris Interactive Annual 2006 RQ study, released February 1, 2007; press release available at www.harrisinteractive.com/news/ allnewsbydate.asp?NewsID=1170.

24. "Philip Morris annual meeting draws most extensive protest in corporation's history," *PR Newswire*, April 25, 2002.

25. Garbett, *Corporate Advertising*, p. 120.

26. GE company Web site, www.ge.com/campaign.htm. Retrieved May 7, 2002.

CHAPTER 7

1. Harshad Mehta was barred from dealing in the stock market because of his involvement in the share price manipulation in 1993.

2. A scandal during the Kargil War. Coffins were priced at an exorbitant amount by the government.

3. Unfair granting of telecom licenses to HFCL (Himachal Futuristic Communications Ltd.) by former Minister of Communication Sukh Ram, 1996.

4. Defense deal exposed by *Tehelka*, an Indian weekly magazine.

5. "Bad news: Another study finds media really has problems," *PR Reporter*, April 7, 1997, p. 1.

6. eReleases Web site, www.ereleases.com. Retrieved April 4, 2002.

7. Alridge, Ron, "A few tips for having good media relations," *Electronic Media*, December 7, 1992, p. 48.

8. Bilefsky, Dan, "Join the sultans of spin media relations," *The Financial Times*, July 13, 2000, p. 19.

9. Adapted from Mary Munter, "How to conduct a successful media interview," *California Management Review*, Summer 1983, pp. 143–150.

10. "How do your PR efforts measure up in the wired world?" *Interactive PR* and *Marketing News*, November 26, 1999.

11. "Measurement helps telecom giant think quicker," *PR News*, September 27, 1999, p. 1.

12. For more information see www.domain-b.com/people/profiles/20030907_lubna_markar.html. Retrieved August 12, 2004.

13. For more information see www.domain-b.com/people/interviews/20030711_vismaya_firodia.htm. Retrieved August, 2004.

14. "Measurement helps telecom giant think quicker," p. 1.

15. Interview by author with Rai Publications on the role of Corp Comm on May 12, 2004.

16. Peterson, Iver, "Journalism education less focused on the news," *New York Times*, May 5, 1996, p. D7.

17. Beck, Rachel, "Disgruntled voices in cyberspace heard loud and clear," *AP Online*, May 4, 1999.

18. "Cyber snipers underscore need for PR intelligence on the Web," *PR News*, September 20, 1999.

19. Kassel, Amelia, "Guide to Internet monitoring and clipping," CyberAlert white paper, www.cyberalert.com/whitepaper.html.

20. Beck, "Disgruntled voices."

CHAPTER 8

1. Collins, James C., and Jerry I. Porras, *Built to Last*, Harper Business, New York, 1994, p. 8.

2. National Investor Relations Institute corporate Web site, www.niri.org/about/index.cfm. Retrieved April 28, 2002.

3. Nelson, Brett, "So what's your story?" *Forbes*, October 30, 2000, p. 274.

4. Light, David A., "Performance measurement: Investors' balanced scorecards," *Harvard Business Review*, November–December 1998, pp. 17–20.

5. Editorial staff, "2000: A look back at the year that was," *Investor Relations Business*, January 8, 2001, pp. 12–13.

6. For details see www.indiainfoline.com/nevi/iire.html. Retrieved September 11, 2004.

7. Davidson, Steve, "Understanding the SEC's new regulation FD," *Community Banker*, March 2001, p. 40.

8. http://money.cnn.com/2008/02/08/news/economy/world_markets/. Downloaded February 9, 2008.

9. Datt, Ruddar, and K. P. M. Sundaram, *Indian Economy*, S. Chand and Company Ltd., New Delhi, 2003, p. 865.

10. Adapted from *Securities Market (Basic) Module Workbook*, National Stock Exchange's Certification in Financial Markets, National Stock Exchange of India Ltd., November 2003, Mumbai, India.

11. Vaish, Manoj, "Towards global standards," *The Hindu Survey of Indian Industry*, 2004.

12. Adapted from *Securities Market (Basic) Module Workbook*, National Stock Exchange's Certification in Financial Markets, National Stock Exchange of India Ltd., November 2003, Mumbai, India.

13. Securities Exchange Board of India.

14. "Flows and outstandings fourth quarter 2001," Board of Governors of the Federal Reserve, p. 90.

15. 2007 Institutional Investment Report, the Conference Board. Released January 22, 2007.

16. Ibid.

17. "What price reputation?" *BusinessWeek*, July 9, 2007.

18. From FRB/Weber Shandwick corporate Web site, www.frbinc.com/servicesdescripts.html. Retrieved April 11, 2002.

19. Barnett, Tommye M., "To speak or not to speak," *Oil and Gas Investor*, September 2001, pp. 73–75.

20. Byrne, John A., et al., "How to fix corporate governance," *BusinessWeek*, May 6, 2002, pp. 69–78.

21. Munk, Nina, "In the final analysis," *Vanity Fair*, August 2001, p. 100.

22. Nelson, Brett, "So what's your story?" *Forbes*, October 30, 2000, p. 274.

23. Londner, Robin, "Street cleaning," *PR Week*, July 23, 2001, p. 17.

24. Elkind, Peter, "Can we ever trust Wall St. again?" *Fortune*, May 14, 2001, p. 69.

25. For more information visit www.icraindia.com/. Retrieved September 11, 2004.

26. Statement by Chairman Joseph Lieberman, "Rating the raters: Enron and the credit rating agencies," U.S. Senate Committee on Governmental Affairs, March 20, 2002, Web site: www.senate.gov/~gov_affairs/03202002lieberman.htm. Retrieved April 30, 2002.

27. Visit Web site: www.domain-b.com/companies/companies_t/tata%20group/20030516_rating.html. Retrieved September 11, 2004.

28. Visit Web site: www.domain-b.com/finance/banks/ifci/20030423_ratings.htm. Retrieved September 11, 2004.

29. "Fitch downgrades bond insurer FGIC," CNNMondey.com, January 31, 2008. Downloaded February 10, 2008.

30. "Investor relations: Corporate," *PRWeek*, September 24, 2001, p. 19.

31. Ibid.

32. "Understanding IR," *PR Week*, September 24, 2001, p. 17.

33. Londner, Robin, "IR-PR link not seen in chain of command," *PR Week*, March 4, 2002.

34. "Business wire announces survey results on the consolidation of communications in IR and PR," *Business Wire*, March 21, 2002.

35. "Corporate cyberspace communication vs. paper-based communication: The impact of media choice on cost and benefit," *Issues in Information Systems*, vol. VIII, no. 2, 2007.

36. Ibid.

37. "Are annual reports still relevant?" *Journal of Business and Design*, vol. 6, no. 2, pp. 26–31.

38. McGuire, Craig, "Companies devote more money to publications than ever before," *PR Week*, June 26, 2000.

39. "The Best and the rest: CFO Asia's annual reports survey: Truth and consequences," CFO Asia, March 2003, Web site: www.cfoasia.com/archives/200303-02.htm. Retrieved September 10, 2004.

40. For more information visit www.domain-b.com/companies/ companies_r/reliance_industries/20020718_creditworthy_firms. html. Retrieved September 11, 2004.

41. Byrne, John A., "Investor relations: When capital gets antsy," *BusinessWeek*, September 13, 1999, p. 72.

42. Ibid.

43. Coyne, Kevin P., and Jonathan W. Witter, "What makes your stock price go up and down," *McKinsey Quarterly*, no. 2, 2002.

44. Ibid.

45. Byrne, John A., "Investor relations."

46. "Understanding IR."

47. Garbett, Thomas F., *How to Build a Corporation's Identity and Project Its Image*, Lexington Books, Lexington, MA, 1988, p. 99.

48. Investment Decisions, January 1986.

49. Ibid.

50. From CCBN company Web site: www.ccbn.com/about/faqs.html. Retrieved April 11, 2002.

51. Business/technology editors, "Shareholder.com clients showcase strength at IR magazine U.S. awards," *Business Wire*, April 3, 2002.

52. Scherreik, Susan, "Finding stocks you can trust," *BusinessWeek*, March 25, 2002, p. 128.

53. Ibid.

54. Gandel, Stephen, "Posse pursues Wall St.," *Crain's New York Business*, April 12, 2002.

55. Chatterjee, Sumeet, "Middle class left in the lurch by US-64 freeze," July 5, 2001, IANS. Web site: http://newsarchives

.indiainfo.com/2001/07/05/05uti.html. Retrieved September 10, 2004.

56. Bacani, Cesar, and Shirish Nadkarni, "Bombay, business conglomerates unreliable? Troubles at Reliance worry investors," *Asiaweek*, January 19, 1996, Web site: www.asiaweek.com/asiaweek/96/0119/biz1.html. Retrieved September 10, 2004.

57. www.asiaweek.com/asiaweek/96/0119/biz1.html. Retrieved April 28, 2005.

58. Nath Sa, Sambhu, "Tech meltdown worse than market fall," IndiaInfoLine, February 23, 2004, Web site: www.indiainfoline.com/nevi/melt.html. Retrieved September 11, 2004.

59. White, Ben, "Enron-related fears take toll on other firms' stocks," *The Washington Post*, February 13, 2002, p. E01.

60. Cordasco, Paul, "Tyco ends 'boring' investor calls, claiming IR success," *PR Week*, April 8, 2002, p. 3.

61. Adapted from "India's most investor friendly companies," *Business Today*, March 14, 2004.

CHAPTER 9

1. Adapted from Datt, Ruddar, and K. P. M. Sundharam, *Indian Economy*, 48th rev. ed., S. Chand & Company, New Delhi, 2003.

2. Ibid.

3. Hansen, Wendy L., and Neil J. Mitchell, "Disaggregating and explaining corporate political activity: Domestic and foreign corporations in national politics," *American Political Science Review*, December 1, 2000, p. 891.

4. Pinkham, Douglas G., "How'd we get to be the bad guys?" *Public Relations Quarterly*, July 22, 2001, p. 12.

5. Weidenbaum, Murray L., *Business, Government, and the Public*, Prentice Hall, Englewood Cliffs, NJ, 1977.

6. Ibid.

7. Broder, John M., "FTC rejects deal to join two giants of office supplies," *The New York Times*, April 5, 1997, p. 7.

8. "Legislative roundup," *The American Banker*, July 11, 2002, p. 5.

9. For more information see http://nppaindia.nic.in/frequent.html. Retrieved September 23, 2004.

10. For more information see http://fcamin.nic.in/ecpbacts.htm. Retrieved September 23, 2004.

11. For more information see http://pib.nic.in/feature/feyr2003/ fjan2003/f080120032.html. Retrieved September 23, 2004.

12. Hansen and Mitchell, "Disaggregating and explaining corporate political activity."

13. Ibid.

14. Adams, Walter, and James W. Brock, *The Bigness Complex: Industry, Labor, and Government in the American Economy*, Pantheon Books, New York, 1986.

15. Levitan, Sar A., and Martha R. Cooper, *Business Lobbies: The Public Good and the Bottom Line*, The Johns Hopkins University Press, Baltimore, 1984, pp. 4–5.

16. Zeller, Shawn, "Lobbying: Saying so long to D.C. outposts," *National Journal*, December 1, 2001.

17. "Survey shows public affairs emerging as top management function," *Public Relations Quarterly*, July 22, 2000, p. 30.

18. Ibid.

19. Zeller, Shawn. "Lobbying."

20. Birnbaum, Jeffrey H, "How Microsoft conquered Washington," *Fortune*, April 29, 2002, pp. 95–96.

21. Pinkham. "How'd we get to be the bad guys?"

22. Mayer, Jane, "The accountant's war," *The New Yorker*, April 22 and 29, 2002, pp. 64–71.

23. See Web site of CII, www.ciionline.org/Common/91/Images/ Featur.pdf. Retrieved August 6, 2004.

24. See Web site of FICCI, www.ficci.com/ficci/index.htm. Retrieved August 6, 2004.

25. Singer, James W., "Business and government: A new 'quasi-public' role," *National Journal*, April 15, 1978, p. 596.

26. Steel, Michael, "FedEx flies high," *National Journal*, February 24, 2001.

27. Ibid.

28. Ibid.

29. "Industry has big agenda for new government," BS Corporate Bureau in Mumbai, May 14, 2004, http://inhome.rediff.com/money/2004/may/14industry.htm?zcc=rl. Retrieved September 25, 2004.

30. Wilson, Graham, *Interest Groups in the United States*, Oxford University Press, New York, 1981.

31. American Chamber of Commerce Web site, www.uschamber.com. Retrieved June 10, 2002.

32. Ibid.

33. Gerry, Keim, "Corporate grassroots program in the 1980s," *California Management Review*, vol. 28, no. 1, fall 1985, p. 117.

34. "CII opposes some provisions of the Companies Bill," IndiaInfoLine, Web site: www.indiainfoline.com/news/news.asp?dat=24291. Retrieved September 25, 2004.

35. Dalal, Sucheta, "Lessons for drafting legislation," *The Financial Express*, October 27, 2003.

36. "Software piracy . . . losses in India at $245mn in '01," IndiaInfoLine, June 26, 2002, Web site: www.indiainfoline.com/cyva/feat/sopi.html. Retrieved September 25, 2004.

37. Hansen and Mitchell, "Disaggregating and explaining corporate political activity."

38. Handler, Edward, and John R. Mulkern, *Business in Politics*, Lexington Books, Lexington, MA, 1982.

39. Birnbaum, Jeffrey H., et al., "The influence market: Capitol clout," *Fortune*, October 26, 1998, p. 177.

40. Ibid.

41. Mayer, "The accountant's war."

42. Pinkham, "How'd we get to be the bad guys?"

43. Former Chief Justice of India and advisor of the Birla electoral trust.

44. Neogi, Saikat, "The boardroom votes for state funding," *The Financial Express*, Internet edition, April 04, 2004. See Web site, www.financialexpress.com/fe_full_story.php?content_id=56234. Retrieved September 24, 2004.

45. Abhimanyu, "The capitalist class, the media, and exit polls, people's democracy," April 29, 2001, Web site: http://pd.cpim.org/ 2001/april29/april29_media.htm. Retrieved September 24, 2004.

46. Kaplan, Lawrence F., "Why trade won't bring democracy to China," *The New Republic*, July 9, 2001.

47. Mikkelsen, Randall, "Update 4: Bush seeks 'new era of corporate integrity,'" Reuters, July 9, 2002. Retrieved July 12, 2002 from Forbes.com, www.forbes.com/home/newswire/2002/07/09/ rtr655891.html.

48. Pinkham, "How'd we get to be the bad guys?"

49. Pinkham, Douglas G., "Corporate public affairs: running faster, jumping higher," *Public Relations Quarterly*, vol. 43, 1998, p. 33.

CHAPTER 10

1. From a presentation by Ray O'Rourke to Corporate Reputation Conference, New York University, January 1997. At the time of this presentation, Mr. O'Rourke was with the public relations firm of Burson-Marsteller.

2. Leavitt, Harold J., "Hot groups," *Harvard Business Review*, July 1, 1995, p. 109.

3. O'Reilly, Brian, "Managing: J&J is on a roll," *Fortune*, December 26, 1994, p.109.

4. Ibid.

5. "Special report: The best global brands," *BusinessWeek*, August 6, 2001, p. 64.

6. Perrier press release, The Perrier Group, February 10, 1990.

7. "When the bubble burst," *The Economist*, August 3, 1991, p. 67.

8. Ibid.

9. "Handling corporate crises; total recall," *The Economist*, June 3, 1995, p. 61.

10. Ibid.

11. "Poor Perrier, it's gone to water," *Sydney Morning Herald*, February 15, 1990, p. 34.

12. Ibid.

13. Birkland, David, "Couple say they found used needle in Pepsi," *The Seattle Times*, June 11, 1993, p. 18.

14. Sonnenfeld, Sandi, "Media policy—what media policy?" *Harvard Business Review*, July 1, 1994, p. 18.

15. Ibid.

16. Kessler, Glenn, and Theodore Spencer, "How the media put the fizz into the Pepsi scare story," *Newsday*, June 20, 1993, p. 69.

17. Schwartz, John, "Pepsi punches back with PR blitz; crisis team worked around the clock," *The Washington Post*, June 19, 1993, p. C1.

18. Leith, Scott, "Cola wars: A gain for Pepsi; No. 1 Coke's U.S. market share down in '01," *The Atlanta Journal and Constitution*, March 1, 2002, p. F1.

19. Mayer, Caroline E., and Frank Swoboda, "A corporate collision; Ford-Firestone feud accelerated after effort to head it off failed," *The Washington Post*, June 20, 2001, p. E1.

20. Halliday, Jean, "Ford, Firestone suffer damage in tire blowout; both lose consumer trust, while Firestone faces 'survival challenge,'" *Advertising Age*, May 28, 2001, p. 57.

21. "Who's up who's down," *Fortune*, February 19, 2001, p. 104.

22. Frank, John, *PRWeek*, February 19, 2001.

23. Ibid.

24. Muller, Joann, David Welch, and Jeff Green, "A crisis of confidence: CEO Nasser scrambles to contain the tire problem," *BusinessWeek*, September 18, 2000, pp. 40–42.

25. See www.domainb.com/people/interviews/20040302kssusindar.htm. Retrieved May 11, 2005.

26. See www.domainb.com/people/interviews/20040302_k_s_susindar.htm. Retrieved August 10, 2004.

27. See www.domain-b.com/companies/companies_i/infosys/20020731_lawsuit.htm. Retrieved October 9, 2004.

28. See www.domain-b.com/companies/companies_i/i-Flex_solutions/20030516_sex_harassment.html. Retrieved August 10, 2004.

29. See www.tata.com/tata_sons/media/20030105.htm. Retrieved August 11, 2004.

30. See www.domainb.com/management/general/20040720_
    perception.html. Retrieved August 11, 2004.

31. Chatterjee, Uday, "Runaway fiery," April 20, 2003. See
    www.domain-b.com/finance/banks/icici_bank/20030420_
    runaway_fiery.html. Retrieved August 10, 2004.

32. Jagannathan, Venkatachari, "A crisis tale and two banks: Global Trust
    Bank, ICICI Bank, April 15, 2003." See www.domain-b.com/
    finance/banks/200304apr/20030415_banks.html. Retrieved
    August 10, 2004.

33. Markoff, John, "Thief reveals credit card data when Web extortion
    plot fails," *The New York Times*, January 10, 2000, p. A1.

34. Weiss, Joanna, "Dunkin' Donuts complaint-site saga shows business
    power of Internet," *The Boston Globe*, August 25, 1999.

35. Ibid.

36. "PRWeek/Burson-Marsteller CEO Survey," 2001, *PRWeek*,
    November 26, 2001, pp. 20–29.

37. Carey, Carol, "World Trade Center," *Access Control & Security
    Systems Integration*, July 1, 1997.

38. Fonda, Daren, "Girding against new risks: Global executives are
    working to better protect their employees and businesses from
    calamity," *Time*, October 8, 2001, p. B8.

39. Bloom, Jonah, "CEOs: Leadership through communication,"
    PRWeek, November 26, 2001, pp. 20–29.

40. "Corporate America's reaction," *PRWeek*, September 24, 2001, p. 10.

41. Bloom, Jonah, "CEOs: Leadership through communication."

42. Corrado, Frank, *Media for Managers*, Prentice Hall, New York, 1984.

43. "Crises: in-house, in hand," *PRWeek*, January 21, 2002, p. 13.

44. Frank, John, "What can we learn from the Ford/Firestone tire
    recall? As John Frank explains, unlike the Tylenol crisis, the
    problem is that they just can't seem to put a lid on it," *PRWeek*,
    October 9, 2000, p. 31.

45. Huxley, Aldous, *Grey Eminence; a Study in Religion and Politics*,
    Chatto & Windus, London, 1941.

Index

About the Author

Paul A. Argenti is Professor of Corporate Communication at the Tuck School of Business at Dartmouth College. He provides management and corporate communication consulting to such clients as Goldman Sachs, Sony, and Novartis.